To Sarah,
Merry Christmas 1976.
Love,
Aunt Jan & Uncle Eric

The Golden Treasury

OF

POETRY

The Golden Treasury
OF
POETRY

Selected and with a Commentary

by LOUIS UNTERMEYER

Illustrated by JOAN WALSH ANGLUND

GOLDEN PRESS
NEW YORK

Western Publishing Company, Inc.
Racine, Wisconsin

ACKNOWLEDGMENTS The editor and publisher have made every effort to trace the ownership of all copyrighted material and to secure permission from holders of such poems. In the event of any question arising as to the use of any material the publisher and editor, while expressing regret for inadvertent error, will be pleased to make the necessary corrections in future printings. Thanks are due to the following authors, publishers, publications, and agents for permission to use the material indicated.

APPLETON-CENTURY-CROFTS, INC., for "The Elf and the Dormouse" by Oliver Herford, from *Artful Anticks*, copyright 1894 by The Century Company, 1922, by Oliver Herford.

EDWARD ANTHONY for the poems printed under the pseudonym, A. C. Gate, and for those in *Every Dog Has His Say* by Edward Anthony, copyright 1947 by Watson-Guptill Publications, Inc.

WILLIAM BLACKWOOD & SONS, LTD., for "The Highwayman" from *Collected Poems of Alfred Noyes*, copyright 1909, 1913.

THE BOBBS-MERRILL COMPANY for "The Raggedy Man" from *Rhymes of Childhood* by James Whitcomb Riley, reprinted by permission of the Bobbs-Merrill Company.

BRANDT & BRANDT for "God's World" from *Collected Poems of Edna St. Vincent Millay*, published by Harper & Bros., copyright © 1913, 1941 by Edna St. Vincent Millay; for "In Just—" from *Poems: 1923-1954* by E. E. Cummings, published by Harcourt, Brace and Company, copyright © 1923, 1951 by E. E. Cummings.

MELVILLE H. CANE for "Bed-Time Story" from *And Pastures New*, published by Harcourt, Brace and Company, copyright 1947, 1956 by Melville H. Cane.

JONATHAN CAPE LIMITED for "A Windy Day" from *Collected Poems of Andrew Young*.

ELIZABETH COATSWORTH for "The Barn," "On a Night of Snow," "Country Cat," "The Complete Hen," and "Conquistador."

COWARD-MCCANN, INC., for "The Barn" from *Compass Rose* by Elizabeth Coatsworth, copyright 1929 by Coward-McCann, Inc.

NATHALIA CRANE for "The Janitor's Boy," "Destiny," and "Standards," from *The Janitor's Boy*, copyright 1924 and *Lava Lane*, copyright 1925 by Nathalia Crane.

THE JOHN DAY COMPANY, INC., for "The Old Coon-Dog Dreams" from *No Rain From These Clouds*, by Kenneth Porter, copyright 1946 by Kenneth Porter, and reprinted by permission of The John Day Company, Inc.

DODD, MEAD & COMPANY, INC., for "I Meant To Do My Work To-day" from *The Lonely Dancer* by Richard LeGallienne, copyright 1913, 1941 by Richard LeGallienne, and reprinted by permission of Dodd, Mead & Company, Inc.

DOUBLEDAY & COMPANY, INC., for "If—" from *Rewards and Fairies* by Rudyard Kipling, copyright 1910, 1938, reprinted by permission of Mrs. George Bambridge and Doubleday & Company, Inc.; "The Bat" from *The Waking: Poems 1933-1953* by Theodore Roethke, copyright 1938, 1939, 1953 by Theodore Roethke. Reprinted by permission of Doubleday & Company, Inc.

KENNETH DURANT for "Millions of Strawberries" by Genevieve Taggard, originally published in *The New Yorker*.

E. P. DUTTON & CO., INC., for "The Four Friends" from *When We Were Very Young* by A. A. Milne. Copyright 1924 by E. P. Dutton & Co., Inc., renewal, 1952 by A. A. Milne. Reprinted by permission of the publishers.

EXPOSITION PRESS for "Only the Wind Says Spring" from *Song After War and Other Poems* by Helen Janet Miller, copyright 1947 by the author.

FABER AND FABER LTD. for "The Old Gumbie Cat" and "The Ad-Dressing of Cats" from *Old Possum's Book of Practical Cats*, copyright 1939 by T. S. Eliot; for "Nod," "Silver," "Tartary," and "Jim Jay" by Walter de la Mare.

ELEANOR FARJEON for "Minnie" and "Griselda" from *The Children's Bells*, copyright 1957.

ROSALIE GRAYER for "Altar Smoke."

HARCOURT, BRACE AND COMPANY, INC., for "The Old Gumbie Cat" and "The Ad-Dressing of Cats" from *Old Possum's Book of Practical Cats* by T. S. Eliot, copyright 1939 by T. S. Eliot; for "Yarns" from *The People, Yes* by Carl Sandburg, copyright 1936 by Harcourt, Brace and Company, Inc.; for the poems from *Selected Poems and Parodies of Louis Untermeyer*, copyright 1917, 1935. All of these are reprinted by permission of Harcourt, Brace and Company, Inc.

HARPER & BROTHERS for "The Gastronomic Guile of Simple Simon" from *Mother Goose for Grown-Ups* by Guy Wetmore Carryl. Copyright 1900 by Harper & Brothers; copyright 1928 by Constance C. Sargent.

SARA HENDERSON HAY for "The Shape God Wears."

WILLIAM HEINEMANN LTD. for "The Doze" and "The Chickamungus" from *Prefabulous Animiles* by James Reeves, copyright 1957.

HENRY HOLT & COMPANY, INC., for "The Runaway" and "Goodbye and Keep Cold" from *Collected Poems of Robert Frost*, copyright 1930, 1939 by Henry Holt & Company, Inc., copyright 1936 by Robert Frost; for "Four Little Foxes" from *The Collected Poems of Lew Sarett*, copyright 1941 by Henry Holt & Company,

Inc.; for "Tartary" from *Collected Poems by Walter de la Mare*, copyright 1920; for "Fog" from *Chicago Poems* by Carl Sandburg, copyright 1916 by Henry Holt & Company, Inc.; copyright 1944 by Carl Sandburg. All of these are reprinted by permission of Henry Holt & Company, Inc.

HOUGHTON MIFFLIN COMPANY for "The Camel's Complaint" from *The Admiral's Caravan* by Charles E. Carryl, and "The Walloping Window-Blind" from *Davy and the Goblin* by Charles E. Carryl, copyright 1913; for "The Fish" from *Poems* by Elizabeth Bishop, copyright 1955 by Elizabeth Bishop.

ALFRED A. KNOPF, INC., for "George" from *Cautionary Tales for Children* by Hilaire Belloc.

JOSEPH LAUREN AND MICHAEL LEWIS are pseudonyms. Poems by these authors are printed by permission of Louis Untermeyer.

J. B. LIPPINCOTT COMPANY for "The Highwayman" from *Collected Poems: Volume One* by Alfred Noyes, copyright 1913, 1941 by Alfred Noyes; for "Minnie" and "Griselda" by Eleanor Farjeon from *Poems for Children*, copyright 1926, 1927, 1933, 1938, 1951. Reprinted by permission of J. B. Lippincott Company.

LITTLE, BROWN & COMPANY for "The Rhinoceros," "An Introduction to Dogs," "The Tale of Custard the Dragon" from *The Face Is Familiar* by Ogden Nash, copyright 1931, 1933, 1935, 1936, 1937, 1939, 1940 by Ogden Nash; for "Yak," "Opossum," and "Seal" from *Boy Blue's Book of Beasts* by William Jay Smith, copyright © 1957 by William Jay Smith; for "Every Time I Climb a Tree" from *Far and Few* by David McCord, copyright 1952 by David McCord. All these poems are reprinted by permission of Little, Brown & Company.

THE MACMILLAN COMPANY for "The Moon's the North Wind's Cooky" from *Collected Poems* by Vachel Lindsay, copyright 1914, 1923; for "The Song of Wandering Aengus" from *Collected Poems of William Butler Yeats*, copyright 1933; for "Country Cat" and "On a Night of Snow" from *Night and the Cat* by Elizabeth Coatsworth, copyright 1950. All these poems are reprinted by permission of The Macmillan Company.

THE MACMILLAN COMPANY OF CANADA for "The Song of Wandering Aengus" from *Collected Poems of William Butler Yeats*.

DAVID McCORD for "Isabel Jones & Curabel Lee."

McINTOSH & OTIS, INC., for "Andrew Jackson" from *Brady's Bend* by Martha Keller, published by Rutgers University Press, copyright 1946 by Martha Keller Rowland.

MRS. HAROLD MONRO for "Dogs," "Milk for the Cat," and "Bird at Dawn" by Harold Monro.

ROSALIE MOORE for "Catalog" and "Gnat."

EARL L. NEWTON for "The Skippery Boo."

OXFORD UNIVERSITY PRESS for "Pied Beauty" from *Poems of Gerard Manley Hopkins*, published by Oxford University Press, copyright 1918, and reprinted by permission of the Hopkins Estate and Oxford University Press.

MARCELLA POWERS for "Cat" by Sinclair Lewis.

RINEHART & COMPANY, INC., for "Was Worm" and "The Cloud-Mobile" from *A Cage of Spines* by May Swenson, copyright 1958 by May Swenson, published by Rinehart & Company, Inc.

TED ROBINSON for "April."

G. SCHIRMER, INC., for "Wind" from *The Children* by Leonard Feeney, copyright 1946 by G. Schirmer, Inc.

CHARLES SCRIBNER'S SONS for "Wynken, Blynken, and Nod" and "Orkney Lullaby" from *A Little Book of Western Verse* by Eugene Field, and "The Fly-Away Horse" from *Love Songs of Childhood* by Eugene Field, copyright 1894 by Eugene Field, 1922 by Julia Sutherland Field, and reprinted by permission of Charles Scribner's Sons.

THE SOCIETY OF AUTHORS for "Nod," "Silver," "Tartary" and "Jim Jay" from *Collected Poems by Walter de la Mare*, reprinted by permission of Faber & Faber Ltd. and The Literary Trustees of Walter de la Mare.

PEARL STRACHAN for "Morning Overture: Chorus of Dogs."

THE VIKING PRESS, INC., for "Christmas Morning," "The Hens," and "The Rabbit" from *Under the Tree* by Elizabeth Madox Roberts, copyright 1922 by B. W. Huebsch, Inc., 1950 by Ivor S. Roberts, and reprinted by permission of The Viking Press, Inc.

A. P. WATT & SON for "If—" from *Rewards and Fairies* by Rudyard Kipling, reprinted by permission of Doubleday & Company, Inc., and Mrs. George Bambridge; for "The Song of Wandering Aengus" from *Collected Poems of William Butler Yeats* reprinted by permission of Mrs. Yeats and The Macmillan Company of Canada; for "The Highwayman" from *Collected Poems of Alfred Noyes*, reprinted by permission of William Blackwood and Sons, Ltd., and Alfred Noyes.

CONTENTS

UNFORGETTABLE STORIES

LAUGHTER HOLDING BOTH HIS SIDES

FOREWORD

This is a book to grow on.

It is also a book to grow with.

In these pages are poems that will become favorites;

you will never lose your taste for them. They will be part of you

as long as you live. These verses—the nimble and the nonsensical

as well as the greatly meaningful—delighted me

when I was young. They still delight me today.

You will laugh at some of these poems; you will learn

from others. Some of them will be exciting new experiences;

some will let you see familiar things as though you had never seen

them before. But all of them were meant primarily

to be enjoyed. Enjoyment is the essence.

Poetry is written in many moods and on many levels, each of which

provides its own particular pleasure. Come along

through these pages and let me show you what I mean.

Let us begin at the beginning.

LOUIS UNTERMEYER

IN THE BEGINNING

In the beginning, they tell us, there was nothing but joy in the world. Everything was bright and new. Earth and sky had just been made. Man was a child, living in a Paradise which was a cross between a great garden and a divine playground. Every morning was a fresh surprise.

All beginnings have this same radiance. "Heaven," said Wordsworth, "lies about us in our infancy." The poems in this first section recapture that early freshness and innocent joy. Each one pipes a happy song, an echo of a young and untroubled world.

Pirate Story

Three of us afloat in the meadow by the swing,
    Three of us aboard in the basket on the lea.
Winds are in the air, they are blowing in the spring;
    And waves are on the meadow like the waves there are at sea.

Where shall we adventure, to-day that we're afloat,
    Wary of the weather and steering by a star?
Shall it be to Africa, a-steering of the boat,
    To Providence, or Babylon, or off to Malabar?

Hi! but here's a squadron a-rowing on the sea—
    Cattle on the meadow a-charging with a roar!
Quick, and we'll escape them, they're as mad as they can be,
    The wicket is the harbor and the garden is the shore.

ROBERT LOUIS STEVENSON

Infant Joy

"I have no name,
  I am but two days old."
What shall I call thee?
"I happy am,
  Joy is my name."
Sweet joy befall thee!

Pretty Joy!
Sweet Joy, but two days old,
Sweet Joy I call thee:
Thou dost smile,
I sing the while;
Sweet joy befall thee!

WILLIAM BLAKE

10

Happy Songs

Piping down the valleys wild,
    Piping songs of pleasant glee,
On a cloud I saw a child,
    And he, laughing, said to me,

"Pipe a song about a lamb,"
    So I piped with merry cheer;
"Piper, pipe that song again,"
    So I piped, he wept to hear.

"Drop thy pipe, thy happy pipe,
    Sing thy songs of happy cheer."
So I sang the same again,
    While he wept with joy to hear.

"Piper, sit thee down and write
    In a book that all may read."
So he vanish'd from my sight;
    And I pluck'd a hollow reed,

And I made a rural pen,
    And I stained the water clear,
And I wrote my happy songs
    Every child may joy to hear.

WILLIAM BLAKE

The Shepherd

How sweet is the shepherd's sweet lot!
From the morn to the evening he strays;
He shall follow his sheep all the day,
And his tongue shall be filled with praise.

For he hears the lamb's innocent call,
And he hears the ewe's tender reply;
He is watchful while they are in peace,
For they know when their shepherd is nigh.

WILLIAM BLAKE

Nurse's Song

When the voices of children are heard on the green
    And laughing is heard on the hill,
My heart is at rest within my breast,
    And everything else is still.

"Then come home, my children, the sun is gone down,
    And the dews of the night arise;
Come, come, leave off play, and let us away
    Till the morning appears in the skies."

"No, no, let us play, for it is yet day,
    And we cannot go to sleep;
Besides in the sky the little birds fly,
    And the hills are all covered with sheep."

"Well, well, go and play till the light fades away,
    And then go home to bed."
The little ones leaped and shouted and laughed;
    And all the hills echoéd.

WILLIAM BLAKE

Laughing Song

When the green woods laugh with the voice of joy,
And the dimpling stream runs laughing by;
When the air does laugh with our merry wit,
And the green hill laughs with the noise of it;

When the meadows laugh with lively green,
And the grasshopper laughs in the merry scene,
When Mary and Susan and Emily
With their sweet round mouths sing "Ha, Ha, He!"

When the painted birds laugh in the shade,
When our table with cherries and nuts is spread,
Come live and be merry, and join with me,
To sing the sweet chorus of "Ha, Ha, He!"

WILLIAM BLAKE

Robert Louis Stevenson was a sickly child; he had to spend much of his time indoors, often alone. He entertained himself by making up stories. Later on, his little world of make-believe grew into such famous books as Treasure Island *and* Kidnapped, *as well as* A Child's Garden of Verses, *from which* Pirate Story *and the next two poems are taken. They capture the secret life of childhood for everyone.*

The Land of Story-Books

At evening when the lamp is lit,
Around the fire my parents sit;
They sit at home and talk and sing,
And do not play at anything.

Now, with my little gun I crawl
All in the dark along the wall,
And follow round the forest track
Away behind the sofa back.

There, in the night, where none can spy,
All in my hunter's camp I lie,
And play at books that I have read
Till it is time to go to bed.

These are the hills, these are the woods,
These are my starry solitudes;
And there the river by whose brink
The roaring lions come to drink.

I see the others far away.
As if in firelit camp they lay,
And I, like to an Indian scout,
Around their party prowled about.

So, when my nurse comes in for me,
Home I return across the sea,
And go to bed with backward looks
At my dear land of Story-Books.

ROBERT LOUIS STEVENSON

Escape at Bedtime

The lights from the parlor and kitchen shone out
   Through the blinds and the windows and bars;
And high overhead and all moving about,
   There were thousands of millions of stars.
There ne'er were such thousands of leaves on a tree,
   Nor of people in church or the park,
As the crowds of the stars that looked down upon me,
   And that glittered and winked in the dark.

The Dog, and the Plough, and the Hunter, and all,
   And the star of the sailor, and Mars,
These shone in the sky, and the pail by the wall
   Would be half full of water and stars.
They saw me at last, and they chased me with cries,
   And they soon had me packed into bed;
But the glory kept shining and bright in my eyes,
   And the stars going round in my head.

ROBERT LOUIS STEVENSON

It is obviously a girl who is speaking in the next poem, letting us in on what she dreams of doing if no one ever marries her. The author, by the way, was a celebrated nineteenth-century English painter.

If No One Ever Marries Me

If no one ever marries me—
   And I don't see why they should,
For nurse says I'm not pretty,
   And I'm seldom very good—

If no one ever marries me
   I shan't mind very much,
I shall buy a squirrel in a cage
   And a little rabbit-hutch;

I shall have a cottage near a wood,
   And a pony all my own,
And a little lamb, quite clean and tame,
   That I can take to town.

And when I'm getting really old—
   At twenty-eight or nine—
I shall buy a little orphan-girl
   And bring her up as mine.

LAWRENCE ALMA-TADEMA

13

Seven Times One

There's no dew left on the daisies and clover,
    There's no rain left in heaven.
I've said my "seven times" over and over:
    Seven times one are seven.

I am old—so old I can write a letter;
    My birthday lessons are done.
The lambs play always—they know no better;
    They are only one times one.

O Moon! in the night I have seen you sailing
    And shining so round and low.
You were bright—ah, bright—but your light is failing;
    You are nothing now but a bow.

You Moon! have you done something wrong in heaven,
    That God has hidden your face?
I hope, if you have, you will soon be forgiven,
    And shine again in your place.

O velvet Bee! you're a dusty fellow—
    You've powdered your legs with gold.
O brave marsh Mary-buds, rich and yellow,
    Give me your money to hold!

O Columbine! open your folded wrapper,
    Where two twin turtle-doves dwell!
O Cuckoo-pint! tell me the purple clapper
    That hangs in your clear green bell!

And show me your nest, with the young ones in it—
    I will not steal them away;
I am old, you may trust me, linnet, linnet!
    I am seven times one to-day.

JEAN INGELOW

14

In the beginning there must have been elves. The young world seems to have been full of pixies and fairies, goblins and wizards. Long after we have stopped believing in their actual existence, we still delight in the thought of their free and fantastic activities.

The Elf Singing

An Elf sat on a twig,
He was not very big,
He sang a little song,
He did not think it wrong;
But he was on a Wizard's ground,
Who hated all sweet sound.

Elf, Elf,
Take care of yourself,
He's coming behind you,
To seize you and bind you
And stifle your song.
The Wizard! the Wizard!
He changes his shape
In crawling along.
An ugly old ape,
A poisonous lizard,

A spotted spider,
A wormy glider,
The Wizard! the Wizard!
He's up on the bough;
He'll bite through your gizzard.
He's close to you now!

The Elf went on with his song,
It grew more clear and strong,
    It lifted him into air,
    He floated singing away,
    With rainbows in his hair;
While the Wizard-worm from his creep
    Made a sudden leap,
    Fell down into a hole,
And, ere his magic word he could say,
    Was eaten up by a Mole.

The Elf and the Dormouse   WILLIAM ALLINGHAM

Under a toadstool
Crept a wee elf
Out of the rain
To shelter himself.

Under the toadstool
Sound asleep
Sat a big dormouse
All in a heap.

Trembled the wee elf
Frightened, and yet
Fearing to fly away
Lest he got wet.

To the next shelter
Maybe a mile!
Sudden the wee elf
Smiled a wee smile,

Tugged till the toadstool
Toppled in two,
Holding it over him
Gaily he flew.

Soon he was safe home,
Dry as could be;
Soon woke the dormouse—
"Good gracious me!

"Where is my toadstool?"
Loud he lamented.

And that's how umbrellas
First were invented.

OLIVER HERFORD

15

The Little Elf

I met a little Elf-man, once,
    Down where the lilies blow.
I asked him why he was so small,
    And why he didn't grow.

He slightly frowned, and with his eye
    He looked me through and through.
"I'm quite as big for me," said he,
    "As you are big for you."

JOHN KENDRICK BANGS

The writing of light verse is frequently a relief and a relaxation to the poet. Many writers have repeatedly turned from the difficult problems of their serious work to the ease of pleasant versifying. Thackeray, author of Vanity Fair *and other novels, was one of these. In* Fairy Days, *he writes about old times and uses old-fashioned words. A "palfrey" is a saddle-horse; "paynim" means pagan or heathen; a "falchion" is a short sword.*

Fairy Days

Beside the old hall-fire—upon my nurse's knee,
Of happy fairy days, what tales were told to me!
I thought the world was once all peopled with princesses,
And my heart would beat to hear their loves and their distresses;
And many a quiet night, in slumber sweet and deep,
The pretty fairy people would visit me in sleep.

I saw them in my dreams, come flying east and west,
With wondrous fairy gifts the new-born babe they blessed:
One has brought a jewel and one a crown of gold,
And one has brought a curse, but she is wrinkled and old.
The gentle queen turns pale to hear those words of sin,
But the king he only laughs and bids the dance begin.

The babe has grown to be the fairest of the land,
And rides the forest green, a hawk upon her hand,
An ambling palfrey white, a golden robe and crown;
I've seen her in my dreams, riding up and down,
And heard the ogre laugh, as she fell into his snare,
At the little tender creature who wept and tore her hair!

16

But ever when it seemed her need was at the sorest,
A prince in shining mail comes prancing through the forest,
A waving ostrich plume; a buckler burnished bright!
I've seen him in my dreams—good sooth! a gallant knight.
His lips are coral red beneath his dark moustache;
See how he waves his hand, and how his blue eyes flash!

"Come forth, thou paynim knight!" he shouts in accents clear.
The giant and the maid both tremble his voice to hear.
Saint Mary guard him well!—he draws his falchion keen,
The giant and the knight are fighting on the green.
I see them in my dreams—his blade gives stroke for stroke,
The giant pants and reels—and tumbles like an oak!

With what a blushing grace he falls upon his knee,
And takes the lady's hand and whispers, "You are free!"
Ah! happy childish tales, of knight and faerie!
I waken from my dreams—but there's ne'er a knight for me.
I waken from my dreams and wish that I could be
A child by the old hall-fire, upon my nurse's knee.

WILLIAM MAKEPEACE THACKERAY

Out of the fun and frolic of childhood have come countless jingles, including the old Mother Goose rhymes. On the streets and in the backwoods of America new and lively "play poems" are continually being made. Here are a few of what we might call American Father Gander.

American Father Gander

Cry-baby, cry;
Wipe your little eye;
Go tell your mammy
To give you a piece of pie.

* * *

Way down yonder in the maple swamp
The wild geese gather and the ganders honk.
The mares kick up and the ponies prance;
The old sow whistles and the little pigs dance.

Monkey was a-settin' on a railroad track,
Pickin' his teeth with a carpet tack;
The train came suddenly around the bend,
And the monkey reached his journey's end.

* * *

When I am the President
    Of these United States,
I'll eat up all the candy
    And swing on all the gates.

17

A little old man came riding by.
Said I, "Old man, your horse will die."
Said he, "If he dies I'll tan his skin,
And if he lives I'll ride him again."

*   *   *

Old Joe Brown, he had a wife,
  She was all of eight feet tall.
She slept with her head in the kitchen,
  And her feet stuck out in the hall.

*   *   *

I asked my mother for fifty cents
To see the elephant jump the fence.
He jumped so high he touched the sky
And never came back till the Fourth of July.

*   *   *

"What's your name?"
"Puddintame!
Ask me again and
I'll tell you the same!"

*   *   *

The boy stood on the burning deck
Eating peanuts by the peck.
His father called; he would not go,
Because he loved those peanuts so.

*   *   *

Every time I come to town
The boys all kick my dog around.
Makes no difference if he *is* a hound,
They gotta stop kicking my dog around.

*   *   *

Fishy-fishy in the brook
Daddy caught him with a hook;
Mammy fried him in the pan
And baby ate him like a man.

*   *   *

There was an old woman sat spinning—
And that's the beginning.
She had a calf—
And that's half.
The old woman started to sing;
The calf started to bawl.
And that's all.

Went to the river, couldn't get across,
Paid five dollars for an old gray hoss.
Hoss wouldn't pull so I traded for a bull.
Bull wouldn't holler so I traded for a dollar.
Dollar wouldn't pass so I threw it on the grass.
Grass wouldn't grow so I traded for a hoe.
Hoe wouldn't dig so I traded for a pig.
Pig wouldn't squeal so I traded for a wheel.
Wheel wouldn't run so I traded for a gun.
Gun wouldn't shoot so I traded for a boot.
Boot wouldn't fit so I thought I'd better quit.
So I quit.

*   *   *

Fuzzy Wuzzy was a bear,
  A bear was Fuzzy Wuzzy.
When Fuzzy Wuzzy lost his hair
  He wasn't fuzzy, was he?

*   *   *

All I need to make me happy:
Two little boys to call me Pappy;
One named Biscuit, the other named Gravy—
If I had another I'd call him Davy.

*   *   *

I'll eat when I'm hungry
And drink when I'm dry;
If a tree don't fall on me,
I'll live till I die.

*   *   *

The funniest sight that ever I saw
Was a little old man in Arkansaw.
He put his vest on over his coat,
And his britches were buttoned up over his throat.

*   *   *

There was an old man named Michael Finnegan,
A long beard grew out of his chin again—
Along came a wind and blew it right in again—
Poor old Michael Finnegan.

*   *   *

Jay-bird, jay-bird, settin' on a rail,
Pickin' his teeth with the end of his tail;
Mulberry leaves and calico sleeves—
All school teachers are hard to please.

Frog Went A-Courtin'

Mr. Froggie went a-courtin' an' he did ride;
Sword and pistol by his side.

He went to Missus Mousie's hall,
Gave a loud knock and gave a loud call.

"Pray, Missus Mousie, air you within?"
"Yes, kind sir, I set an' spin."

He tuk Miss Mousie on his knee,
An' sez, "Miss Mousie, will ya marry me?"

Miss Mousie blushed an' hung her head,
"You'll have t'ask Uncle Rat," she said.

"Not without Uncle Rat's consent
Would I marry the Pres-i-dent."

Uncle Rat jumped up an' shuck his fat side,
To think his niece would be Bill Frog's bride.

Nex' day Uncle Rat went to town,
To git his niece a weddin' gown.

Whar shall the weddin' supper be?
'Way down yander in a holler tree.

First come in was a Bumble-bee,
Who danced a jig with Captain Flea.

Next come in was a Butterfly,
Sellin' butter very high.

An' when they all set down to sup,
A big gray goose come an' gobbled 'em all up.

An' this is the end of one, two, three,
The Rat an' the Mouse an' the little Froggie.

19

To be young is to be carefree—but also to be curious. No child can tell where curiosity may lead him...except from one "why" to another.

Questions at Night

Why
Is the sky?

What starts the thunder overhead?
Who makes the crashing noise?
Are the angels falling out of bed?
Are they breaking all their toys?

Why does the sun go down so soon?
Why do the night-clouds crawl
Hungrily up to the new-laid moon
And swallow it, shell and all?

If there's a Bear among the stars,
As all the people say,
Won't he jump over those pasture-bars
And drink up the Milky Way?

Does every star that happens to fall
Turn into a firefly?
Can't it ever get back to Heaven at all?
And why
Is the sky?

LOUIS UNTERMEYER

The Child's Hymn

We are poor and lowly born;
  With the poor we bide;
Labor is our heritage,
  Care and want beside.
What of this?—Our blesséd Lord
  Was of lowly birth,
And poor toiling fishermen
  Were His friends on earth!

We are ignorant and young,
  Simple children all;
Gifted with but humble powers,
  And of learning small.
What of this?—Our blesséd Lord
  Lovéd such as we;
How He blessed the little ones
  Sitting on His knee!

MARY HOWITT

RHYME WITH REASONS

There are many reasons for rhyme. Rhyme rounds out the rhythm with a pleasant sound. It punctuates the lines with music, little bells that ring in the mind. One sound furnishes the key to another — and it is this magic of rhyme that makes poetry easier to remember than prose. That is why, since earliest times, much wisdom was stored in little rhyming syllables, and people learned to say them when they wanted to recall how many days there were in each month, or weather signs, or homely proverbs, or bits of folklore, or merely counting-out rhymes...Whenever there was danger of forgetting the sense, the rhyme came to the rescue.

Signs, Seasons, and Sense

Thirty days hath September,
April, June, and November.
All the rest have thirty-one,
Except February alone,
Which has four and twenty-four
Till leap-year gives it one day more.

* * *

A sunshiny shower
Won't last an hour.

* * *

When the days begin to lengthen,
Then the cold begins to strengthen.

* * *

Rainbow at night
Is the sailor's delight;
Rainbow at morning,
Sailor, take warning!

* * *

Birds of a feather will flock together,
    And so will pigs and swine.
Rats and mice will have their choice,
    And so will I have mine.

* * *

Blue is true,
Yellow's jealous,
Green's forsaken,
Red's brazen,
White is love's breath,
And black is death.

* * *

Evening red and morning gray
Are the signs of a bonny day.
Evening gray and morning red
Bring down rain on the farmer's head.

* * *

Cocks crow in the morn
    To tell us to rise,
And he who lies late
    Will never be wise;
For early to bed
    And early to rise
Is the way to be healthy,
    And wealthy, and wise.

Needles and pins, needles and pins,
When a man marries his trouble begins.

* * *

Now you're married you must obey;
You must be true to all you say;
You must be kind; you must be good;
And keep your wife in kindling wood.

* * *

God made the bees,
    And the bees make honey.
The miller's man does all the work—
    But the miller makes the money.

* * *

I do not love thee, Doctor Fell,
    The reason why I cannot tell;
But this I know, I know full well:
    I do not love thee, Doctor Fell.

* * *

Mirror, mirror, tell me,
    Am I pretty or plain?
Or am I downright ugly
    And ugly to remain?
Shall I marry a gentleman?
    Shall I marry a clown?
Or shall I marry old Knives-and-Scissors
    Shouting through the town?

* * *

There was an old owl who lived in an oak;
The more he heard, the less he spoke.
The less he spoke, the more he heard.
Why aren't we like that wise old bird!

* * *

Small skill is gained by those who cling to ease;
The hardy sailor hails from stormy seas.

* * *

Monday's child is fair of face,
Tuesday's child is full of grace,
Wednesday's child is full of woe,
Thursday's child has far to go,
Friday's child is loving and giving,
Saturday's child works hard for its living,
And a child that's born on the Sabbath day
Is fair and wise and good and gay.

When clouds appear like rocks and towers,
The earth's refreshed by frequent showers.
If woolly fleeces spread the heavenly way,
No rain, be sure, disturbs the summer's day.

* * *

When the wind is in the East,
'Tis neither good for man nor beast;
When the wind is in the North,
The skillful fisher goes not forth;
When the wind is in the South,
It blows the bait in the fishes' mouth;
When the wind is in the West,
Then 'tis at the very best.

* * *

One, two,
Buckle my shoe;
Three, four,
Shut the door;
Five, six,
Pick up sticks;
Seven, eight,
Lay them straight;
Nine, ten,
A big fat hen;
Eleven, twelve,
Who will delve?
Thirteen, fourteen,
Maids a-courting;
Fifteen, sixteen,
Maids a-kissing;
Seventeen, eighteen,
Maids a-waiting;
Nineteen, twenty,
My stomach's empty.

* * *

St. Swithin's Day, if thou dost rain,
  For forty days it will remain;
St. Swithin's Day, if thou be fair,
  For forty days 'twill rain nae mair.

* * *

See a pin and pick it up,
All the day you'll have good luck.
See a pin and let it lie,
You'll be sorry by and by.

Winter's thunder
Is the world's wonder.

* * *

Rain before seven,
Clear by eleven.

* * *

March winds and April showers
Bring forth May flowers.

* * *

If bees stay at home,
Rain will soon come.
If they fly away,
Fine will be the day.

* * *

Multiplication is vexation,
Division is as bad;
The Rule of Three it puzzles me,
And Fractions drive me mad.

* * *

Matthew, Mark, Luke and John,
Bless the bed that I lay on;
Four corners to my bed,
Four angels round my head,
One to watch and one to pray,
And two to bear my soul away.

* * *

I see the moon,
And the moon sees me.
God bless the moon,
And God bless me.

23

Hours of Sleep

Nature needs five;
Custom takes seven;
Laziness takes nine;
And wickedness eleven.

The Difference

'Twixt optimist and pessimist
    The difference is droll:
The optimist sees the doughnut;
    The pessimist sees the hole.

Pedigree

The pedigree of honey
Does not concern the bee;
A clover, any time, to him
Is aristocracy.

EMILY DICKINSON

Comparisons

As wet as a fish—as dry as a bone;
As live as a bird—as dead as a stone;
As plump as a partridge—as poor as a rat;
As strong as a horse—as weak as a cat;
As hard as a flint—as soft as a mole;
As white as a lily—as black as a coal;
As plain as a staff—as rough as a bear;
As light as a drum—as free as the air;
As heavy as lead—as light as a feather;
As steady as time—uncertain as weather;
As hot as an oven—as cold as a frog;
As gay as a lark—as sick as a dog;
As savage as tigers—as mild as a dove;
As stiff as a poker—as limp as a glove;
As blind as a bat—as deaf as a post;
As cool as a cucumber—as warm as toast;
As flat as a flounder—as round as a ball;
As blunt as a hammer—as sharp as an awl;
As brittle as glass—as tough as gristle;
As neat as a pin—as clean as a whistle;
As red as a rose—as square as a box;
As bold as a thief—as sly as a fox.

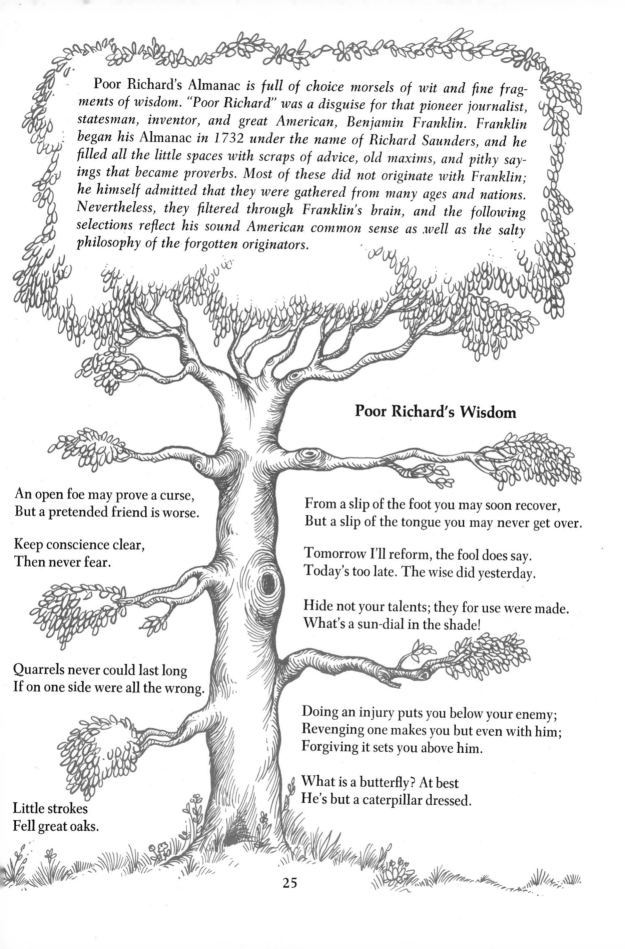

Poor Richard's Almanac *is full of choice morsels of wit and fine fragments of wisdom. "Poor Richard" was a disguise for that pioneer journalist, statesman, inventor, and great American, Benjamin Franklin. Franklin began his* Almanac *in 1732 under the name of Richard Saunders, and he filled all the little spaces with scraps of advice, old maxims, and pithy sayings that became proverbs. Most of these did not originate with Franklin; he himself admitted that they were gathered from many ages and nations. Nevertheless, they filtered through Franklin's brain, and the following selections reflect his sound American common sense as well as the salty philosophy of the forgotten originators.*

Poor Richard's Wisdom

An open foe may prove a curse,
But a pretended friend is worse.

Keep conscience clear,
Then never fear.

Quarrels never could last long
If on one side were all the wrong.

Little strokes
Fell great oaks.

From a slip of the foot you may soon recover,
But a slip of the tongue you may never get over.

Tomorrow I'll reform, the fool does say.
Today's too late. The wise did yesterday.

Hide not your talents; they for use were made.
What's a sun-dial in the shade!

Doing an injury puts you below your enemy;
Revenging one makes you but even with him;
Forgiving it sets you above him.

What is a butterfly? At best
He's but a caterpillar dressed.

Take this remark from Richard, poor and lame,
Whate'er's begun in anger, ends in shame.

He that goes a-borrowing
Soon goes a-sorrowing.

Vessels large may venture more,
But little boats should keep near shore.

If you would reap praise, sow the seeds:
Gentle words and useful deeds.

Haste
Makes waste.

When you're an anvil, hold still.
When you're a hammer, strike your fill!

BENJAMIN FRANKLIN

The following four rhymes to remember have serious titles and contain serious ideas. Don't be alarmed by them. You don't have to take them too seriously. The author didn't.

Let Others Share

Let others share your toys, my son,
Do not insist on *all* the fun.
For if you do it's certain that
You'll grow to be an adult brat.

Character Building

Spanking is something that must go,
Say some psychologists, although
Character building is a feat
Sometimes accomplished through the seat.

Duty of the Student

It is the duty of the student
Without exception to be prudent.
If smarter than his teacher, tact
Demands that he conceal the fact.

Advice to Small Children

Eat no green apples or you'll droop,
Be careful not to get the croup,
Avoid the chicken-pox and such,
And don't fall out of windows much.

EDWARD ANTHONY

CREATURES OF EVERY KIND

Man has always shared the world with creatures of every kind, and he has learned to love them. In the pages of the Bible—in the midst of the book of Job—God reveals the mystery of creation and the wonder of living things: the wild goats bearing their young among the cruel rocks, the proud peacock warming her eggs in the dust, the ravens fed by a miracle, the lonely eagle, lord of the sky, the hippopotamus with his tail "like a cedar," the monstrous Leviathan, a marvel and a mystery. Perhaps Job's most vivid tribute is this majestic picture of the horse, who "rejoiceth in his strength" and whose neck is "clothed with thunder."

27

The Horse

Hast thou given the horse strength?
Hast thou clothed his neck with thunder?
Canst thou make him afraid as a grasshopper?
The glory of his nostrils is terrible.
He paweth in the valley and rejoiceth in his strength:
He goeth to meet the armed men;
He mocketh at fear and is not affrighted,
Neither turneth he back from the sword.
The quiver rattleth against him,
The glittering spear and the shield—
He swalloweth the ground with fierceness and rage,
Neither believeth he that it is the sound of the trumpet—
He saith among the trumpets, "Ha! ha!"
And he smelleth the battle afar off,
The thunder of the captains, and the shouting.

The Bible: Job, 39

In the play, King Henry V, *Shakespeare writes with pure eloquence about the beauty and power of the horse. In Shakespeare's words, the horse becomes another Pegasus, that flying steed who makes the earth sing when he touches it and whose hoofs beat out a god-like music. Although the description is fantastically poetic, it suggests the thrill that any rider feels as his mount gallops down the road and across the landscape.*

The Horse

I will not change my horse with any that treads...
When I bestride him, I soar, I am a hawk.
He trots the air; the earth sings when he touches it.
The basest horn of his hoof is more musical than the pipe of Hermes...
He's of the color of the nutmeg and of the heat of the ginger...
He is pure air and fire, and the dull elements
Of earth and water never appear in him,
But only in patient stillness while his rider mounts him...
It is the prince of palfreys. His neigh is like
The bidding of a monarch, and his countenance
Enforces homage.

WILLIAM SHAKESPEARE

A far different horse appears in The Runaway. *This is a young American breed, a Morgan, raised in Vermont, a few miles from the farm of the poet, Robert Frost. Typically New England is the picture of the mountain pasture with the first snowfall which strikes Vermont sometimes as early as September. Startled, the little colt, who has never known snow and is not "winter-broken," "shudders his coat" as if to shrug off the white and coldly stinging flies. A restrained tenderness concludes the poem as the speaker hopes that someone will notice the plight of the frightened little Morgan and will "come and take him in."*

The Runaway

Once when the snow of the year was beginning to fall,
We stopped by a mountain pasture to say, "Whose colt?"
A little Morgan had one forefoot on the wall,
The other curled at his breast. He dipped his head
And snorted at us. And then he had to bolt.
We heard the miniature thunder where he fled,
And we saw him, or thought we saw him, dim and grey
Like a shadow against the curtain of falling flakes.
"I think the little fellow's afraid of the snow.
He isn't winter-broken. It isn't play
With the little fellow at all. He's running away.
I doubt if even his mother could tell him, 'Sakes,
It's only weather.' He'd think she didn't know!
Where is his mother? He can't be out alone."
And now he comes again with a clatter of stone,
And mounts the wall again with whited eyes
And all his tail that isn't hair up straight.
He shudders his coat as if to throw off flies.
"Whoever it is that leaves him out so late,
When other creatures have gone to stall and bin,
Ought to be told to come and take him in."

ROBERT FROST

29

Near the end of The Rime of the Ancient Mariner, *the author, Samuel Taylor Coleridge, has the speaker declare:*

> He prayeth best who loveth best
> All things both great and small;
> For the dear God who loveth us,
> He made and loveth all.

Nature, like the God of Nature, makes no distinction between great and small. Even the littlest things have their own way of surviving: the industrious ants that learn to store their food for the winter, the conies (or rabbits) that make homes for themselves in the stoniest fields, the locusts whose strength is in their numbers, the fragile spiders spinning their powerful webs.

Four Things

There be four things which are little upon the earth, but they are exceeding wise:

The ants are a people not strong, yet they prepare their meat in the summer;

The conies are but a feeble folk, yet they make their houses in the rocks;

The locusts have no king, yet go they forth all of them by bands.

The spider taketh hold with her hands, and is in kings' palaces.

The Bible: PROVERBS, 30

Although A. A. Milne has written serious novels, plays, and even murder mysteries, he is best known as the creator of an unreal animal, Winnie-the-Pooh. Even when this author deals with real creatures, he gives them a touch of oddity never found in any zoo.

The Four Friends

Ernest was an elephant, a great big fellow,
  Leonard was a lion with a six-foot tail,
George was a goat, and his beard was yellow,
  And James was a very small snail.

Leonard had a stall, and a great big strong one,
  Ernest had a manger, and its walls were thick,
George found a pen, but I think it was the wrong one,
  And James sat down on a brick.

Ernest started trumpeting, and cracked his manger,
　　Leonard started roaring, and shivered his stall,
James gave the huffle of a snail in danger
　　And nobody heard him at all.

Ernest started trumpeting and raised such a rumpus,
　　Leonard started roaring and trying to kick,
James went a journey with the goat's new compass
　　And he reached the end of his brick.

Ernest was an elephant and very well-intentioned,
　　Leonard was a lion with a brave new tail,
George was a goat, as I think I have mentioned,
　　But James was only a snail.

A. A. Milne

Here is a poem about four animals that is utterly different from Milne's amusing lines about the four queer friends. Four Little Foxes is filled with tenderness, and is a suspenseful short story that makes the reader hope for a happy ending.

Four Little Foxes

Speak gently, Spring, and make no sudden sound;
For in my windy valley yesterday I found
New-born foxes squirming on the ground—
　　　　Speak gently.

Walk softly, March, forbear the bitter blow;
Her feet within a trap, her blood upon the snow,
The four little foxes saw their mother go—
　　　　Walk softly.

Go lightly, Spring, Oh, give them no alarm;
When I covered them with boughs to shelter them from harm,
The thin blue foxes suckled at my arm—
　　　　Go lightly.

Step softly, March, with your rampant hurricane;
Nuzzling one another, and whimpering with pain,
The new little foxes are shivering in the rain—
　　　　Step softly.

Lew Sarett

31

Song-stories about foxes have been made up by many ballad singers. One ballad in particular has been favored ever since it was composed a century ago in the south of England by some now-forgotten minstrel. The song traveled across the water, took a native twist, and many generations of Americans have listened with pleasure to the tale of the fearless fox and his raid on the poultry-yard of Mother Slipper-Slopper (sometimes known as Old Mother Flipper-Flopper), and of his successful return to his hungry children.

Ballad of the Fox

A fox went out one chilly night,
And he begged of the moon to give him light
For he'd a long way to trot that night
Before he could reach his den, O.

At first he came to the farmer's fence
Where the hedge was thick and the shadows dense
He saw the barns, and he hied him hence
All on a summer's night, O.

He took the gray goose by the sleeve.
Says he: "Madam Goose, by your gracious leave
I'll take you away, I do believe,
And carry you home to my den, O."

He seized the black duck by the neck
And swung her back across his back;
The black duck cried out: "Quack, quack, quack,"
With her legs hanging dangling a-down, O.

Then Old Mother Slipper-Slopper jumped out of b
And out of the window she popped her head:
"John! John! the gray goose is gone,
And the fox is off to his den, O."

Then John went up to the top of the hill
And he blew a blast both loud and shrill.
Says the fox: "The music is pretty; still
I'd rather be in my den, O."

At last the fox got home to his den,
To his dear little foxes eight, nine, ten;
Says he: "You're in luck; here's a good fat duck
With her legs hanging dangling a-down, O."

He then sat down with his hungry wife
(And they did very well, with no fork and knife);
They never ate better duck in their life
In their snug little foxes' den, O.

32

Wolves have always been feared by men; legends have told of their fierce hate and savage hunger. But here is a situation where a man and beast were thrown together—and forgot they were enemies. This story may recall to you the ancient tale of Romulus and Remus who were nursed by a wolf, and Rudyard Kipling's Mowgli, who was brought up in the jungle by Mother Wolf and her cubs.

A Night with a Wolf

High up on the lonely mountains,
    Where the wild men watched and waited;
Wolves in the forest, and bears in the bush,
    And I on my path belated.

The rain and the night together
    Came down, and the wind came after,
Bending the props of the pine-tree roof,
    And snapping many a rafter.

I crept along in the darkness,
    Stunned, and bruised, and blinded;
Crept to a fir with thick-set boughs,
    And a sheltering rock behind it.

There, from the blowing and raining,
    Crouching, I sought to hide me.
Something rustled; two green eyes shone;
    And a wolf lay down beside me!

His wet fur pressed against me;
    Each of us warmed the other;
Each of us felt, in the stormy dark,
    That beast and man were brother.

And when the falling forest
    No longer crashed in warning,
Each of us went from our hiding place
    Forth in the wild, wet morning.

BAYARD TAYLOR

33

The lamb, the mildest of creatures, is the subject of the two following famous poems. Each considers the lamb in an entirely different way. In the first, it becomes the symbol of all that is gentle and pure, a synonym for the love of Jesus and of his Father. In the second, it is shown as the familiar pet, childhood's devoted companion.

The Lamb

Little lamb, who made thee?
  Dost thou know who made thee,
Gave thee life, and made thee feed
By the stream and o'er the mead?
Gave thee clothing of delight,
Softest clothing, woolly, bright?
Gave thee such a tender voice,
Making all the vales rejoice?
  Little lamb, who made thee?
  Dost thou know who made thee,

  Little lamb, I'll tell thee;
  Little lamb, I'll tell thee:
He is calléd by thy name,
For He calls Himself a lamb.
He is meek, and He is mild;
He became a little child:
I a child, and thou a lamb,
We are calléd by His name.
  Little lamb, God bless thee!
  Little lamb, God bless thee!

WILLIAM BLAKE

Mary's Lamb

Mary had a little lamb,
  Its fleece was white as snow;
And everywhere that Mary went,
  The lamb was sure to go.

He followed her to school one day—
  That was against the rule;
It made the children laugh and play,
  To see a lamb at school.

So the teacher turned him out,
  But still he lingered near,
And waited patiently about,
  Till Mary did appear.

Then he ran to her, and laid
  His head upon her arm,
As if he said, "I'm not afraid—
  You'll keep me from all harm."

"What makes the lamb love Mary so?"
  The eager children cry.
"Oh, Mary loves the lamb, you know,"
  The teacher did reply.

SARAH JOSEPHA HALE

34

Young Lambs

The spring is coming by a many signs;
The trays are up, the hedges broken down
That fenced the haystack, and the remnant shines
Like some old antique fragment weathered brown.
And where suns peep, in every sheltered place,
The little early buttercups unfold
A glittering star or two—till many trace
The edges of the blackthorn clumps in gold.
And then a little lamb bolts up behind
The hill, and wags his tail to meet the yoe;[1]
And then another, sheltered from the wind,
Lies all his length as dead—and lets me go
Close by, and never stirs, but basking lies,
With legs stretched out as though he could not rise.

yoe: ewe

JOHN CLARE

William Blake's The Lamb *represents everything that is mild and loving.* The Tiger *is its opposite, a symbol of force, savagery, and almost terrifying power. Yet Blake finds the lamb and the tiger equally beautiful works of God, both framed by the "immortal hand or eye."*

The Tiger

Tiger! Tiger! burning bright
In the forests of the night,
What immortal hand or eye
Could frame thy fearful symmetry?

In what distant deeps or skies
Burnt the fire of thine eyes?
On what wings dare he aspire?
What the hand dare seize the fire?

And what shoulder, and what art,
Could twist the sinews of thy heart?
And when thy heart began to beat,
What dread hand? and what dread feet?

What the hammer? what the chain?
In what furnace was thy brain?
What the anvil? what dread grasp
Dare its deadly terrors clasp?

When the stars threw down their spears
And watered heaven with their tears,
Did he smile his work to see?
Did he who made the Lamb make thee?

Tiger! Tiger! burning bright
In the forests of the night,
What immortal hand or eye
Dare frame thy fearful symmetry?

WILLIAM BLAKE

Nobody knows quite what the Leviathan was. He is mysteriously mentioned in the Bible, but he is never described. Perhaps he was a water-dragon, a fabulous whale, or some other enormous sea-monster. It is hard to think about the Leviathan without wonder or exaggeration.

Leviathan

God's deathless plaything rolls an eye
Five hundred thousand cubits high.
The smallest scale upon his tail
Could hide six dolphins and a whale.
His nostrils breathe, and on the spot
The churning waves turn seething hot.
If he be hungry, one huge fin

Drives seven thousand fishes in;
And when he drinks what he may need,
The rivers of the earth recede.
Yet he is more than huge and strong—
Twelve brilliant colors play along
His sides until, compared to him,
The naked, burning sun seems dim.

LOUIS UNTERMEYER

We know that the camel is remarkably adapted to his life in dry, sun-baked countries. He can travel as much as fifty miles a day over burning sands and go five days without water. Man, who uses their patient "ship of the desert" as a steed and a beast of burden, has reason to be grateful that the camel is constructed the way he is. But is the camel grateful? This might be his wry reply.

The Camel's Lament

"Canary-birds feed on sugar and seed,
    Parrots have crackers to crunch;
And as for the poodles, they tell me the noodles
    Have chickens and cream for their lunch.
      But there's never a question
      About MY digestion—
Anything does for me!

"Cats, you're aware, can repose in a chair,
    Chickens can roost upon rails;
Puppies are able to sleep in a stable,
    And oysters can slumber in pails.
      But no one supposes
      A poor Camel dozes—
Any place does for me!

"Lambs are enclosed where it's never exposed.
    Coops are constructed for hens;
Kittens are treated to houses well heated,
    And pigs are protected by pens.
      But a Camel comes handy
      Wherever it's sandy—
Anywhere does for me!

"People would laugh if you rode a giraffe,
    Or mounted the back of an ox;
It's nobody's habit to ride on a rabbit,
    Or try to bestraddle a fox.
      But as for a Camel, he's
      Ridden by families—
Any load does for me!

"A snake is as round as a hole in the ground,
    And weasels are wavy and sleek;
And no alligator could ever be straighter
    Than lizards that live in a creek,
      But a Camel's all lumpy
      And bumpy and humpy—
ANY shape does for me!"

CHARLES EDWARD CARRYL

The Rhinoceros

The Rhino is a homely beast,
For human eyes he's not a feast,
But you and I will never know
Why Nature chose to make him so.
Farewell, farewell, you old rhinoceros,
I'll stare at something less prepoceros.

OGDEN NASH

37

The dog, says everyone, is man's best friend. But Ogden Nash says it better—and funnier. Nash does everything differently. He entertains readers with odd sentences and startles them with queer rhymes. In order to make two unlikely words rhyme, he mangles one of them or makes up an entirely new word. In the previous poems, for example, he takes liberties with the word "preposterous" so that it appears to rhyme with "rhinoceros."

Who else but Nash could couple "hideaways" with "sideaways"!

An Introduction to Dogs

The dog is man's best friend.
He has a tail on one end.
Up in front he has teeth.
And four legs underneath.

Dogs like to bark.
They like it best after dark.
They not only frighten prowlers away
But also hold the sandman at bay.

A dog that is indoors
To be let out implores.
You let him out and what then?
He wants back in again.

Dogs display reluctance and wrath
If you try to give them a bath.
They bury bones in hideaways
And half the time they trot sideaways.

They cheer up people who are frowning,
And rescue people who are drowning,
They also track mud on beds,
And chew people's clothes to shreds.

Dogs in the country have fun.
They run and run and run.
But in the city this species
Is dragged around on leashes.

Dogs are upright as a steeple
And much more loyal than people.

OGDEN NASH

38

Harold Monro is another modern poet who does strange things with words. He does not, like Ogden Nash, distort them for humor. Instead, he combines them to give us a sharper sense of awareness. We feel how a dog must feel when we come across phrases like "four-legged brain of a walk-ecstatic dog" and "bed-delicious hours."

Dogs

O little friend, your nose is ready; you sniff,
Asking for that expected walk,
(Your nostrils full of the happy rabbit-whiff)
And almost talk..

And so the moment becomes a moving force;
Coats glide down from their pegs in the humble dark;
You scamper the stairs,
Your body informed with the scent and the track and the mark
Of stoats and weasels, moles and badgers and hares.

We are going *Out.* You know the pitch of the word,
Probing the tone of thought as it comes through fog
And reaches by devious means (half-smelt, half-heard)
The four-legged brain of a walk-ecstatic dog.

Out through the garden your head is already low.
You are going your walk, you know,
And your limbs will draw
Joy from the earth through the touch of your padded paw.

Now, sending a look to us behind,
Who follow slowly the track of your lovely play,
You fetch our bodies forward away from mind
Into the light and fun of your useless day.

HAROLD MONRO

Thus, for your walk, we took ourselves, and went
Out by the hedge, and tree, to the open ground.
You ran, in delightful strata of wafted scent,
Over the hill without seeing the view;
Beauty is hinted through primitive smells to you:
And that ultimate Beauty you track is but rarely found.

Home...and further joy will be waiting there:
Supper full of the lovely taste of bone,
You lift up your nose again, and sniff, and stare
For the rapture known
Of the quick wild gorge of food, then the still lie-down;
While your people will talk above you in the light
Of candles, and your dreams will merge and drown
Into the bed-delicious hours of night.

HAROLD MONRO

The effect the moon might have on a dog suggests dissimilar images to poets. Instead of the alarming intrusion of a silver moon, as in Dog at Night, *here a golden harvest moon seems, to an old hunting dog, like something to be tracked down and caught.*

The Old Coon-Dog Dreams

The moon...the moon...the moon...the moon—
a giant golden-furred raccoon—
    curls in the topmost crotch of a cottonwood.

I'll paw at the trunk and bay
till the Master comes that way,
    and swings his keen-edged ax as a woodsman should.

When the tree at last shall fall
and down comes 'coon and all,
    my jaws will have his life in three shakes or four!

Come, all you hunters! Soon
you'll see the pelt of the moon
    stretched broad and bright and proud on our smoke-house door!

KENNETH PORTER

40

Thomas Campbell, the author of My Dog Tray, *was not a "blithe Irish lad," but a Scotsman who lived most of his life—he was born in 1777— in England. And, far from being merry, he was considered rather grim by those who knew him. He was renowned not only for his poetry but for his absentmindedness. One evening he was invited to dine at a house near the tavern "The Green Man" at Dulwich. Instead of going there, Campbell went instead to Greenwich, where he looked vainly for the sign of "The Dull Man."*

My Dog Tray

On the green banks of Shannon when Sheelah was nigh,
No blithe Irish lad was so happy as I;
No harp like my own could so cheerily play,
And wherever I went was my poor dog Tray.

When at last I was forced from my Sheelah to part,
She said, (while the sorrow was big at her heart,)
Oh! remember your Sheelah when far, far away:
And be kind, my dear Pat, to our poor dog Tray.

Poor dog! he was faithful and kind to be sure,
And he constantly loved me although I was poor;
When the sour-looking folk sent me heartless away,
I had always a friend in my poor dog Tray.

When the road was so dark, and the night was so cold,
And Pat and his dog were grown weary and old,
How snugly we slept in my old coat of grey,
And he licked me for kindness—my old dog Tray.

Though my wallet was scant I remembered his case,
Nor refused my last crust to his pitiful face;
But he died at my feet on a cold winter day,
And I played a sad lament for my poor dog Tray.

Where now shall I go, poor, forsaken, and blind?
Can I find one to guide me, so faithful and kind?
To my sweet native village, so far, far away,
I can never more return with my poor dog Tray.

THOMAS CAMPBELL

Anyone who has lived in the country has heard one dog rousing another until the voices develop into a full orchestra of barking, bellowing, and baying. The next two poems are different impressions—at different times of the day—of this resounding effect.

Dog at Night

At first he stirs uneasily in sleep
And, since the moon does not run off, unfolds
Protesting paws. Grumbling that he must keep
Both eyes awake, he whimpers; then he scolds
And, rising to his feet, demands to know
The stranger's business. You who break the dark
With insolent light, who are you? Where do you go?
But nothing answers his indignant bark.
The moon ignores him, walking on as though
Dogs never were. Stiffened to fury now,
His small hairs stand upright, his howls come fast,
And terrible to hear is the bow-wow
That tears the night. Stirred by this bugle-blast,
The farmer's bitch grows active; without pause
Summons her mastiff and the hound that lies
Three fields away to rally to the cause.
And the next county wakes. And miles beyond
Throats tear themselves and brassy lungs respond
With threats, entreaties, bellowings and cries,
Chasing the white intruder down the skies.

LOUIS UNTERMEYER

Morning Overture: Chorus of Dogs

The cock had first performed and roused the dogs.
His saxophone had rent the whispering folds
Of country darkness. Up from east and west,
North, south, and in between the voices came
Of all the village dogs—the high, the low,
Deep-belled and lighter like a thin soprano
High up the scale; the feminine contralto
Of the she-collie, and the throaty tenor
Of an excited chow. The Saint Bernard
Added the minor notes. A spaniel flung
A recitative into the program. Then,
Full-chested baritone, the Belgian hound
Boomed a defiance to the world and set
The bulldog's bass. If I had only known
How to write music on that summer morn
I might have given you a thing to keep,
A fitting overture to such a day.

PEARL STRACHAN

42

Edward Anthony has put the characteristics of many breeds of dogs into light-hearted verse. The Bloodhound, The Collies, *and* The Dachshund *are from his collection punningly entitled* Every Dog Has His Say.

The Collies

In fiction tales we keep performing
Heroics that are most heart-warming.
We rescue babies left to smother
In burning houses. There's no other
Dog in the world so oft selected
To save the child that's unprotected.
We like that kind of reputation
Because it brings us adoration,
But wish that folks would not forget
We also like the role of pet
And love to stretch out on the floor,
And fall asleep and even snore,
And dream of canine heroes breezy
While we—by collie!—take life easy.

The Bloodhound

I am the dog world's best detective.
My sleuthing nose is so effective
I sniff the guilty at a distance
And then they lead a doomed existence.
My well-known record for convictions
Has earned me lots of maledictions
From those whose trail of crime I scented
And sent to prison, unlamented.
Folks either must avoid temptation
Or face my nasal accusation.

The Dachshund

Because I waddle when I walk,
Should this give rise to silly talk
That I'm ungainly? What's ungainly?
I'm really rather graceful—mainly.
The experts have been known to state
That there's a twinkle in our gait.
One said, "They have a clumsy grace,"
Which after all is no disgrace.

My funny features may abound:
Short legs, long body, low-to-ground,
But I'm about the perfect pal
For man or woman, boy or gal.
I'm gentle, very playful, kind,
I housebreak fast 'cause I'm refined,
I'm smart but never sly or foxy—
No, do not underrate the dachsie!

EDWARD ANTHONY

43

T. S. Eliot is one of the great writers of our day. His poems, plays, and essays have been praised throughout the world; he was awarded the Nobel Prize in 1948. Most of his work is extremely serious and, to many, extremely difficult. But when he writes about cats, he writes with liveliness and loving simplicity. His playful Old Possum's Book of Practical Cats includes amusing tributes to such favorite felines as Growltiger, Griddlebone, Old Deuteronomy, the mysterious Macavity, and the enterprising and exemplary Jennyanydots.

The Old Gumbie Cat

I have a Gumbie Cat in mind, her name is Jennyanydots;
Her coat is of the tabby kind, with tiger stripes and leopard spots.
All day she sits upon the stair or on the steps or on the mat:
She sits and sits and sits and sits—and that's what makes a Gumbie Cat!

But when the day's hustle and bustle is done,
Then the Gumbie Cat's work is but hardly begun.
And when all the family's in bed and asleep,
She tucks up her skirts to the basement to creep.

44

She is deeply concerned with the ways of the mice—
Their behavior's not good and their manners not nice;
So when she has got them lined up on the matting,
She teaches them music, crocheting and tatting.

I have a Gumbie Cat in mind, her name is Jennyanydots;
Her equal would be hard to find, she likes the warm and sunny spots.
All day she sits beside the hearth or on the bed or on my hat:
She sits and sits and sits and sits—and that's what makes a Gumbie Cat!

But when the day's hustle and bustle is done,
Then the Gumbie Cat's work is but hardly begun.
As she finds that the mice will not ever keep quiet,
She is sure it is due to irregular diet;
And believing that nothing is done without trying,
She sets right to work with her baking and frying.
She makes them a mouse-cake of bread and dried peas,
And a *beautiful* fry of lean bacon and cheese.

I have a Gumbie Cat in mind, her name is Jennyanydots;
The curtain-cord she likes to wind, and tie it into sailor-knots.
She sits upon the window-sill, or anything that's smooth and flat:
She sits and sits and sits and sits—and that's what makes a Gumbie Cat!

But when the day's hustle and bustle is done,
Then the Gumbie Cat's work is but hardly begun.
She thinks that the cockroaches just need employment
To prevent them from idle and wanton destroyment.
So she's formed, from that lot of disorderly louts,
A troop of well-disciplined helpful boy-scouts,
With a purpose in life and a good deed to do—
And she's even created a Beetles' Tattoo.

So for Old Gumbie Cats let us now give three cheers—
On whom well-ordered households depend, it appears.

T. S. ELIOT

Of all creatures, I prefer cats. That's one reason why there are more poems about cats in this section than about any other four-legged animal. Another reason is that there seem to be more charming cat poems written. This must be because the cat is a complex personality—beautiful to behold, lovely in motion, happy in front of any hearth, useful as a mouser, whimsical, teasing, perhaps fickle, but always fascinating.

In a long and curious poem entitled Rejoice in the Lamb *an eighteenth-century poet, Christopher Smart, went out of his way to tell how much his cat meant to him. In one particularly happy passage, where every line begins with "For," the poem sums up the virtues, the tricks, and the characteristics of the entire feline tribe.*

My Cat Jeoffry

For I will consider my cat Jeoffry.
For he is the servant of the Living God, duly and daily serving him . . .
For first he looks upon his fore-paws to see if they are clean.
For secondly he kicks up behind to clear away there.
For thirdly he works it upon stretch with the fore-paws extended.
For fourthly he sharpens his paws by wood.
For fifthly he washes himself.
For sixthly he rolls upon wash.
For seventhly he fleas himself, that he may not be interrupted upon the beat.
For eighthly he rubs himself against a post.
For ninthly he looks up for his instructions.
For tenthly he goes in quest of food.
For having considered God and himself he will consider his neighbor.
For if he meets another cat he will kiss her in kindness.
For when he takes his prey he plays with it to give it chance.
For one mouse in seven escapes by his dallying.
For when his day's work is done his business more properly begins.
For he keeps the Lord's watch in the night against the adversary.
For he counteracts the powers of darkness by his electrical skin and glaring
    eyes.
For he counteracts the Devil, who is death, by brisking about the life.
For in his morning orisons he loves the sun and the sun loves him.
For he is of the tribe of Tiger.
For the Cherub Cat is a term of the Angel Tiger.
For he has the subtlety and hissing of a serpent, which in goodness he
    suppresses.
For he will not do destruction if he is well-fed, neither will he spit without
    provocation.
For he purrs in thankfulness, when God tells him he's a good Cat.

CHRISTOPHER SMART

A few pages back you met Dog. *Its author, Harold Monro, a lover of every kind of creature, shows himself equally capable of understanding the mind and desires of a cat.*

Milk for the Cat

When the tea is brought at five o'clock,
And all the neat curtains are drawn with care,
The little black cat with bright green eyes
Is suddenly purring there.

At first she pretends, having nothing to do,
She has come in merely to blink by the grate,
But, though tea may be late or the milk may be sour,
She is never late.

And presently her agate eyes
Take a soft large milky haze,
And her independent casual glance
Becomes a stiff hard gaze.

Then she stamps her claws or lifts her ears
Or twists her tail and begins to stir,
Till suddenly all her little body becomes
One breathing trembling purr.

The children eat and wriggle and laugh;
The two old ladies stroke their silk:
But the cat is grown small and thin with desire,
Transformed to a creeping lust for milk.

The white saucer like some full moon descends
At last from the clouds of the table above;
She sighs and dreams and thrills and glows,
Transfigured with love.

She nestles over the shining rim,
Buries her chin in the creamy sea;
Her tail hangs loose; each drowsy paw
Is doubled under each bending knee.

A long dim ecstasy holds her life;
Her world is an infinite shapeless white,
Till her tongue has curled the last holy drop,
Then she sinks back into the night.

Draws and dips her body to heap
Her sleepy nerves in the great arm-chair,
Lies defeated and buried deep
Three or four hours unconscious there.

HAROLD MONRO

Little Pussy

I love little Pussy,
　Her coat is so warm;
And if I don't hurt her,
　She'll do me no harm.

So I'll not pull her tail,
　Nor drive her away,
But Pussy and I
　Very gently will play.

She shall sit by my side,
　And I'll give her some food;
And she'll love me, because
　I am gentle and good.

I'll pat little Pussy,
　And then she will purr,
And thus show her thanks
　For my kindness to her.

I'll not pinch her ears,
　Nor tread on her paw,
Lest I should provoke her
　To use her sharp claw.

I never will vex her,
　Nor make her displeased,
For Puss doesn't like
　To be worried or teased.

JANE TAYLOR

On a Night of Snow is a half-solemn, half-playful dialogue. The form of the poem is a sonnet, a fourteen-line structure, usually divided into eight and six lines. In the first eight lines, the cat's mistress pleads with her pet to remain indoors. The cat replies in the answering six lines. And, while it speaks, the little hearth kitten is transformed into the ancient cat of mystery, in league with dark and powerful spirits, "intoning strange lore," who call from the great unknown.

On a Night of Snow

Cat, if you go outdoors you must walk in the snow.
You will come back with little white shoes on your feet,
Little white slippers of snow that have heels of sleet.
Stay by the fire, my Cat. Lie still, do not go.
See how the flames are leaping and hissing low,
I will bring you a saucer of milk like a marguerite,
So white and so smooth, so spherical and so sweet—
Stay with me, Cat. Outdoors the wild winds blow.

Outdoors the wild winds blow, Mistress, and dark is the night.
Strange voices cry in the trees, intoning strange lore;
And more than cats move, lit by our eyes' green light,
On silent feet where the meadow grasses hang hoar—
Mistress, there are portents abroad of magic and might,
And things that are yet to be done. Open the door!

ELIZABETH COATSWORTH

48

Sinclair Lewis was an outstanding novelist; he was awarded the Nobel Prize in 1930 for his important contributions to literature. Few people know that, besides his close attachment to the American scene, he deeply loved two other things: poetry and cats. Some say that the kitten called "Cleo" is one of the best characters in his story, Cass Timberlane. The following poem, hitherto unpublished, was given to me, as a fellow cat-lover, by the novelist shortly before he died.

Cat

This is a cat that sleeps at night,
That takes delight
In visions bright,
And not a vagrant that creeps at night
On box-cars by the river.
This is a sleepy cat to purr
And rarely stir
Its shining fur;
This is a cat whose softest purr
Means salmon, steaks, and liver.

That is a cat respectable,
Connectable
With selectable
Feline families respectable,
Whose names would make you quiver.
That is a cat of piety,
Not satiety,
But sobriety.

Its very purr is of piety
And thanks to its Feline Giver.

And this is how it prays:

"Ancient of days
With whiskers torrendous,
Hark to our praise,
Lick and defend us.
Lo, how we bring to Thee
Sweet breasts of mouses;
Hark how we sing to Thee,
Filling all houses
With ardent miaouses,
Until it arouses
All mankind to battery.
Thou of the golden paws,
Thou of the silver claws,
Thy tail is the comets' cause,
King of all cattery!"

SINCLAIR LEWIS

Here is a thumb-nail (or should I say toe-nail?) portrait of all cats by one who has lovingly noted the habits of these tigers of the house. See how a California poet, Rosalie Moore, has observed the way they curl up in velvet balls to "sleep fat" or shrink themselves "to walk thin," and how they can fit themselves anywhere, whether it is in the narrowest opening or the most inconvenient box.

Catalog

Cats sleep fat and walk thin.
Cats, when they sleep, slump;
When they wake, pull in—
And where the plump's been
There's skin.
Cats walk thin.

Cats wait in a lump,
Jump in a streak.
Cats, when they jump, are sleek
As a grape slipping its skin—
They have technique.
Oh, cats don't creak.
They sneak.

Cats sleep fat.
They spread comfort beneath them
Like a good mat,
As if they picked the place
And then sat.
You walk around one
As if he were the City Hall
After that.

If male,
A cat is apt to sing upon a major scale:
This concert is for everybody, this
Is wholesale.
For a baton, he wields a tail.

(He is also found,
When happy, to resound
With an enclosed and private sound.)

A cat condenses.
He pulls in his tail to go under bridges,
And himself to go under fences.
Cats fit
In any size box or kit;
And if a large pumpkin grew under one,
He could arch over it.

When everyone else is just ready to go out,
The cat is just ready to come in.
He's not where he's been.
Cats sleep fat and walk thin.

ROSALIE MOORE

Here is another novelist who loved cats and poetry. Jan Struther, who wrote the immensely popular Mrs. Miniver, *expresses the curious notion that a cat might be alarmed by this thing called a soul which They, her owners, so often talk about.*

Cat

I am exceedingly rich:
    I have several toys.
Some of them are silent,
    Some make a noise.

Item, a scrap of string;
    A wooden spool;
Item, the loosened braid
    At the edge of a stool;

Item, a rustling leaf
    Which fell to the floor;
Item, a safety-pin
    Which one of Them wore.

Item, a pellet of paper,
    Brisk as a mouse—
All of the unwanted clutter
    Of a casual house.

And if these should be thrown away
    And all else fail,
I have, attached to me,
    My own proud tail;

Tail, Me and yet not Me,
    Tail beyond price,
Tail worth a dozen spools
    Or a hundred mice;

Tail unpredictable,
    Now gay, now serious;
Tail all familiar
    Yet all mysterious.

I lead a pleasant life;
    Toil not, nor spin.
In, I want swiftly out:
    Out, I want in.

They are my willing slaves:
    I have Them by the fur.
When He's off duty, I
    Just call for Her.

And yet, I sometimes feel
    A vague unease.
It is dangerous to dwell
    With such as These.

It seems They too possess,
    If toys should fail,
Some Thing as much Their own
    As this, my tail.

But Thing not safely joined
    To rippling spine—
A treasure less secure
    Than this of mine;

Thing which may one day steal
    From me, perhaps,
Their smoothly-stroking hands,
    Their useful laps.

They talk and talk; and I,
    Crouching and watching,
Think, with a dim disquiet,
    "Souls may be catching."

To live with such as These—
    Friends and yet strangers—
Has, for one of my race,
    Uncharted dangers.

And yet, what choice have I?
    A tamed, wild thing,
I live by Their bowls of milk,
    Their scraps of string.

So, if this strange disease
    Should take its toll,
And I should die, sick
    Of an unwanted soul,

This is my testament;
    To my successors
(Since *They,* being once possessed,
    Must stay possessors,)

I leave a scrap of string;
    A wooden spool;
I leave the loosened braid
    At the edge of a stool;

I leave a rustling leaf
    Which fell to the floor;
I leave a safety-pin
    Which one of Them wore;

I leave a pellet of paper,
    Brisk as a mouse—
All the unwanted clutter
    Of a casual house.

JAN STRUTHER

The Kitten Playing with the Falling Leaves

See the kitten on the wall
Sporting with the leaves that fall!
Withered leaves, one, two, and three,
From the lofty elder-tree.
Through the calm and frosty air
Of this morning bright and fair
Eddying round and round they sink
Softly, slowly.—One might think,
From the motions that are made,
Every little leaf conveyed
Some small fairy, hither tending,
To this lower world descending.
—But the kitten how she starts!
Crouches, stretches, paws, and darts:
First at one, and then its fellow,
Just as light, and just as yellow:
There are many now—now one—
Now they stop and there are none.
What intentness of desire
In her up-turned eye of fire!
With a tiger-leap half way,
Now she meets the coming prey.
Lets it go at last, and then
Has it in her power again.

WILLIAM WORDSWORTH

Country Cat

"Where are you going, Mrs. Cat,
  All by your lonesome lone?"
"Hunting a mouse, or maybe a rat
  Where the ditches are overgrown."

"But you're very far from your house and home,
  You've come a long, long way—"
"The further I wander, the longer I roam
  The more I find mice at play."

"But you're very near to the dark pinewood
  And foxes go hunting too."
"I know that a fox might find me good,
  But what is a cat to do?

I have my kittens who must be fed,
  I *can't* have them skin and bone!"
And Mrs. Cat shook her brindled head
  And went off by her lonesome lone.

ELIZABETH COATSWORTH

53

The Ad-Dressing of Cats

You've read of several kinds of Cat,
And my opinion now is that
You should need no interpreter
To understand their character.
You now have learned enough to see
That Cats are much like you and me
And other people whom we find
Possessed of various types of mind.
For some are sane and some are mad
And some are good and some are bad
And some are better, some are worse—
But all may be described in verse.
You've seen them both at work and games,
And learnt about their proper names,
Their habits and their habitat:
But
   How would you ad-dress a Cat?

So first, your memory I'll jog,
And say: A CAT IS NOT A DOG.

Now Dogs pretend they like to fight;
They often bark, more seldom bite;
But yet a Dog is, on the whole,
What you would call a simple soul.
Of course I'm not including Pekes,
And such fantastic canine freaks.
The usual Dog about the Town
Is much inclined to play the clown,
And far from showing too much pride
Is frequently undignified.
He's very easily taken in—
Just chuck him underneath the chin
Or slap his back or shake his paw,
And he will gambol and guffaw.
He's such an easy-going lout,
He'll answer any hail or shout.

Again I must remind you that
A Dog's a Dog—a CAT'S A CAT.

With Cats, some say, one rule is true:
Don't speak till you are spoken to.
Myself, I do not hold with that—
I say, you should ad-dress a Cat.
But always keep in mind that he
Resents familiarity.
I bow, and taking off my hat,
Ad-dress him in this form: O CAT!
But if he is the Cat next door,
Whom I have often met before
(He comes to see me in my flat)
I greet him with an OOPSA CAT!
I think I've heard them call him James—
But we've not got so far as names.

Before a Cat will condescend
To treat you as a trusted friend,
Some little token of esteem
Is needed, like a dish of cream;
And you might now and then supply
Some caviare, or Strassburg Pie,
Some potted grouse, or salmon paste—
He's sure to have his personal taste.
(I know a Cat, who makes a habit
Of eating nothing else but rabbit,
And when he's finished, licks his paws
So's not to waste the onion sauce.)
A Cat's entitled to expect
These evidences of respect.
And so in time you reach your aim,
And finally call him by his NAME.

So this is this, and that is that:
And there's how you AD-DRESS A CAT.

T. S. ELIOT

54

Marjory (christened Margaret) Fleming was a Scottish girl born in 1803. She died a few weeks before her ninth birthday. As soon as she could write, she began a diary and composed poems, including one on Mary, Queen of Scots. To a Monkey was written when she was seven. With its quaint misspellings and errors in grammar it has become a minor classic because of its charm and unconscious humor.

To a Monkey

O lovely O most charming pug
Thy gracefull air and heavenly mug
The beauties of his mind do shine
And every bit is shaped so fine
Your very tail is most devine
Your teeth is whiter than the snow
You are a great buck and a bow
Your eyes are of so fine a shape
More like a christains than an ape
His cheeks is like the roses blume
Your hair is like the ravens plume
His noses cast is of the roman
He is a very pretty weoman
I could not get a rhyme for roman
And was oblidged to call it weoman.

MARJORY FLEMING

The Rabbit

When they said the time to hide was mine,
I hid back under a thick grape vine.

And while I was still for the time to pass
A little gray thing came out of the grass.

He hopped his way through the melon bed
And sat down close by a cabbage head.

He sat down close where I could see,
And his big still eyes looked hard at me,

His big eyes bursting out of the rim,
And I looked back very hard at him.

ELIZABETH MADOX ROBERTS

Yak

The long-haired Yak has long black hair,
He lets it grow—he doesn't care.
He lets it grow and grow and grow,
He lets it trail along the stair.
Does he ever go to the barbershop? No!
How wild and woolly and devil-may-care
A long-haired Yak with long black hair
Would look when perched in a barber chair!

WILLIAM JAY SMITH

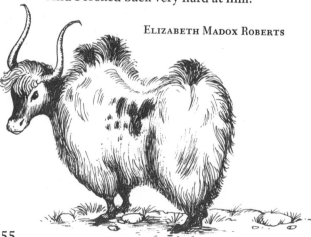

55

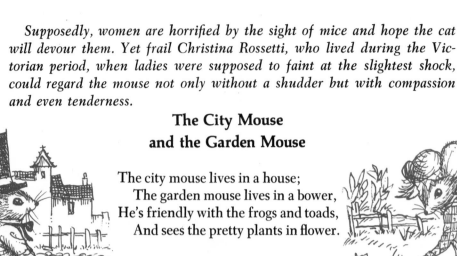

Supposedly, women are horrified by the sight of mice and hope the cat will devour them. Yet frail Christina Rossetti, who lived during the Victorian period, when ladies were supposed to faint at the slightest shock, could regard the mouse not only without a shudder but with compassion and even tenderness.

The City Mouse
and the Garden Mouse

The city mouse lives in a house;
   The garden mouse lives in a bower,
He's friendly with the frogs and toads,
   And sees the pretty plants in flower.

The city mouse eats bread and cheese;
   The garden mouse eats what he can;
We will not grudge him seeds and stalks,
   Poor little, timid, furry man.

Christina Georgina Rossetti

The Bat

By day the bat is cousin to the mouse;
He likes the attic of an aging house.

His fingers make a hat about his head.
His pulse-beat is so slow we think him dead.

He loops in crazy figures half the night
Among the trees that face the corner light.

But when he brushes up against a screen,
We are afraid of what our eyes have seen:

For something is amiss or out of place
When mice with wings can wear a human face.

Theodore Roethke

Opossum

Have you ever in your life seen a Possum play possum?
Have you ever in your life seen a Possum play dead?
When a Possum is trapped and can't get away
He turns up his toes and lays down his head,
Bats both his eyes and rolls over dead.
But then when you leave him and run off to play,
The Possum that really was just playing possum
Gets up in a flash and scurries away.

William Jay Smith

Ralph Waldo Emerson, one of the chief New England poets of the nineteenth century, called the following poem "A Fable." Just as Aesop made animals the characters in his fables, so Emerson lets the squirrel, familiarly called "Bun," talk—and talk back to a mountain.

The Mountain and the Squirrel

The mountain and the squirrel
Had a quarrel;
And the former called the latter "Little Prig."
Bun replied,
"You are doubtless very big;
But all sorts of things and weather
Must be taken in together,
To make up a year
And a sphere.
And I think it no disgrace
To occupy my place.
If I'm not so large as you,
You are not so small as I,
And not half so spry,
I'll not deny you make
A very pretty squirrel track;
Talents differ; all is well and wisely put;
If I cannot carry forests on my back,
Neither can you crack a nut."

RALPH WALDO EMERSON

The Squirrel

The squirrel, flippant, pert, and full of play,
Drawn from his refuge in some lonely elm
That age or injury hath hollowed deep,
Where, on his bed of wool and matted leaves,
He has out-slept the winter, ventures forth
To frisk awhile, and bask in the warm sun:
He sees me, and at once, swift as a bird,
Ascends the neighboring beech: there whisks his brush,
And perks his ears, and stamps, and cries aloud,
With all the prettiness of feigned alarm,
And anger insignificantly fierce.

WILLIAM COWPER

Poets have celebrated birds more often than any other of God's creatures. This is natural enough. Birds are known for their songs—and so are poets. Birds are winged symbols of flight and freedom—and poets, speaking for most men and women, have always sought liberty and have longed to leave the everyday world to soar into limitless space. The following poems bring together birds of many a feather, from the mighty eagle to the homely hen, from the common crow to the ruby-throated hummingbird and the flame-tipped oriole.

Bird at Dawn

What I saw was just one eye
In the dawn as I was going:
A bird can carry all the sky
In that little button glowing.

Never in my life I went
So deep into the firmament.

He was standing on a tree,
All in blossom overflowing;
And he purposely looked hard at me,
At first, as if to question merrily:
"Where are you going?"
But next some far more serious thing to say:
I could not answer, could not look away.

Oh, that hard, round, and so distracting eye:
Little mirror of all the sky!
And then the after-song another tree
Held, and sent radiating back on me.

If no man had invented human word,
And a bird-song had been
The only way to utter what we mean,
What would we men have heard,
What understood, what seen,
Between the trills and pauses, in between
The singing and the silence of a bird?

The Eagle

He clasps the crag with crooked hands:
Close to the sun in lonely lands,
Ringed with the azure world, he stands.

The wrinkled sea beneath him crawls;
He watches from his mountain walls,
And like a thunderbolt he falls.

ALFRED, LORD TENNYSON

HAROLD MONRO

58

The Blackbird

A slender young Blackbird built in a thorn-tree,
A spruce little fellow as ever could be;
His bill was so yellow, his feathers so black,
So long was his tail, and so glossy his back,
That good Mrs. B., who sat hatching her eggs,
And only just left them to stretch her poor legs,
And pick for a minute the worm she preferred,
Thought there never was seen such a beautiful bird.

And such a kind husband! How early and late
He would sit at the top of the old garden gate,
And sing, just as merry as if it were June,
Being ne'er out of patience, or temper, or tune.
"So unlike those rooks, dear; from morning till night
They seem to do nothing but quarrel and fight,
And wrangle and jangle, and plunder—while we
Sit, honest and safe, in our pretty thorn-tree."

"O dear Mrs. Blackbird," in turn warbled he,
"How happy we are in our humble thorn-tree.
How gayly we live, living honest and poor;
How sweet are the May blossoms over our door."
"And then our dear children," the mother replied,
As she nestled them close to her warm feathered side.
And with a soft twitter of drowsy content,
In the quiet May moonlight to sleep they all went.

DINAH MULOCK CRAIK

Oriole

How falls it, oriole, thou hast come to fly
In tropic splendor through our Northern sky?
At some glad moment was it nature's choice
To dower a scrap of sunset with a voice?
Or did some orange tulip, flaked with black,
In some forgotten garden, ages back,
Yearning toward Heaven until its wish was heard,
Desire unspeakably to be a bird?

EDGAR FAWCETT

Emily Dickinson was born in 1830 in Amherst, Massachusetts, lived there all her life, never married, and died, practically unknown, in 1886. She wrote eighteen hundred poems, scribbled them on small scraps of paper, on the backs of recipes, on brown paper bags from the grocer, and hid them away. Only seven were published during her lifetime. Today she is recognized as one of the most daring and original of poets. The form of her poetry is simple enough, but the rhymes and the images are startling. "A route of evanescence," for example, immediately pictures the darting flight of the hummingbird which disappears almost as soon as it is seen. Its incredibly fast wings whir like "a revolving wheel." The green of its back is so brilliant that it appears to vibrate like sound—"a resonance of emerald"—and its ruby throat is so vivid that it seems to be a flash of "cochineal," a scarlet dye. If, as the poet imagines, this tiny bird could carry a letter, it could bring it from Tunis, half-way around the world, in a couple of hours.

The Hummingbird

A route of evanescence
With a revolving wheel;
A resonance of emerald,
A rush of cochineal;
And every blossom on the bush
Adjusts its tumbled head—
The mail from Tunis, probably,
An easy morning's ride.

EMILY DICKINSON

The Robin and the Cows

The robin sings in the elm;
    The cattle stand beneath,
Sedate and grave with great brown eyes,
    And fragrant meadow-breath.

They listen to the flattered bird,
    The wise-looking, stupid things!
And they never understand a word
    Of all the robin sings.

WILLIAM DEAN HOWELLS

Bob White

There's a plump little chap in a speckled coat,
And he sits on the zigzag rails remote,
Where he whistles at breezy, bracing morn,
When the buckwheat is ripe, and stacked is the corn
    "Bob White!   Bob White!   Bob White!"

Is he hailing some comrade as blithe as he?
Now I wonder where Robert White can be!
O'er the billows of gold and amber grain
There is no one in sight—but, hark again:
    "Bob White!   Bob White!   Bob White!"

Ah! I see why he calls; in the stubble there
Hide his plump little wife and babies fair!
So contented is he, and so proud of the same,
That he wants all the world to know his name,
    "Bob White!   Bob White!   Bob White!"

GEORGE COOPER

60

The Skylark

The earth was green, the sky was blue:
   I saw and heard one sunny morn
A skylark hang between the two,
   A singing speck above the corn;

A stage below, in gay accord,
   White butterflies danced on the wing,
And still the singing skylark soared,
   And silent sank, and soared to sing.

The cornfield stretched a tender green
   To right and left beside my walks;
I knew he had a nest unseen
   Somewhere among the million stalks.

And as I paused to hear his song,
   While swift the sunny moments slid,
Perhaps his mate sat listening long,
   And listened longer than I did.

CHRISTINA GEORGINA ROSSETTI

William Wordsworth, born in England in 1770, is considered one of the great nature poets; he has even been called the poet of nature. You have already read one of his poems, The Kitten Playing with the Falling Leaves, *and you will find a number of others in these pages.* To the Cuckoo *illustrates several of Wordsworth's characteristics: his descriptive power, his singing sense of delight, and his easy, almost conversational manner.*

To the Cuckoo

O blithe new-comer! I have heard,
   I hear thee and rejoice.
O cuckoo! shall I call thee bird,
   Or but a wandering voice?

While I am lying on the grass
   Thy twofold shout I hear;
From hill to hill it seems to pass,
   At once far off and near.

Though babbling only to the vale
   Of sunshine and of flowers,
Thou bringest unto me a tale
   Of visionary hours.

Thrice welcome, darling of the spring!
   Even yet thou art to me
No bird, but an invisible thing,
   A voice, a mystery;

The same whom in my school-boy days
   I listened to; that cry
Which made me look a thousand ways,
   In bush and tree and sky.

To seek thee did I often rove
   Through woods and on the green;
And thou wert still a hope, a love;
   Still longed for, never seen.

And I can listen to thee yet;
   Can lie upon the plain
And listen, till I do beget
   That golden time again.

O blesséd bird! the earth we pace
   Again appears to be
An unsubstantial, fairy place;
   That is fit home for thee!

WILLIAM WORDSWORTH

Although Cock Robin *is often included among nursery rhymes, it is more than a mere jingle. It is a set of verses which tells a little story and which, at the same time, characterizes various creatures in a light but memorable way.*

Cock Robin

Who killed Cock Robin?
  "I," said the Sparrow,
  "With my bow and arrow,
I killed Cock Robin."

Who saw him die?
  "I," said the Fly,
  "With my little eye,
I saw him die."

Who'll be the parson?
  "I," said the Rook,
  "With my little book.
I'll be the parson."

Who'll be the clerk?
  "I," said the Lark,
  "I'll say Amen in the dark;
I'll be the clerk."

Who caught his blood?
  "I," said the Fish,
  "With my little dish,
I caught his blood."

Who'll make his shroud?
  "I," said the Beetle,
  "With my thread and needle,
I'll make his shroud."

Who'll dig his grave?
  "I," said the Owl,
  "With my spade and trowel,
I'll dig his grave."

Who'll be chief mourner?
  "I," said the Dove,
  "I mourn for my love;
I'll be chief mourner."

Who'll bear the torch?
  "I," said the Linnet,
  "I'll come in a minute,
I'll bear the torch."

Who'll sing his dirge?
  "I," said the Thrush,
  "As I sing in the bush
I'll sing his dirge."

Who'll bear the pall?
  "We," said the Wren,
  Both the Cock and the Hen;
"We'll bear the pall."

Who'll carry his coffin?
  "I," said the Kite,
  "If it be in the night,
I'll carry his coffin."

Who'll toll the bell?
  "I," said the Bull,
  "Because I can pull,
I'll toll the bell."

All the birds of the air
  Fell to sighing and sobbing
When they heard the bell toll
  For poor Cock Robin.

The Thrush's Song

Dear, dear, dear,
In the rocky glen,
Far away, far away, far away
The haunts of men;
There shall we dwell in love
With the lark and the dove,
Cuckoo and corn-rail,
Feast on the bearded snail,
Worm and gilded fly,
Drink of the crystal rill
Winding adown the hill
Never to dry.
With glee, with glee, with glee
   Cheer up, cheer up, cheer up here;
Nothing to harm us, then sing merrily,
   Sing to the loved one whose nest is near.

From the Gaelic
Translated by W. MacGillivary

The Swallow

Fly away, fly away, over the sea,
   Sun-loving swallow, for summer is done.
Come again, come again, come back to me,
   Bringing the summer and bringing the sun.

Christina Georgina Rossetti

The Thrush's Nest

Within a thick and spreading hawthorn bush,
   That overhung a mole-hill large and round,
I heard from morn to morn a merry thrush
   Sing hymns of rapture, while I drank the sound
With joy; and oft, an unintruding guest,
   I watch'd her secret toils from day to day,
How true she warp'd the moss to form her nest,
   And modell'd it within with wool and clay.
And bye and bye, like heath-bells gilt with dew,
   There lay her shining eggs as bright as flowers,
Ink-spotted over, shells of green and blue;
   And there I witness'd, in the summer hours,
A brood of nature's minstrels chirp and fly,
Glad as the sunshine and the laughing sky.

John Clare

The Pheasant

See! from the brake the whirring pheasant springs,
And mounts exulting on triumphant wings;
Short is his joy! he feels the fiery wound,
Flutters in blood, and panting beats the ground.
Ah! what avails his glossy varying dyes,
His purple crest, and scarlet-circled eyes,
The vivid green his shining plumes unfold,
His painted wings, and breast that shines with gold.

Alexander Pope

The owl was the bird chosen by Minerva, Goddess of Wisdom, to be her symbol. People still refer to "the wise old owl." Alfred, Lord Tennyson, who became Poet Laureate of England in 1850, remembers this as he depicts the owl "warming his five wits," the five senses, alone and aloof, under the roof of an old windmill.

The Crow

The Owl

When cats run home and light is come,
    And dew is cold upon the ground,
And the far-off stream is dumb,
    And the whirring sail goes round,
    And the whirring sail goes round;
        Alone and warming his five wits,
        The white owl in the belfry sits.

When merry milkmaids click the latch,
    And rarely smells the new-mown hay,
And the cock hath sung beneath the thatch
    Twice or thrice his roundelay,
    Twice or thrice his roundelay;
        Alone and warming his five wits,
        The white owl in the belfry sits.

ALFRED, LORD TENNYSON

With rakish eye and 'plenished crop,
    Oblivious of the farmer's gun,
Upon the naked ash-tree top
    The crow sits basking in the sun.

An old ungodly rogue, I wot!
    For, perched in black against the blue,
His feathers, torn with beak and shot,
    Let woeful glints of April through.

The year's new grass and, golden-eyed,
    The daisies sparkle underneath,
And chestnut-trees on either side
    Have opened every ruddy sheath.

But doubtful still of frost and snow,
    The ash alone stands stark and bare,
And on its topmost twig the crow
    Takes the glad morning's sun and air.

WILLIAM CANTON

Wild Geese

I have heard the curlew crying
    On a lonely moor and mere;
And the sea-gull's shriek in the gloaming
    Is a lonely sound in the ear:
And I've heard the brown thrush mourning
    For her children stolen away; —
But it's O for the homeless wild geese
    That sailed ere the dawn of day!

For the curlew out on the moorland
    Hath five fine eggs in the nest;
And the thrush will get her a new love
    And sing her song with the best.
As the swallow flies to the summer
    Will the gull return to the sea:
But never the wings of the wild geese
    Will flash over seas to me.

KATHERINE TYNAN

65

The hen might seem a prosaic barnyard subject, with few possibilities for poetry. But observe what different things different poets see in her: Elizabeth Madox Roberts looks at the hen with the eyes of a wondering child; Elizabeth Coatsworth gives the hen a mature, machine-age treatment; the unknown author of Five Little Chickens *makes the mother bird the heroine of a brief lesson-story.*

The Hens

The night was coming very fast;
It reached the gate as I ran past.

The pigeons had gone to the tower of the church
And all the hens were on their perch,

Up in the barn, and I thought I heard
A piece of a little purring word.

I stopped inside, waiting and staying,
To try to hear what the hens were saying.

They were asking something, that was plain,
Asking it over and over again.

One of them moved and turned around,
Her feathers made a ruffled sound,

A ruffled sound, like a bushful of birds,
And she said her little asking words.

She pushed her head close into her wing,
But nothing answered anything.

ELIZABETH MADOX ROBERTS

The Complete Hen

Now and again I like to see
A hen who still runs wide and free,

Who crosses roads and flies o'er ditches,
Who cackles till she gets the stitches,

Who hunts for grasshoppers in the stubble,
And scratches merrily in old rubble,

Who cocks her head when roosters crow,
Who knows all things that hens should know:

When to obey the housewife's call
And when to pay no heed at all,

Where grubs grow best, and how to roost
On some low branch without a boost;

And last of all, to prove her worth
(Her nearness to the rights of earth)

Let her become an agitator,
Fixed enemy to the incubator,

And obstinately steal her nest
And shelter chicks beneath her breast.

ELIZABETH COATSWORTH

66

Five Little Chickens

Said the first little chicken,
With a queer little squirm,
"Oh, I wish I could find
A fat little worm!"

Said the next little chicken,
With an odd little shrug,
"Oh, I wish I could find
A fat little bug!"

Said the third little chicken,
With a sharp little squeal,
"Oh, I wish I could find
Some nice yellow meal!"

Said the fourth little chicken,
With a small sigh of grief,
"Oh, I wish I could find
A green little leaf!"

Said the fifth little chicken,
With a faint little moan,
"Oh, I wish I could find
A wee gravel-stone!"

"Now, see here," said the mother,
From the green garden-patch,
"If you want any breakfast,
You must come and scratch."

As you get to know more and more poems by Emily Dickinson you will begin to recognize her extraordinary way of thinking about things and what they seem like to her. No one else would say, as the snake slithers along, that "the grass divides as with a comb," or that, when a coiled snake straightens out, it is a "whip-lash unbraiding in the sun," or that the chill felt when coming suddenly upon a snake is cold as "zero at the bone."

The Snake

A narrow fellow in the grass
Occasionally rides;
You may have met him,—did you not,
His notice sudden is.

The grass divides as with a comb,
A spotted shaft is seen;
And then it closes at your feet
And opens further on.

He likes a boggy acre,
A floor too cool for corn.
Yet when a child, and barefoot,
I more than once, at morn,

Have passed, I thought, a whip-lash
Unbraiding in the sun,—
When, stooping to secure it,
It wrinkled, and was gone.

Several of nature's people
I know, and they know me;
I feel for them a transport
Of cordiality;

But never met this fellow,
Attended or alone,
Without a tighter breathing,
And zero at the bone.

EMILY DICKINSON

Seal

See how he dives
From the rocks with a zoom!
See how he darts
Through his watery room
Past crabs and eels
And green seaweed,
Past fluffs of sandy
Minnow feed!
See how he swims
With a swerve and a twist,
A flip of the flipper,
A flick of the wrist!
Quicksilver-quick,
Softer than spray,

Down he plunges
And sweeps away;
Before you can think,
Before you can utter
Words like "Dill pickle"
Or "Apple butter,"
Back up he swims
Past sting-ray and shark,
Out with a zoom,
A whoop, a bark;
Before you can say
Whatever you wish,
He plops at your side
With a mouthful of fish!

WILLIAM JAY SMITH

The Whale

—Warm and buoyant in his oily mail
Gambols on seas of ice the unwieldy whale,
Wide waving fins round floating islands urge
His bulk gigantic through the troubled surge.

O'er the white wave he lifts his nostril bare,
And spouts transparent columns into air;
The silvery arches catch the setting beams,
And transient rainbows tremble o'er the streams.

ERASMUS DARWIN

Son of a seventeenth-century English schoolmaster, Isaac Watts wrote many lines that we may still remember. For example:

Let dogs delight to bark and bite,
For God hath made them so.

In 1715 Watts put together a collection of thoughts like the one just quoted and called them Divine Songs for Children. *They were much admired—so much so that when he died a monument to his memory was placed in Westminster Abbey. His lines about the busy little bee were sung all over the English-speaking world.*

The Bee

How doth the little busy bee
  Improve each shining hour,
And gather honey all the day
  From every opening flower!

How skillfully she builds her cell!
  How neat she spreads the wax!
And labors hard to store it well
  With the sweet food she makes.

In works of labor or of skill
  I would be busy too;
For Satan finds some mischief still
  For idle hands to do.

In books, or work, or healthful play,
  Let my first years be past;
That I may give for every day
  Some good account at last.

ISAAC WATTS

Somewhat more than a hundred years after the death of the good Dr. Watts, a young Oxford teacher, the Reverend Charles Lutwidge Dodgson went rowing with the small daughters of the Dean; to pass away the time, he made up a story about a little girl who fell down a rabbit-hole. When the story was finished and printed, it carried the title Alice's Adventures in Wonderland *and it was signed "Lewis Carroll." In it the author made fun of many things, mixing sense and nonsense. He even turned the famous rhymes of Isaac Watts topsy-turvy—and the busy little bee became (in Alice's confused memory) a lazy crocodile.*

69

The Crocodile

How doth the little crocodile
   Improve his shining tail,
And pour the waters of the Nile
   On every golden scale!

How cheerfully he seems to grin,
   How neatly spreads his claws,
And welcomes little fishes in,
   With gently smiling jaws!

LEWIS CARROLL

The Lobster

As a young lobster roamed about,
Itself and mother being out,
Their eyes at the same moment fell
On a boiled lobster's scarlet shell.
"Look," said the younger; "is it true
That we might wear so bright a hue?
No coral, if I trust mine eye,
Can with its startling brilliance vie;
While you and I must be content
A dingy aspect to present."
"Proud heedless fool," the parent cried;
"Know'st thou the penalty of pride?
The tawdry finery you wish,
Has ruined this unhappy fish.
The hue so much by you desired
By his destruction was acquired—
So be contented with your lot,
Nor seek to change by going to pot."

70

Herman Melville, born in New York City in 1819, wrote many books of grim adventure. One of them, Moby Dick, an American saga of whaling, became a universal classic. Practically everything Melville wrote had a profound and tragic significance. But there was humor in Melville, too —a lighter side that is seldom recognized. Even his most serious work is veined with irony as well as poetry, to which he was devoted. We Fish, for example, is from his obscure novel, Mardi.

We Fish

We fish, we fish, we merrily swim,
We care not for friend nor for foe.
   Our fins are stout,
   Our tails are out,
As through the seas we go.

Fish, fish, we are fish with red gills;
  Naught disturbs us, our blood is at zero:
We are buoyant because of our bags,
  Being many, each fish is a hero.
We care not what is it, this life

   That we follow, this phantom unknown;
To swim, it's exceedingly pleasant—
   So swim away, making a foam.
This strange looking thing by our side,
   Not for safety, around it we flee: —
Its shadow's so shady, that's all—
   We only swim under its lee.
And as for the eels there above,
   And as for the fowls of the air,
We care not for them nor their ways,
   As we cheerily glide afar!

HERMAN MELVILLE

The poetry of John Keats, who lived in the beginning of the nineteenth century, is pure enchantment. The magic grows once we are under its spell. As he wrote:

   A thing of beauty is a joy for ever:
   Its loveliness increases; it will never
   Pass into nothingness . . .

Minnows is full of delightful details which combine observation with imagination. The lines are part of a long poem by Keats beginning:

   I stood tip-toe upon a little hill,
   The air was cooling, and so very still,
   That the sweet buds which with a modest pride
   Pull droopingly, in slanting curve aside,
   Their scantly leaved and finely tapering stems,
   Had not yet lost those starry diadems . . .

Minnows

Swarms of minnows show their little heads,
Staying their wavy bodies 'gainst the streams,
To taste the luxury of sunny beams
Tempered with coolness. How they ever wrestle
With their own sweet delight, and ever nestle
Their silver bellies on the pebbly sand.
If you but scantily hold out the hand,
That very instant not one will remain;
But turn your eye, and they are there again.
The ripples seem right glad to reach those cresses,
And cool themselves among the em'rald tresses;
The while they cool themselves, they freshness give,
And moisture, that the bowery green may live.

JOHN KEATS

In one of our childhood games we used to repeat a cruel rhyme that ran:

Lady-bug, lady-bug! fly away home!
Your house is on fire, your children will burn.

The poet, Caroline Southey, knew these unhappy lines, but, she changed them lovingly and made a captivating fantasy out of them. In her verses the house is not on fire, the children fortunately do not burn, and the lady-bug becomes a lady-bird.

Lady-Bird

Lady-bird, lady-bird! fly away home!
    The field-mouse has gone to her nest,
The daisies have shut up their sleepy red eyes,
    And the bees and the birds are at rest.

      Lady-bird, lady-bird! fly away home!
        The glow-worm is lighting her lamp,
      The dew's falling fast, and your fine speckled wings
        Will flag with the close-clinging damp.

            Lady-bird, lady-bird! fly away home!
              The fairy bells tinkle afar!
            Make haste, or they'll catch you, and harness you fast
              With a cobweb, to Oberon's car.

CAROLINE SOUTHEY

The Caterpillar

Brown and furry
Caterpillar in a hurry;
Take your walk
To the shady leaf or stalk.

May no toad spy you,
May the little birds pass by you;
Spin and die,
To live again a butterfly.

CHRISTINA GEORGINA ROSSETTI

May Swenson, a contemporary American poet, writes in an unconventional but graphic style. She likes stimulating suggestion rather than flat statement. She frequently leaves out words in order to condense her thought and telegraph the meaning. Reminding us a little of Emily Dickinson, she sees things in her own unique way. Once a caterpillar in its colorless cocoon, the butterfly emerges resplendent in a "sequin coat." Its boldly patterned wings are "little chinks of mosaic," and their fluttering motion recalls "applauding hands."

Was Worm

Was worm
swaddled in white.

Now, tiny queen
in sequin coat
peacock-bright,
drinks the wind and feeds
on sweat of the leaves.

Is little chinks
of mosaic floating,
a scatter of colored beads.

Alighting, pokes
with her new black wire,
the saffron yokes.

On silent hinges
open-folds her wings'
applauding hands.

Weaned
from coddling white
to lake-deep air,
to blue and green,
is queen.

MAY SWENSON

To a Butterfly

I've watched you now a full half-hour,
Self-poised upon that yellow flower;
And, little butterfly! indeed
I know not if you sleep or feed.
How motionless! Not frozen seas
More motionless! And then
What joy awaits you, when the breeze
Has found you out among the trees,
And calls you forth again!

This plot of orchard-ground is ours;
My trees they are, my sister's flowers;
Here rest your wings when they are weary,
Here lodge as in a sanctuary!
Come often to us, fear no wrong;
Sit near us on the bough!
We'll talk of sunshine and of song,
And summer days, when we are young;
Sweet childish days, that were as long
As twenty days are now.

WILLIAM WORDSWORTH

The Butterfly's Ball

Come take up your hats, and away let us haste
To the butterfly's ball and the grasshopper's feast;
The trumpeter gadfly has summoned the crew,
And the revels are now only waiting for you.
On the smooth shaven grass, by the side of the wood,
Beneath a broad oak that for ages has stood,
See the children of earth, and the tenants of air,
For an evening's amusement together repair.

And there came the beetle so blind and so black,
Who carried the emmet,[1] his friend, on his back;
And there was the gnat, and the dragon-fly too,
With all their relations, green, orange, and blue.

And there came the moth in his plumage of down,
And the hornet in jacket of yellow and brown,
Who with him the wasp his companion did bring,
But they promised that evening to lay by their sting.

74

And the sly little dormouse crept out of his hole,
And led to the feast his blind brother the mole,
And the snail, with his horns peeping out from his shell,
Came from a great distance—the length of an ell.[2]

A mushroom their table, and on it was laid
A water-dock leaf, which a table-cloth made;
The viands were various, to each of their taste,
And the bee brought his honey to crown the repast.

There, close on his haunches, so solemn and wise,
The frog from a corner looked up to the skies;
And the squirrel, well pleased such diversions to see,
Sat cracking his nuts overhead in a tree.

Then out came the spider, with fingers so fine,
To show his dexterity on the tight line;
From one branch to another his cobwebs he slung,
Then, quick as an arrow, he darted along.

But just in the middle, oh! shocking to tell!
From his rope in an instant poor Harlequin[3] fell;
Yet he touched not the ground, but with talons outspread,
Hung suspended in air at the end of a thread.

Then the grasshopper came with a jerk and a spring,
Very long was his leg, though but short was his wing;
He took but three leaps, and was soon out of sight,
Then chirped his own praises the rest of the night.

With step so majestic, the snail did advance,
And promised the gazers a minuet to dance;
But they all laughed so loud that he pulled in his head,
And went in his own little chamber to bed.

Then as evening gave way to the shadows of night
Their watchman, the glowworm, came out with his light;
Then home let us hasten while yet we can see,
For no watchman is waiting for you and for me.

WILLIAM ROSCOE

[1] emmet: ant
[2] ell: generally speaking,
  less than four feet
[3] Harlequin: a tricky dancer
  and acrobat; in this case,
  the spider

Poets have praised not only the larger creations of nature but the smaller creatures, even the insects. Two thousand five hundred years ago, the Greek poet Anacreon celebrated the happy grasshopper drinking "the dewy morning's gentle wine" at the end of the summer.

More than two thousand years later, two Englishmen were discussing the nimble grasshopper of the fields and comparing it to the cricket, "the cheerful little grasshopper of the fireside." They challenged each other to a contest: each was to write a poem of exactly fourteen lines on the two insects. The young John Keats won the contest. His poem was finished first. Yet, though it was judged the more beautiful in expression, Keats modestly preferred Leigh Hunt's sonnet to his own.

The Grasshopper

Happy insect, what can be
In happiness compared to thee?
Fed with nourishment divine,
The dewy morning's gentle wine!
Nature waits upon thee still,
And thy verdant cup does fill;
Thou dost drink, and dance, and sing,
Happier than the happiest king!
All the fields which thou dost see,
All the plants belong to thee;
All the summer hours produce,
Fertile made with early juice.
Man for thee does sow and plow,
Farmer he, and landlord thou!

Thou dost innocently enjoy;
Nor does thy luxury destroy.
The shepherd gladly heareth thee,
More harmonious than he.
Thee country folk with gladness hear,
Prophet of the ripened year!
To thee, of all things upon earth,
Life is no longer than thy mirth.
Happy insect! happy thou,
Dost neither age nor winter know;
But when thou'st drunk, and danced, and sung
Thy fill, the flowery leaves among,
Sated with thy summer feast,
Thou retir'st to endless rest.

From the Greek of Anacreon
Translated by ABRAHAM COWLEY

76

On the Grasshopper and Cricket

The poetry of earth is never dead:
When all the birds are faint with the hot sun
And hide in cooling trees, a voice will run
From hedge to hedge about the new-mown mead.
That is the grasshopper's—he takes the lead
In summer luxury,—he has never done
With his delights; for, when tired out with fun,
He rests at ease beneath some pleasant weed.

The poetry of earth is ceasing never.
On a lone winter evening, when the frost
Has wrought a silence, from the stove there shrills
The cricket's song, in warmth increasing ever,
And seems, to one in drowsiness half lost,
The grasshopper's among some grassy hills.

JOHN KEATS

On the Grasshopper and Cricket

Green little vaulter in the sunny grass,
Catching your heart up at the feel of June,
Sole voice that's heard amidst the lazy noon,
When even the bees lag at the summoning brass;
And you, warm little housekeeper, who class
With those who think the candles come too soon,
Loving the fire, and with your tricksome tune,
Nick the glad, silent moments as they pass;
O sweet and tiny cousins, that belong
One to the fields, the other to the hearth,
Both have your sunshine; both, though small, are strong
At your clear hearts; and both seem given to earth
To sing in thoughtful ears this natural song,
In doors and out, summer and winter—mirth.

LEIGH HUNT

A Centipede

A centipede was happy quite,
    Until a frog in fun
Said, "Pray, which leg comes after which?"
This raised her mind to such a pitch,
She lay distracted in the ditch
    Considering how to run.

77

The Ant and the Cricket

A silly young cricket, accustomed to sing
Through the warm, sunny months of gay summer and spring,
Began to complain when he found that, at home,
His cupboard was empty, and winter was come.
        Not a crumb to be found
        On the snow-covered ground;
        Not a flower could he see,
        Not a leaf on a tree.
"Oh! what will become," says the cricket, "of me?"

At last, by starvation and famine made bold,
All dripping with wet, and all trembling with cold,
Away he set off to a miserly ant,
To see if, to keep him alive, he would grant
        Him shelter from rain,
        And a mouthful of grain.
        He wished only to borrow;
        He'd repay it to-morrow;
If not, he must die of starvation and sorrow.

Says the ant to the cricket, "I'm your servant and friend,
But we ants never borrow; we ants never lend.
But tell me, dear cricket, did you lay nothing by
When the weather was warm?" Quoth the cricket, "Not I!
        My heart was so light
        That I sang day and night,
        For all nature looked gay."
        "You sang, sir, you say?
Go, then," says the ant, "and dance winter away!"

Thus ending, he hastily lifted the wicket,
And out of the door turned the poor little cricket.
Folks call this a fable. I'll warrant it true:
Some crickets have four legs, and some have but two.

Adapted from Aesop

78

The Snail

The frugal snail, with forecast of repose,
Carries his house with him where'er he goes;
Peeps out—and if there comes a shower of rain,
Retreats to his small domicile again.
Touch but a tip of him, a horn—'tis well—
He curls up in his sanctuary shell.
He's his own landlord, his own tenant; stay

Long as he will, he dreads no Quarter Day.
Himself he boards and lodges; both invites
And feasts himself; sleeps with himself o'nights.
He spares the upholsterer trouble to procure
Chattels; himself is his own furniture,
And his sole riches. Wheresoe'er he roam—
Knock when you will—he's sure to be at home.

CHARLES LAMB

The Snail

To grass, or leaf, or fruit, or wall
The snail sticks fast, nor fears to fall,
As if he grew there, house and all,
        together.

Within that house secure he hides
When danger imminent betides,
Or storms, or other harms besides
        of weather.

Give but his horns the slightest touch,
His self-collecting power is such,
He shrinks into his house with much
        displeasure.

Where'er he dwells, he dwells alone,
Except himself, has chattels none,
Well satisfied to be his own
        whole treasure.

Thus, hermit-like, his life he leads,
Nor partner of his banquet needs,
And if he meets one, only feeds
        the faster.

(Who seeks him must be worse than blind,
He and his house are so combined)
finding it he fails to find
        its master.

WILLIAM COWPER

The Nightingale
and the Glowworm

A Nightingale that all day long
Had cheer'd the village with his song,
Nor yet at eve his note suspended,
Nor yet when eventide was ended,
Began to feel, as well he might,
The keen demands of appetite;
When looking eagerly around,
He spied far off, upon the ground,
A something shining in the dark,
And knew the Glowworm by his spark;
So, stooping down from hawthorn top,
He thought to put him in his crop.
The worm, aware of his intent,
Harangued him thus, right eloquent:
"Did you admire my lamp," quoth he,
"As much as I your minstrelsy,
You would abhor to do me wrong,
As much as I to spoil your song:
For 'twas the self-same Power Divine
Taught you to sing, and me to shine;
That you with music, I with light,
Might beautify and cheer the night."
The songster heard this short oration,
And warbling out his approbation,
Released him, as my story tells,
And found a supper somewhere else.

WILLIAM COWPER

79

As we have already seen in The Lamb *and other poems, William Blake (born in London in 1757) had the gift of making trifling things tremendous. In the most commonplace objects he saw the hand of the Creator and felt a kinship with the meanest of God's works, even with a fly.*

In On a Fly Drinking from His Cup, *William Oldys, who was born sixty years before Blake, makes a similar, and charming, comparison. His somewhat elaborate language is a contrast to Blake's tiny lines which consist mainly of one-syllable words.*

Gnat

People simper and drawl
Over anything small.
They look at it, and can't believe
That's all.
So they drawl.

Even the most ardent disputer
Will agree, of most things, that the minuter
The cuter.

Oh people might—say, be
Interested in a celebrity, but they'd be
More interested in him if he were a baby.

You usually suppose
That a large nose
Is not as attractive as
A small rose-
Bud of a nose.

And the expression on Pekes and Chows,
Though sulkier,
Is valued more than that on cows,
Which are bulkier.

Yet if a thing is *too* pat,
Concise, or flat—
That's that.

Nobody admires a gnat
But a gnat.

ROSALIE MOORE

On a Fly Drinking from His Cup

Busy, curious, thirsty fly,
Drink with me, and drink as I.
Freely welcome to my cup,
Couldst thou sip, and sip it up;
Make the most of life you may,
Life is short and wears away.

Just alike, both mine and thine,
Hasten quick to their decline.
Thine's a summer, mine no more,
Though repeated to three-score.
Three-score summers, when they're gone
Will appear as short as one.

WILLIAM OLDY

Kindness to Animals

Little children, never give
Pain to things that feel and live;
Let the gentle robin come
For the crumbs you save at home;
As his meat you throw along
He'll repay you with a song.
Never hurt the timid hare
Peeping from her green grass lair,
Let her come and sport and play
On the lawn at close of day.
The little lark goes soaring high
To the bright windows of the sky,
Singing as if 'twere always spring,
And fluttering on an untired wing—
Oh! let him sing his happy song,
Nor do these gentle creatures wrong

The Fly

Little fly,
Thy summer's play
My thoughtless hand
Has brushed away.

Am not I
A fly like thee?
Or art not thou
A man like me?

For I dance
And drink and sing,
Till some blind hand
Shall brush my wing.

If thought is life
And strength and breath,
And the want
Of thought is death,

Then am I
A happy fly,
If I live
Or if I die.

WILLIAM BLAKE

Melville Cane in Bed-Time Story *compares his animals who unite for common cause, with the United Nations. In the last two lines an important question is asked which "daddy" neatly sidetracks. Perhaps the future will provide the right and happy answer.*

Bed-Time Story

Once there was a spaniel
By the name of Daniel,
And a pig,
Sig,
And a pussy,
Gussie—
She chased a mouse,
Klaus;
And a squirrel,
Errol,
And a white she-bear,
Claire,
And a Scotch lion,
Ian,
And a very fierce shark,
Mark.

You'll agree, my dear,
They were rather a queer
Assortment
Of temperament and deportment.

And yet,
My pet,
In spite of their diversities
And perversities
Both zoological
And ideological,
They all gathered together
One day, when the weather
Was especially frightful, and decided
It wasn't safe to stay divided
Any longer, and that they should,
For their common good,
(Rather than risk another calamity)
Try amity.

And that's the way there began to dawn a
Plan they christened UNITED FAUNA.

"And did they live happily ever after, daddy?"
"I'll tell you the rest tomorrow. Good-night, dear."

81   MELVILLE CANE

A common weakness among human beings is to see everything from their own particular point of view. The Blind Men and the Elephant, *the first poem in the section "Laughter Holding Both His Sides," treats this thought with broad humor. Sara Henderson Hay develops the idea, whimsically but seriously, that every living creature—even the snail—believes God is made in his own image.*

The Shape God Wears

But ask now the beasts, and they shall teach thee; and the fowls of the air, and they shall tell thee . . . JOB 12, 7.

So questioning, I was bold to dare
The sinewy tiger in his lair.
"Come forth, striped sir, make known to me
What God it was who fashioned thee."

Out leapt he like a muscled blaze,
Patterned in black and gold he was.
"Jehovah is his name," he cried,
"Tiger of Tigers, beryl-eyed,

"Flat flanked and sleek, His paws are curled
About the margins of the world.
He stalketh in His jungles grim—
I, even I, am like to Him!"

I sought that moving mountain side,
The elephant, with ears fanned wide,
Treading the forests. "Sir, tell me
What manner of a God made thee?"

He swirled his trunk about the oak
And wrenched it up before he spoke,
Then answered in a trumpet blast,
"Old Super-Pachyderm, that vast

"Lord of the Elephants, the great
Trampler upon the worm's estate.
Crag-shouldered, terrible is He
Who of His substance fashioned me!"

I scaled the precipice, to seek
The eagle on his drafty peak.
"Tell me, O Gazer at the sun,
The nature of that Mighty One,

Your Lord." He turned his crested head
And screamed athwart the wind and said,
"Ancient of Eagles, wild and free,
Rider of tempests, He made me!

"His wing is stretched above the thunder,
His claws can rip the hills asunder.
His beak of two hooked knives is made—
Look on His likeness. Be afraid!"

Then turned I to the whorléd snail
Whose house is exquisite and frail,
Most deftly wrought. "Sir, I would know
What God it was Who shaped thee so."

Then cried he proudly to my face,
"Eternal Snail, God of my race.
The lightning is His silvery track,
He wears the world upon His back.

"He is most beautiful and wise,
He dwelleth in the moisty skies,
In the gray wall at heaven's rim,
And He has made me after Him!"

82

Then laughed I in superior mirth,
"Attend, ye creatures of the earth,
Misled, mistaken, all undone
And self-deceivers, every one.

"Hear ye, deluded beasts, while I
Explain the shape God wears, and why.
Self-evident the truth's displayed:
He is *my* Father, sirs," I said,
"And in my image He is made!"

Sara Henderson Hay

GALLERY OF PEOPLE

Some of the greatest portraits have been painted by poets. And here is a whole gallery of personalities. Some of them are simple, everyday people; some, like the hag astride a bramble lash, would hardly go riding down the main street of your town. But, whether they have warm blood or moonlight magic in their veins, I think you will find that they all breathe, move, and come alive as you read about them.

The section opens with two descriptions by Shakespeare. The first, which spans a lifetime, is from As You Like It; the second is from Julius Caesar.

All the World's a Stage

All the world's a stage
And all the men and women merely players:
They have their exits and their entrances;
And one man in his time plays many parts,
His acts being seven ages. At first the infant,
Mewling and puking in the nurse's arms.
Then the whining school-boy, with his satchel
And shining morning face, creeping like snail
Unwillingly to school. And then the lover,
Sighing like furnace, with a woeful ballad
Made to his mistress' eyebrow. Then a soldier,
Full of strange oaths, and bearded like the pard,[1]
Jealous in honor, sudden and quick in quarrel,
Seeking the bubble reputation
Even in the cannon's mouth. And then the justice,
In fair round belly with good capon lined,
With eyes severe and beard of formal cut,
Full of wise saws and modern instances;
And so he plays his part. The sixth age shifts
Into the lean and slippered pantaloon,
With spectacles on nose and pouch on side,
His youthful hose, well saved, a world too wide
For his shrunk shank; and his big manly voice,
Turning again toward childish treble, pipes
And whistles in his sound. Last scene of all,
That ends this strange eventful history,
Is second childishness and mere oblivion,
Sans[2] teeth, sans eyes, sans taste, sans every thing.

WILLIAM SHAKESPEARE

Brutus

This was the noblest Roman of them all:
All the conspirators, save only he,
Did that they did in envy of great Caesar;
He only, in a general honest thought
And common good to all, made one of them.
His life was gentle, and the elements
So mixed in him that Nature might stand up
And say to all the world "This was a man!"

WILLIAM SHAKESPEARE

[1] Pard: leopard
[2] Sans: without

85

The Canterbury Tales *is a collection of marvelous stories supposedly told to each other by a mixed group of pilgrims on their way to the shrine at Canterbury. The year is 1388 and, behind the story, Geoffrey Chaucer, called the "father of English poetry," gives us a panorama of fourteenth-century life in England. There are thirty pilgrims, each one of whom is sharply individualized with vivid details. Prominent among them are a quiet but courageous Knight; his son, the Squire, a young lover; and a thickset, muscular Miller who plays the bagpipe and roars his jokes out of a mouth "broad as a great furnace door."*

From the Canterbury Tales

A Knight there was, and that a worthy man,
Who, from the moment when he first began
To ride forth, loved the code of chivalry:
Honor and truth, freedom and courtesy.
His lord's war had established him in worth;
He rode—and no man further—ends of earth
In heathen parts as well as Christendom,
Honored wherever he might go or come . . .
Of mortal battles he had seen fifteen,
And fought hard for our faith at Tramassene
Thrice in the lists, and always slain his foe.
This noble knight was even led to go
To Turkey where he fought most valiantly
Against the heathen hordes for Palaty.

Renowned he was; and, worthy, he was wise—
Prudence, with him, was more than mere disguise;
He was as meek in manner as a maid.
Vileness he shunned, rudeness he never said
In all his life, respecting each man's right.
He was a truly perfect, noble knight.

A SQUIRE

With him there was his son, a youthful Squire,
A merry blade, a lover full of fire;
With locks as curled as though laid in a press—
Scarce twenty years of age was he, I guess.
In stature he was of an average length,
Wondrously active, bright, and great in strength.
He proved himself a soldier handsomely
In Flanders, in Artois and Picardy,
Bearing himself so well, in so short space,
Hoping to stand high in his lady's grace.
Embroidered was his clothing, like a bed
Full of gay flowers, shining white and red.
Singing he was, or fluting, all the day—
He was as fresh as is the month of May.
Short was his gown; his sleeves were long and wide;
Well did he sit his horse, and nimbly ride,
He could make songs, intone them or indite,
Joust, play and dance, and also draw and write.
So well could he repeat love's endless tale,
He slept no more than does the nightingale.
Yet he was humble, courteous and able,
And carved before his father when at table.

A MILLER

The Miller, stout and sturdy as the stones,
Delighted in his muscles and big bones;
They served him well; at fair and tournament
He took the wrestling prize where'er he went.
He was short-shouldered, broad, knotty
                               and tough;
He'd tear a door down easily enough
Or break it, charging thickly with his head.
His beard, like any sow or fox, was red,
And broadly built, as though it were a spade.
Upon the tiptop of his nose he had
A wart, and thereon stood a tuft of hairs,
Bright as the bristles of a red sow's ears.

His nostrils matched the miller, black and wide.
He bore a sword and buckler by his side.
His mouth was broad as a great furnace door.
He loved to tell a joke, and boast, and roar
About his many sins and deviltries;
He stole, and multiplied his thefts by threes.
And yet he had a thumb of gold, 'tis true.
He wore a white coat and a hood of blue,
And he could blow the bagpipe up and down—
And with a tune he brought us out of town.

GEOFFREY CHAUCER
Modern Version by Louis Untermeyer

87

Born about a hundred years later than Chaucer, the fifteenth-century John Skelton was a lively if erratic poet. His rhythms were rough, his style was ragged, and he delighted in catch-as-catch-can rhymes. Everything he did was done in high spirits; even such a graceful tribute as the verses to Merry Margaret *are playfully helter-skelter. It is not necessary to know that the "fair Isyphill" was originally Hypsipyle, a legendary Greek girl who saved her father's life; that "good Cassander" was Cassandra, the Trojan prophetess; that "coriander" is an aromatic herb; and that "sweet pomander" is a ball of perfume which used to be worn as a charm. Such information may enhance appreciation of the poem but, even without the meaning, the sound of the words makes a pretty music.*

Merry Margaret

Merry Margaret,
As midsummer flower,
Gentle as falcon
Or hawk of the tower;
With solace and gladness,
Much mirth and no madness,
All good and no badness;
So joyously,
So maidenly,
So womanly,
Her demeaning;
In every thing
Far, far passing
That I can indite
Or suffice to write
Of merry Margaret,
As midsummer flower,
Gentle as falcon
Or hawk of the tower.

As patient and as still,
And as full of good will,
As the fair Isyphill,
Coriander,
Sweet pomander,
Good Cassander;
Steadfast of thought,
Well made, well wrought.
Far may be sought
Ere than ye can find
So courteous, so kind,
As merry Margaret,
This midsummer flower,
Gentle as falcon
Or hawk of the tower.

JOHN SKELTON

The Friar's Hunting Song *immediately recalls Friar Tuck, the good friend and robust companion of Robin Hood. Before settling down to a life of religious contemplation, the friar of our poem was a gallant knight. Even before he put off his armor and went about in a somber cassock, the "Yoicks! hark away! and tally-ho!" cry of the hunters stirred his pulse. He could never hear the horn without a sad, glad tugging at his heart.*

Friar's Hunting Song

Though I be now a gray, gray friar,
    Yet I was once a hale young knight:
The cry of my dogs was the only choir
    In which my spirit did take delight.
Little I recked of matin bell,
    But drowned its toll with my clanging horn
And the only beads I loved to tell
    Were the beads of dew on the spangled thorn.

An archer keen I was withal,
    As ever did lean on greenwood tree;
And could make the fleetest roebuck fall,
    A good three hundred yards from me.
Though changeful time, with hand severe,
    Has made me now these joys forego,
Yet my heart bounds whene'er I hear
    Yoicks! hark away! and tally-ho!

THOMAS LOVE PEACOCK

The author of Snow-Bound *subtitled the poem "A Winter Idyll" and the two together exactly describe the long New England winters which John Greenleaf Whittier experienced over a hundred years ago. The poem is truly autobiographical; its characters are the family and friends who gathered around the Whittier fireplace to talk and trade reminiscences. Whittier seemed particularly fond of "The Uncle" and "The Schoolmaster," and he painted their portraits with the skill of an Old Master.*

From Snow-Bound

THE UNCLE

Our uncle, innocent of books,
Was rich in lore of fields and brooks,
The ancient teachers never dumb
Of Nature's unhoused lyceum.
In moons and tides and weather wise,
He read the clouds as prophecies,
And foul or fair could well divine,
By many an occult hint and sign,
Holding the cunning-warded keys
To all the woodcraft mysteries;
Himself to Nature's heart so near
That all her voices in his ear
Of beast or bird had meanings clear,
Like Apollonius of old,
Who knew the tales the sparrows told,
Or Hermes who interpreted
What the sage cranes of Nilus said;
A simple, guileless, childlike man,
Content to live where life began;
Strong only on his native grounds,
The little world of sights and sounds
Whose girdle was the parish bounds,
Whereof his fondly partial pride
The common features magnified,
As Surrey hills to mountains grew
In White of Selborne's loving view,—
He told how teal and loon he shot,
And how the eagle's eggs he got,
The feats on pond and river done,
The prodigies of rod and gun;
Till, warming with the tales he told,
Forgotten was the outside cold,
The bitter wind unheeded blew,
From ripening corn the pigeons flew,
The partridge drummed i' the wood, the mink
Went fishing down the river-brink.
In fields with bean or clover gay,
The woodchuck, like a hermit gray,
Peered from the doorway of his cell;
The muskrat plied the mason's trade,
And tier by tier his mud-walls laid;
And from the shagbark overhead
The grizzled squirrel dropped his shell.

89

THE SCHOOLMASTER

Brisk wielder of the birch and rule,
The master of the district school
Held at the fire his favored place,
Its warm glow lit a laughing face
Fresh-hued and fair, where scarce appeared
The uncertain prophecy of beard.
He teased the mitten-blinded cat,
Played cross-pins on my uncle's hat,
Sang songs, and told us what befalls
In classic Dartmouth's college halls.
Born the wild Northern hills among,
From whence his yeoman father wrung
By patient toil subsistence scant,
Not competence and yet not want,
He early gained the power to pay
His cheerful, self-reliant way;
Could doff at ease his scholar's gown
To peddle wares from town to town;
Or through the long vacation's reach
In lonely lowland districts teach,
Where all the droll experience found
At stranger hearths in boarding round,
The moonlit skater's keen delight,
The sleigh-drive through the frosty night,
The rustic party, with its rough
Accompaniment of blind-man's-buff,
And whirling plate, and forfeits paid,
His winter task a pastime made.
Happy the snow-locked homes wherein
He tuned his merry violin,
Or played the athlete in the barn,
Or held the good dame's winding-yarn,
Or mirth-provoking versions told
Of classic legends rare and old,
Wherein the scenes of Greece and Rome
Had all the commonplace of home,
And little seemed at best the odds
'Twixt Yankee pedlers and old gods.

JOHN GREENLEAF WHITTIER

I'm Nobody! Who Are You?

I'm nobody! Who are you?
Are you nobody, too?
Then there's a pair of us—don't tell!
They'd banish us, you know.

How dreary to be somebody!
How public, like a frog
To tell your name the livelong day
To an admiring bog!

EMILY DICKINSON

Odd-sounding names stick in our minds; the eccentric beat of their syllables keeps on echoing even after they have lost all meaning. Ucalegon happened to be one of the elders at the siege of Troy, Melchizedek is mentioned in the Bible as a king of Salem. But the poet, Edwin Arlington Robinson, was not much concerned about their history or even their actuality. He just loved the sound of their names, names that pursued him wherever he went.

Two Men

There be two men of all mankind
    That I should like to know about;
But search and question where I will,
    I cannot ever find them out.

Melchizedek he praised the Lord,
    And gave some wine to Abraham;
But who can tell what else he did
    Must be more learned than I am.

Ucalegon he lost his house
    When Agamemnon came to Troy;
But who can tell me who he was—
    I'll pray the gods to give him joy.

There be two men of all mankind
    That I'm forever thinking on:
They chase me everywhere I go—
    Melchizedek, Ucalegon.

EDWIN ARLINGTON ROBINSON

Mother of the House

Strength and dignity are her clothing;
    And she laugheth at the time to come.
She openeth her mouth to wisdom;
    And the law of kindness is in her tongue.
She looketh well to the ways of her household,
    And eateth not the bread of idleness;
Her children rise up and call her blessed,
    Her husband, also, and he praiseth her, saying:
"Many daughters have done virtuously,
    But thou excelleth them all."

The Bible: PROVERBS, 31

In the Carpenter Shop

I wish I had been His apprentice,
  To see Him each morning at seven,
As he tossed His gray tunic about Him,
  The Master of earth and of heaven;

When He lifted the lid of His work-chest
  And opened His carpenter's kit,
And looked at His chisels and augers,
  And took the bright tools out of it;

When He gazed at the rising sun tinting
  The dew on the opening flowers,
And he smiled at the thought of His Father
  Whose love floods this fair world of ours;

When He fastened the apron about Him,
  And put on His workingman's cap,
And grasped the smooth haft of His hammer
  To give the bent woodwork a tap,

Saying, "Lad, let us finish this ox yoke,
  The farmer must finish his crop."
Oh, I wish I had been His apprentice
And worked in the Nazareth shop.

Andrew Jackson, who was twice elected President of the United States, was so tough and stubborn both as man and soldier that he was known as Old Hickory. He lived under fire. He was attacked for having accepted the help of the pirate Lafitte and condemned for having married his wife before it was established that she had a legal divorce. Martha Keller has caught the hardy, gallant spirit of the man who could not be defeated.

Andrew Jackson

He was a man as hot as whiskey.
He was a man whose word was good.
He was a man whose hate was risky—
  Andrew Jackson—hickory wood!

He was in love with love and glory:
His hopes were prospered, but at a price—
The bandying of the ugly story
  He'd had to marry his Rachel twice.

Hot he was and a hasty suitor,
But if he sinned he was poor at sin.
She was plain as a spoon of pewter,
  Plain and good as a safety pin.

Andrew Jackson, man of honor,
Held her name like he held his head..
He stopped a bullet for slurs upon her.
  All his life he carried lead.

All his life wherever he went he
Wore the scar of a pistol shot—
Along with others he had in plenty.
  Hickory wood is hard to rot.

Hard to rot and a fiery fuel—
When faith and freedom both burned dim,
He stood his guns as he fought a duel,
  And heartened others to stand with him.

With any man who was good at sighting,
No ally but the thief Lafitte,
And no campaigns but Indian fighting,
  He brought the British to black defeat.

The odds against him were more than double.
His gunmounts sank like a heart that fails,
Sank in mud and the frosty stubble—
  So he set his cannon on cotton bales.

92

And over the cane and the silver sedges—
The redcoats' coats were as red as flame—
In a hundred rows like a hundred hedges,
    The bayonets of the British came.

The smoke of his cannon rolled and scattered
Like bursting flowers, like cotton blooms.
Like teeth from a comb the red ranks shattered,
    While water lifted in yellow plumes.

White and red on the silver carpet,
Scarlet tunics by crossbelts crossed,
They fell and died—and a flood of scarlet
    Covered over the field of frost.

He was a man whose hand was steady.
He was a man whose aim was good.
He was a man whose guns were ready—
    Andrew Jackson—hickory wood!

MARTHA KELLER

The conquistadors were the early Spanish conquerors of the New World. Elizabeth Coatsworth pictures one of them in all his grandiose pride. Don Juan Gomez so exalts himself that he boasts not only of his power on earth but in heaven.

Conquistador

Let it be understood that I am Don Juan Gomez!
My blood is pure blood from the proudest blood of Spain
And I own hills and valleys beyond a wide day's riding
And heavy lies the silver upon my bridle rein.

Let it be understood that I am Don Juan Gomez!
My saddle cloth is fringed with scalps of Indians I have slain,
And when I see a girl whom I may wish in marriage
I shall demand but once, and need not ask again.

Let it be understood that I am Don Juan Gomez!
Only in prayer to bend the knee and bow the head I deign,
And when I pray, the saints go hurrying to the Virgin
And cry "Don Juan is praying, and must not pray in vain!"

ELIZABETH COATSWORTH

Sir Marmaduke

Sir Marmaduke was a hearty knight—
    Good man! old man!
He's painted standing bolt upright,
    With his hose rolled over his knee;
His periwig's as white as chalk,
And on his fist he holds a hawk;
    And he looks like the head
      Of an ancient family.

His dining-room was long and wide—
    Good man! old man!
His spaniels lay by the fireside;
    And in other parts, d'ye see,
Cross-bows, tobacco pipes old hats,
A saddle, his wife, and a litter of cats;
    And he looked like the head
      Of an ancient family.

He never turned the poor from the gate—
    Good man! old man!
But was always ready to break the pate
    Of his country's enemy.
What knight could do a better thing
Than serve the poor, and fight for his king?
    And so may every head
      Of an ancient family.

GEORGE COLMAN

The Happy Farmer

Let the mighty and great
Roll in splendor and state,
    I envy them not, I declare it.
I eat my own lamb,
My own chicken and ham;
    I shear my own sheep and I wear it.

I have lawns and green bowers,
Fresh fruits and fine flowers,
    The lark is my bright morning charmer.
So God bless the plow
In the future as now—
    A health and long life to the farmer.

OLD ENGLISH RHYME

There Was a Jolly Miller

There was a jolly miller once lived on the river Dee,
He danced and sung from morn till night, no lark so blithe as he;
And this the burden of his song forever used to be:
"I care for nobody, no, not I, if nobody cares for me.

"I live by my mill, God bless her! she's kindred, child, and wife;
I would not change my station for any other in life;
No lawyer, surgeon, or doctor, e'er had a groat from me;
I care for nobody, no, not I, if nobody cares for me."

When spring begins his merry career, oh, how his heart grows gay!
No summer's drought alarms his fears, nor winter's cold decay;
No foresight mars the miller's joy, who's wont to sing and say:
"Let others toil from year to year, I live from day to day."

ISAAC BICKERSTAFFE

94

Thomas Hood began his career writing serious poetry like the significant Song of the Shirt, *the grim* Dream of Eugene Aram, *and the protesting* Bridge of Sighs. *But the public in the early nineteenth century would only buy his light verse. He said punningly but ruefully:*

> I have to be a lively Hood
> If I would earn my livelihood.

I Remember, I Remember, *is the kind of poetry he liked best; in a reminiscent key, it tells some of Hood's own story.*

I Remember I Remember

I remember, I remember
The house where I was born,
The little window where the sun
Came peeping in at morn;
He never came a wink too soon
Nor brought too long a day;
But now, I often wish the night
Had borne my breath away.

I remember, I remember
The fir-trees dark and high;
I used to think their slender tops
Were close against the sky:
It was a childish ignorance,
But now 'tis little joy
To know I'm farther off from Heaven
Than when I was a boy.

THOMAS HOOD

I remember, I remember
The roses, red and white,
The violets, and the lily-cups—
Those flowers made of light!
The lilacs where the robin built,
And where my brother set
The laburnum on his birthday,—
The tree is living yet!

I remember, I remember
Where I was used to swing,
And thought the air must rush as fresh
To swallows on the wing;
My spirit flew in feathers then
That is so heavy now,
The summer pools could hardly cool
The fever on my brow.

95

The longing to leave everything and roam irresponsibly is known as wanderlust. It is a common impulse, and it has never been expressed with more abandon than in The Raggle Taggle Gypsies.

The Raggle Taggle Gypsies

'Twas late last night when my lord came home,
    Inquiring for his lady, O.
The servants said on every hand,
    "She's gone with the Raggle Taggle Gypsies, O."

"Oh, saddle for me my milk-white steed,
    Oh, saddle for me my pony, O,
That I may ride and seek my bride
    Who's gone with the Raggle Taggle Gypsies, O."

Oh, he rode high and he rode low,
    He rode through woods and copses, O,
Until he came to an open field,
    And there he espied his lady, O.

"What makes you leave your house and lands?
    What makes you leave your money, O?
What makes you leave your new-wedded lord
    To go with the Raggle Taggle Gypsies, O?"

"What care I for my house and lands?
    What care I for my money, O?
What care I for my new-wedded lord?
    I'm off with the Raggle Taggle Gypsies, O.'

Last night you slept on a goose-feather bed,
    With the sheet turned down so bravely, O.
Tonight you will sleep in the cold, open field,
    Along with the Raggle Taggle Gypsies, O."

"What care I for your goose-feather bed,
    With the sheet turned down so bravely, O?
For tonight I shall sleep in a cold, open field,
    Along with the Raggle Taggle Gypsies, O."

OLD FOLK SONG

Henry Wadsworth Longfellow was the most widely read of all the nineteenth-century American poets. His poems were quoted everywhere —and still are. He was happiest when writing on homely themes like The Village Blacksmith.

The Village Blacksmith

Under a spreading chestnut tree
    The village smithy stands;
The smith, a mighty man is he,
    With large and sinewy hands;
And the muscles of his brawny arms
    Are strong as iron bands.

His hair is crisp, and black, and long,
    His face is like the tan;
His brow is wet with honest sweat,
    He earns whate'er he can,
And looks the whole world in the face,
    For he owes not any man.

Week in, week out, from morn till night,
    You can hear his bellows blow;
You can hear him swing his heavy sledge,
    With measured beat and slow,
Like a sexton ringing the village bell,
    When the evening sun is low.

And children coming home from school
    Look in at the open door;
They love to see the flaming forge,
    And hear the bellows roar,
And catch the burning sparks that fly
    Like chaff from a threshing floor.

He goes on Sunday to the church,
  And sits among his boys;
He hears the parson pray and preach,
  He hears his daughter's voice,
Singing in the village choir,
  And it makes his heart rejoice.

It sounds to him like her mother's voice,
  Singing in Paradise!
He needs must think of her once more,
  How in the grave she lies;
And with his hard, rough hand he wipes
  A tear out of his eyes.

Toiling—rejoicing—sorrowing,
  Onward through life he goes;
Each morning sees some task begin,
  Each evening sees its close;
Something attempted, something done,
  Has earned a night's repose.

Thanks, thanks to thee, my worthy friend,
  For the lesson thou hast taught!
Thus at the flaming forge of life
  Our fortunes must be wrought;
Thus on its sounding anvil shaped
  Each burning deed and thought!

HENRY WADSWORTH LONGFELLOW

Longfellow's famous picture of his daughters in The Children's Hour *shows why he was called "the household poet." His mention of the Bishop of Bingen refers to the legend about cruel Bishop Hatto who starved his people and whom God punished by sending mice to devour him. Even though the Bishop barricaded himself in a tower, he could not escape the dreadful judgment.*

The Children's Hour

Between the dark and the daylight,
    When the night is beginning to lower,
Comes a pause in the day's occupations,
    That is known as the Children's Hour.

I hear in the chamber above me
    The patter of little feet,
The sound of a door that is opened,
    And voices soft and sweet.

From my study I see in the lamplight,
    Descending the broad hall stair,
Grave Alice, and laughing Allegra,
    And Edith with golden hair.

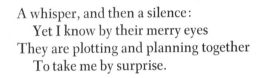

A whisper, and then a silence:
    Yet I know by their merry eyes
They are plotting and planning together
    To take me by surprise.

A sudden rush from the stairway,
    A sudden raid from the hall!
By three doors left unguarded
    They enter my castle wall!

They climb up into my turret
    O'er the arms and back of my chair;
If I try to escape, they surround me;
    They seem to be everywhere.

They almost devour me with kisses,
    Their arms about me entwine,
Till I think of the Bishop of Bingen
    In his Mouse-Tower on the Rhine!

Do you think, O blue-eyed banditti,
    Because you have scaled the wall,
Such an old moustache as I am
    Is not a match for you all!

I have you fast in my fortress,
    And will not let you depart,
But put you down into the dungeon
    In the round-tower of my heart.

And there will I keep you forever,
    Yes, forever and a day,
Till the walls shall crumble to ruin,
    And moulder in dust away!

HENRY WADSWORTH LONGFELLOW

James Whitcomb Riley is usually referred to as the Hoosier poet because he came from Indiana, a state settled mainly by mountaineers, once known as Hoosiers. Most of his poems were written in Hoosier dialect. Dialect verse was little known and not much esteemed until it was popularized by Riley.

The Raggedy Man

O The Raggedy Man! He works fer Pa;
An' he's the goodest man ever you saw!
He comes to our house every day,
An' waters the horses, an' feeds 'em hay;
An' he opens the shed—an' we all ist laugh
When he drives out our little old wobble-ly calf;
An' nen—ef our hired girl says he can—
He milks the cow fer 'Lizabuth Ann.—
  Ain't he a' awful good Raggedy Man?
  Raggedy! Raggedy! Raggedy Man!

W'y, The Raggedy Man—he's ist so good
He splits the kindlin' an' chops the wood;
An' nen he spades in our garden, too,
An' does most things 'at *boys* can't do!—
He clumbed clean up in our big tree
An' shooked a' apple down fer me—
An' nother'n', too, fer 'Lizabuth Ann—
An' nother'n', too, fer The Raggedy Man.—
  Ain't he a' awful kind Raggedy Man?
  Raggedy! Raggedy! Raggedy Man!

An' The Raggedy Man, he knows most rhymes
An' tells 'em, ef I be good, sometimes:
Knows 'bout Giunts, an' Griffuns, an' Elves,
An' the Squidgicum-Squees 'at swallers therselves!
An', wite by the pump in our pasture-lot,
He showed me the hole 'at the Wunks is got,
'At lives 'way deep in the ground, an' can
Turn into me, er 'Lizabuth Ann,
Er Ma er Pa er The Raggedy Man!
  Ain't he a funny old Raggedy Man?
  Raggedy! Raggedy! Raggedy Man!

The Raggedy Man—one time when he
Wuz makin' a little bow-'n'-orry fer me,
Says "When *you're* big like your Pa is,
Air *you* go' to keep a fine store like his—
An' be a rich merchunt—an' wear fine clothes?—
Er what air you go' to be, goodness knows!"
An' nen he laughed at 'Lizabuth Ann,
An' I says "'M go' to be a Raggedy Man!—
  I'm ist go' to be a nice Raggedy Man!
  Raggedy! Raggedy! Raggedy Man!"

JAMES WHITCOMB RILEY

99

Griselda

Griselda is greedy, I'm sorry to say.
She isn't contented with four meals a day,
Like breakfast and dinner and supper and tea
(I've had to put tea after supper—you see
    Why, don't you?)
Griselda is greedy as greedy can be.

She snoops about the larder
For sundry small supplies,
She breaks the little crusty bits
Off rims of apple pies,
She pokes the roast-potato-dish
When Sunday dinner's done,
And if there are two left in it
Griselda snitches one;
Cold chicken and cold cauliflower
She pulls in little chunks—
And when Cook calls:
    "What *are* you doing there?"
    Griselda bunks.

Griselda is greedy. Well, that's how she feels,
She simply can't help eating in-between meals,
And always forgets what it's leading to, though
The Doctor has frequently told her: "You know
    Why, *don't* you?"
When the stomach-ache starts and Griselda says:
    "Oh!"

She slips down to the dining-room
When everyone's in bed,
For cheese-rind on the supper-tray,
And buttered crusts of bread,
A biscuit from the biscuit-box,
Lump sugar from the bowl,
A gherkin from the pickle-jar,
Are all Griselda's toll;
    She tastes the salted almonds,
      And she tries the candied fruits—
And when Dad shouts:
    "Who *is* it down below?"
    Griselda scoots.

Griselda is greedy. Her relatives scold,
And tell her how sorry she'll be when she's old,
She will lose her complexion, she's sure to grow fat,
She will spoil her inside—does she know what she's at?
    (Why *do* they?)
Some people *are* greedy. Leave it at that.

Eleanor Farjeon

100

We all know the first verse of the following rhymes. But did you ever know what happened to this temperamental female? Did you realize that she had a name? Incidentally, the jingle is supposed to have been written by Henry Wadsworth Longfellow in one of his facetious moments.

Jemima

There was a little girl who had a little curl,
Right in the middle of her forehead,
And when she was good, she was very, very good,
But when she was bad she was horrid.

One day she went upstairs, while her parents, unawares,
In the kitchen down below were at their meals,
And she stood upon her head, on her little truckle bed,
And she then began hurraying with her heels.

Her mother heard the noise, and thought it was the boys,
A-playing at a combat in the attic,
But when she climbed the stair and saw Jemima there,
She took and she did spank her most emphatic!

Polly

Brown eyes,
    Straight nose;
Dirt pies,
    Rumpled clothes.

Torn books,
    Spoilt toys;
Arch looks,
    Unlike a boy's.

Little rages,
    Obvious arts;
Three her age is,
    Cakes, tarts.

Falling down
    Off chairs;
Breaking crown
    Down-stairs.

Catching flies
    On the pane;
Deep sighs—
    Cause not plain.

Bribing you
    With kisses,
For a few
    Farthing blisses.

Wide-awake;
    As you hear,
"Mercy's sake,
    Quiet, dear!"

New shoes,
    New frock;
Vague views
    Of what's o'clock.

When it's time
    To go to bed;
Scorn sublime
    For what is said.

Thinks it odd;
    Smiles away;
Yet may God
    Hear her pray!

Bed-gown white;
    Kiss Dolly;
Good night!
    That's Polly.

Fast asleep,
    As you see;
Heaven keep
    My girl for me!

WILLIAM BRIGHTY RANDS

101

Minnie

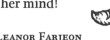

Minnie can't make her mind up,
Minnie can't make up her mind!
   They ask her at tea,
   "Well, what shall it be?"
And Minnie says, "Oh,
Muffins, please! no,
Sandwiches—yes,
Please, egg-and-cress—
I mean a jam one,
Or is there a ham one,
Or is there another kind?
   Never mind!

        Cake
   Is what I will take,
The sort with the citron-rind,
   Or p'r'aps the iced one—
   Or is there a spiced one,
Or is there the currant kind?"
   When tea is done
   She hasn't begun,
She's always the one behind,
Because she can't make her mind up,
Minnie *can't* make up her mind!

ELEANOR FARJEON

Almost everyone knows the words of Old Mother Hubbard *and almost everyone believes them to be a jingle written by an unknown person long before the days of Mother Goose. But a few years ago the author was discovered: she was Sarah Catherine Martin, born in the eighteenth century, daughter of an Admiral of the English fleet. It was said that a young prince, who later became William IV, fell in love with her and that, since the law would not allow them to marry, her family took her off to the country. There, in 1804, the unhappy Sarah comforted herself with verse-making—and* Old Mother Hubbard, *which she not only composed but illustrated herself, was the result. The original manuscript was found by her great-great-niece only a few years ago, and was brought to America where it sold for nearly five thousand dollars....Nobody knows who wrote* The Old Woman.

Old Mother Hubbard

Old Mother Hubbard
   Went to the cupboard,
To get her poor dog a bone:
   But when she got there
   The cupboard was bare,
And so the poor dog had none.

She went to the baker's
   To buy him some bread,
But when she come back
   The poor dog was dead.

She went to the joiner's
   To buy him a coffin,
But when she came back
   The poor dog was laughing.

She took a clean dish
   To get him some tripe,
But when she came back
   He was smoking a pipe.

She went to the fishmonger's
	To buy him some fish,
But when she came back
	He was licking the dish.

She went to the tavern
	For white wine and red,
But when she came back
	The dog stood on his head.

She went to the hatter's
	To buy him a hat,
But when she came back
	He was feeding the cat.

She went to the barber's
	To buy him a wig,
But when she came back
	He was dancing a jig.

She went to the fruiterer's
	To buy him some fruit,
But when she came back
	He was playing the flute.

She went to the tailor's
	To buy him a coat,
But when she came back
	He was riding a goat.

She went to the cobbler's
	To buy him some shoes,
But when she came back
	He was reading the news.

She went to the seamstress
	To buy him some linen,
But when she came back
	The dog was spinning.

She went to the hosier's
	To buy him some hose,
But when she came back
	He was dressed in his clothes.

The dame made a curtsey,
	The dog made a bow,
The dame said, "Your servant,"
	The dog said, "Bow-wow."

This wonderful dog
	Was Dame Hubbard's delight;
He could sing, he could dance,
	He could read, he could write.

She gave him rich dainties
	Whenever he fed,
And built him a monument
	When he was dead.

SARAH CATHERINE MARTIN

The Old Woman

There was an old woman, as I've heard tell,
She went to market her eggs for to sell;
She went to market all on a market day;
And she fell asleep on the king's highway.

There came by a pedlar whose name was Stout,
He cut her petticoats all round about;
He cut her petticoats up to the knees,
Which made the old woman to shiver and freeze.

When this little woman first did wake,
She began to shiver and she began to shake.
She began to wonder and she began to cry,
"Lauk-a-mercy on me, this is none of I.

"But if it be I, as I do hope it be,
I've a little dog at home, and he'll know me;
If it be I, he'll wag his little tail,
And if it be not I, he'll loudly bark and wail!"

Home went the little woman all in the dark,
Up got the little dog, and he began to bark;
He began to bark, so she began to cry,
"Lauk-a-mercy on me, this is none of I!"

103

No one could be simpler than Simple Simon who came to life in a nursery rhyme. His absurdities gave new meaning to the word "simpleton."

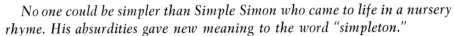

Simple Simon

Simple Simon met a pieman
   Going to the fair;
Says Simple Simon to the pieman,
   "Let me taste your ware."

Says the pieman to Simple Simon,
   "Show me first your penny";
Says Simple Simon to the pieman,
   "Indeed I have not any."

Simple Simon went a-fishing
   For to catch a whale;
All the water he had got
   Was in his mother's pail.

Simple Simon went to look
   If plums grew on a thistle;
He pricked his fingers very much,
   Which made poor Simon whistle.

He went for water in a sieve,
   But soon it all ran through.
And now poor Simple Simon
   Bids you all adieu.

Walter de la Mare seems to speak to us from a mysterious region, the borderland between reality and fantasy. Even when he deals with everyday people, he casts over them a veil of illusion. During his lifetime—he died in 1956—De la Mare wrote and edited more than fifty highly imaginative books. Many of them are about vanished childhood and the ghosts of a forgotten world, a world that is half-juvenile, half-supernatural. Jim Jay belongs to such a world.

Jim Jay

Do diddle di do,
Poor Jim Jay
Got stuck fast
    In Yesterday.
Squinting he was,
    On cross-legs bent,
Never heeding
    The wind was spent.
Round veered the weathercock,
    The sun drew in—
And stuck was Jim
    Like a rusty pin...
We pulled and we pulled
    From seven till twelve,
Jim, too frightened
    To help himself.

But all in vain.
    The clock struck one,
And there was Jim
    A little bit gone.
At half-past five
    You scarce could see
A glimpse of his flapping
    Handkerchee.
And when came noon,
    And we climbed sky-high,
Jim was a speck
    Slip—slipping by.
Come tomorrow,
    The neighbors say,
He'll be past crying for;
    Poor Jim Jay.

WALTER DE LA MARE

To the geographers, Tartary is a vast region of Eastern Europe and Western Asia, cold and barren, once inhabited by wandering Tartar tribes. To Walter de la Mare, it is a realm of golden glamor, an exotic dreamland, a poet's vision.

Tartary

If I were Lord of Tartary,
    Myself and me alone,
My bed should be of ivory,
    Of beaten gold my throne;
And in my court should peacocks flaunt,
And in my forests tigers haunt,
And in my pools great fishes slant
    Their fins athwart the sun.

If I were Lord of Tartary,
    Trumpeters every day
To all my meals should summon me,
    And in my courtyards bray;
And in the evenings lamps should shine
Yellow as honey, red as wine,
While harp and flute and mandoline
    Made music sweet and gay.

If I were Lord of Tartary,
    I'd wear a robe of beads,
White, and gold, and green they'd be—
    And small, and thick as seeds;
And ere should wane the morning star,
I'd don my robe and scimitar,
And zebras seven should draw my car
    Through Tartary's dark glades.

Lord of fruits of Tartary,
    Her rivers silver-pale!
Lord of the hills of Tartary,
    Glen, thicket, wood, and dale!
Her flashing stars, her scented breeze,
Her trembling lakes, like foamless seas,
Her bird-delighting citron-trees
    In every purple vale!

WALTER DE LA MARE

There was a time when people believed in witches, sinister beings far different from the children's Halloween phantom. It was thought there were people who actually dealt in witchcraft, who, it was suspected, could make the milk turn sour, spoil the eggs, sicken the pigs, and put an evil spell on anything. This sort of creature is presented to us by William Barnes in a monologue spoken by a garrulous old farmer full of superstitious fears.

A Country Witch

There's that old hag Moll Brown,
   look, see, just past!
I wish the ugly sly old witch
Would tumble over in the ditch;
I wouldn't pick her out not very fast.
I don't think she's belied, 'tis clear's the sun
That she's a witch if ever there was one.

Yes, I do know just hereabout of two
Or three folk that have learnt
   what Moll can do.
She did, one time, a pretty deal of harm
To Farmer Gruff's folks, down at Lower Farm
One day, you know,
   they happened to offend her,

106

And not a little to their sorrow,
Because they would not give or lend her
The thing she came to beg or borrow;
And so, you know, they soon began to find
That she'd a-left her evil wish behind.
She soon bewitched them;
   and she had such power,
That she did make their milk and ale turn sour,
And addle all the eggs their fowls did lay;
They couldn't fetch the butter in the churn,
And cheeses soon began to turn
All back again to curds and whey.
The little pigs a-running with the sow
Did sicken somehow, nobody knew how,
And fall, and turn their snouts towards the sky,
And only give one little grunt and die;
And all the little ducks and chicken
Were death-struck while they were a-pickin'
Their food, and fell upon their head,
And flapped their wings
   and dropped down dead.

They couldn't fat the calves;
   they wouldn't thrive;
They couldn't save their lambs alive;
Their sheep all took the rot and gave no wool;
Their horses fell away to skin and bones,
And got so weak they couldn't pull
A half a peck of stones;
The dog got dead-alive and drowsy,
The cat fell sick and wouldn't mousey;
And if the wretched souls went up to bed
The hag did come and ride them all half dead.
They used to keep her out o' the house 'tis true,
A-nailing up at door a horse's shoe;
And I've a-heard the farmer's wife did try
To drive a needle or a pin
In through her old hard withered skin
And draw her blood, a-coming by;
But she could never fetch a drop,
She bent the pin and broke the needle's top
Against her skin, you know, and that, of course,
Did only make the hag bewitch them worse!

WILLIAM BARNES

There is more than one kind of witch. There is, first of all, the familiar Halloween symbol that never really frightens anyone, the grotesque, peaked-hat silhouette astride a broomstick. Robert Herrick describes her with mock terror and tripping rhymes.

The Hag

The hag is astride,
  This night for to ride—
The devil and she together;
  Through thick and through thin,
  Now out and then in,
Though ne'er so foul be the weather.

A thorn or a burr
  She takes for a spur;
With a lash of the bramble she rides now
  Through brakes and through briers,
  O'er ditches and mires,
She follows the spirit that guides now.

No beast, for his food,
  Dares now range the wood,
But husht in his lair he lies lurking;
  While mischiefs, by these,
  On land and on seas,
At noon of night are a-working.

The storm will arise,
  And trouble the skies,
This night; and, more the wonder,
  The ghost from the tomb
  Affrighted shall come,
Called out by the clap of the thunder.

ROBERT HERRICK

Of all the fanciful creatures in literature, Shakespeare's Mab, queen of the fairies, is perhaps the most unforgettable. She is a bright apparition, a romantic, mischief-making, frivolous sprite. Her enchanting portrait, occurring as it does in the midst of the tragic Romeo and Juliet, *is like a nimble scherzo in a somber symphony.*

Queen Mab

She is the fairies' midwife, and she comes
In shape no bigger than an agate-stone
On the fore-finger of an alderman,
Drawn with a team of little atomies
Over men's noses as they lie asleep;
Her waggon-spokes made of long spinners' legs.
The cover of the wings of grasshoppers,
Her traces of the smallest spider web,
Her collars of the moonshine's watery beams,
Her whip of cricket's bone, the lash of film,
Her waggoner a small grey-coated gnat,
Not half so big as a round little worm
Prick'd from the lazy finger of a maid;
Her chariot is an empty hazel-nut
Made by the joiner squirrel, or old grub,
Time out o' mind the fairies' coachmakers.
And in this state she gallops night by night
Through lovers' brains, and then they dream of love;
On courtiers' knees, that dream on curtsies straight;
O'er lawyers' fingers, who straight dream on fees;
O'er ladies' lips, who straight on kisses dream,
Which oft the angry Mab with blisters plagues,
Because their breath with sweetmeats tainted are.
Sometimes she gallops o'er a courtier's nose,
And then dreams he of smelling out a suit;
And sometime comes she with a tithe-pig's tail
Tickling a parson's nose as 'a lies asleep,
Then dreams he of another benefice.
Sometime she driveth o'er a soldier's neck,
And then dreams he of cutting foreign throats,
Of breaches, ambuscadoes, Spanish blades,
Of healths five fathom deep: and then anon
Drums in his ear, at which he starts and wakes,

And being thus frightened, swears a prayer or two,
And sleeps again. This is that very Mab
That plats the manes of horses in the night;
And bakes the elf-locks in foul sluttish hairs,
Which once untangled, much misfortune bodes...

WILLIAM SHAKESPEARE

Portraits are very often done in pairs—a husband and wife, for instance, have their pictures painted simultaneously and framed alike to hang opposite each other. Our portrait gallery closes with such a pair, whom Tennyson has painted appropriately—in water colors.

The Mermaid

I

Who would be
A mermaid fair,
Singing alone,
Combing her hair
Under the sea,
In a golden curl
With a comb of pearl,
On a throne?

II

I would be a mermaid fair;
I would sing to myself the whole of the day.
With a comb of pearl I would comb my hair;
And still as I combed I would sing and say,
"Who is it loves me? who loves not me?"
I would comb my hair till my ringlets would fall,
    Low adown, low adown,
And I should look like a fountain of gold
    Springing alone
    With a shrill inner sound,
    Over the throne
    In the midst of the hall.

The Merman

I

Who would be
A merman bold,
Sitting alone,
Singing alone
Under the sea,
With a crown of gold,
On a throne?

II

I would be a merman bold;
I would sit and sing the whole of the day.
I would fill the sea-halls with a voice of power
But at night I would roam abroad and play
With the mermaids in and out of the rocks,
Dressing their hair with the white sea-flower;
And holding them back by their flowing locks
I would kiss them often under the sea,
And kiss them again till they kissed me
        Laughingly, laughingly;
And then we would wander away, away,
To the pale sea-groves straight and high,
        Chasing each other merrily.

ALFRED, LORD TENNYSON

UNFORGETTABLE STORIES

People have always loved heroes—and have loved to make heroes of themselves. The caveman hunter was probably the first story-teller. He boasted how he overcame the mammoth bear and the hairy mastodon, and with each retelling the monsters grew three times as huge as they really were.

Through the ages, deeds of daring and tales of great wars were celebrated by the poets. Their story-poems spread. Wandering minstrels sang them at fairs and taverns, at street corners and market places, as well as in courtyards and castles. These singers were welcome everywhere, for they brought fresh excitement to faraway legends and to the news of the day.

The names of most of these poets are forgotten, but we remember their stories. Such ballads as The Outlandish Knight, Moy Castle, *and* The Bailiff's Daughter of Islington *hold us as intent today as they did the first people who heard them hundreds of years ago.*

110

The Outlandish Knight

An outlandish knight came out of the North
   To woo a maiden fair,
He promised to take her to the North lands,
   Her father's only heir.

"Come, fetch me some of your father's gold,
   And some of your mother's fee;
And two of the best nags out of the stable,
   Where they stand thirty and three."

She fetched him some of her father's gold
   And some of her mother's fee;
And two of the best nags out of the stable,
   Where they stood thirty and three.

She mounted her on her milk-white steed,
   He on the dapple grey;
They rode till they came unto the sea-side,
   Three hours before it was day.

"Light off, light off thy milk-white steed,
   And deliver it unto me;
Six pretty maids have I drowned here,
   And thou the seventh shall be.

"Pull off, pull off thy silken gown,
   And deliver it unto me;
Methinks it looks too rich and too gay
   To rot in the salt sea.

"Pull off, pull off thy silken stays,
   And deliver them unto me;
Methinks they are too fine and gay
   To rot in the salt sea.

"Pull off, pull off thy Holland smock,
   And deliver it unto me;
Methinks it looks too rich and gay
   To rot in the salt sea."

"If I must pull off my Holland smock,
   Pray turn thy back unto me,
For it is not fitting that such a ruffian
   A woman unclad should see."

He turned his back towards her,
   And viewed the leaves so green;
She caught him round the middle so small,
   And tumbled him into the stream.

He dropped high, and he dropped low,
   Until he came to the tide—
"Catch hold of my hand, my pretty maiden,
   And I will make you my bride."

"Lie there, lie there, you false-hearted man,
   Lie there instead of me;
Six pretty maidens have you drowned here,
   And the seventh has drowned thee."

She mounted on her milk-white steed,
   And led the dapple grey.
She rode till she came to her father's hall,
   Three hours before it was day.

111

Moy Castle

There are seven men in Moy Castle
    Are merry men this night;
There are seven men in Moy Castle
    Whose hearts are gay and light.

Prince Charlie came to Moy Castle
    And asked for shelter there,
And down came Lady M'Intosh,
    As proud as she was fair.

"I'm a hunted man, Lady M'Intosh—
    A price is on my head!
If Lord Loudon knew thou'dst sheltered me,
    Both thou and I were sped."

"Come in! come in, my prince!" said she,
    And opened wide the gate;
"To die with Prince Charlie Stuart,
    I ask no better fate."

She's called her seven trusty men,
    The blacksmith at their head:
"Ye shall keep watch in the castle wood,
    To save our prince from dread."

The lady has led the prince away,
    To make him royal cheer;
The seven men of M'Intosh
    Have sought the forest drear.

And there they looked and listened,
    Listened and looked amain;
And they heard the sound of the falling leaves,
    And the soft sound of the rain.

The blacksmith knelt beside an oak,
    And laid his ear to the ground,
And under the noises of the wood
    He heard a distant sound.

He heard the sound of many feet,
    Warily treading the heather—
He heard the sound of many men
    Marching softly together.

"There's no time now to warn the prince,
    The castle guards are few;
'Tis wit will win the play tonight,
    And what we here can do."

112

He's gi'en the word to his six brethren,
    And through the wood they're gone;
The seven men of M'Intosh
    Each stood by himself alone.

"And he who has the pipes at his back,
    His best now let him play;
And he who has no pipes at his back,
    His best word let him say."

It was five hundred Englishmen
    Were treading the purple heather,
Five hundred of Lord Loudon's men
    Marching softly together.

"There's none tonight in Moy Castle
    But servants poor and old;
If we bring the prince to Loudon's lord,
    He'll fill our hands with gold."

They came lightly on their way,
    Had never a thought of ill,
When suddenly from the darksome wood
    Broke out a whistle shrill.

And straight the wood was filled with cries,
    With shouts of angry men,
And the angry skirl of the bagpipes
    Came answering the shouts again.

The Englishmen looked and listened,
    Listened and looked amain,
And nought could they see through the mirk night,
    But the pipes shrieked out again.

"Hark to the slogan of Lochiel,
    To Keppoch's gathering cry!
Hark to the rising swell that tells
    Clanranald's men are nigh!

"Now woe to the men that told us
    Lochiel was far away!
The whole of the Highland army
    Is waiting to bar our way.

"It's little we'll see of Charlie Stuart,
    And little of Loudon's gold,
And but we're away from this armed wood,
    Our lives have but little hold."

It was five hundred Englishmen,
    They turned their faces and ran,
And well for him with the swiftest foot,
    For he was the lucky man.

And woe to him that was lame or slow,
    For they trampled him on the heather!
And back to the place from whence they came
    They're hirpling all together.

Lord Loudon's men, they are gone full far,
    Over the brow of the hill;
The seven men of M'Intosh,
    Their pipes are crying still.

They leaned them to a tree and laughed,
    'Twould do good to hear,
And they are away to Moy Castle
    To tell their lady dear.

And who but Lady M'Intosh
    Would praise her men so bold?
And who but Prince Charlie Stuart
    Would count the good French gold?

There are seven men in Moy Castle
    Are joyful men this night;
There are seven men in Moy Castle
    Whose hearts will aye be light.

 ## The Bailiff's Daughter of Islington

There was a youth, and a well-loved youth,
    And he was a squire's son;
He loved the bailiff's daughter dear,
    That lived in Islington.

Yet she was coy and would not believe
    That he did love her so,
And not at any time would she
    A favor to him show.

But when his friends did understand
    His fond and foolish mind,
They sent him up to London
    An apprentice for to bind.

And when he had been seven long years,
    And never his love could see—
"Many a tear have I shed for her sake,
    When she little thought of me."

Then all the maids of Islington
    Went forth to sport and play,
All but the bailiff's daughter dear;
    She secretly stole away.

She pulled off her gown of green,
    And put on ragged attire,
And to fair London she would go
    Her true love to inquire.

And as she went along the high road,
    The weather being hot and dry,
She sat her down upon a green bank,
    And her true love came riding by.

She started up, with color so red,
    Catching hold of his bridle rein;
"One penny, one penny, kind sir," she said,
    "Will ease me of much pain."

"Before I give you one penny, sweetheart,
    Pray tell me where you were born,"
"At Islington, kind sir," said she,
    "Where I have had many a scorn."

"I pray thee, sweetheart, then tell to me
    O tell me, whether you know
The bailiff's daughter of Islington."
    "She is dead, sir, long ago."

114

"If she be dead, then take my horse,
　My saddle and bridle also;
For I will into some far country,
　Where no man shall me know."

"O stay, O stay, thou goodly youth,
　She standeth by thy side;
She is here alive, she is not dead,
　And ready to be thy bride."

"O farewell grief, and welcome joy,
　Ten thousand times therefore;
For now I have found my own true love,
　Whom I thought I should never see more."

The next two ballads relate some of the exploits of that gay outlaw, Robin Hood, who, they say, stole from the rich to give to the poor. Old though the legends are, they remain as fresh as the green leaves of Sherwood Forest, where Robin and his Merry Men made their home.

Robin Hood and Allan a Dale

Come listen to me, you gallants so free,
　All you that love mirth for to hear,
And I will tell you of a bold outlaw
　That lived in Nottinghamshire.

As Robin Hood in the forest stood,
　All under the greenwood tree,
There he was aware of a brave young man
　As fine as fine might be.

The youngster was cloth'd in scarlet red,
　In scarlet fine and gay;
And he did frisk it over the plain,
　And chanted a roundelay.

As Robin Hood next morning stood
　Amongst the leaves so gay,
There did he espy the same young man,
　Come drooping along the way.

The scarlet he wore the day before
　It was clean cast away;
And at every step he fetch'd a sigh,
　"Alack and a well-a-day!"

Then stepp'd forth brave Little John,
　And Midge, the miller's son,
Which made the young man bend his bow,
　When as he saw them come.

"Stand off, stand off!" the young man said,
　"What is your will with me?"
"You must come before our master straight,
　Under yon greenwood tree."

And when he came bold Robin before,
　Robin asked him courteously,
"O, hast thou any money to spare
　For my merry men and me?"

"I have no money," the young man said,
　"But five shillings and a ring;
And that I have kept this seven long years,
　To have it at my wedding.

"Yesterday I should have married a maid,
　But she from me was ta'en,
And chosen to be an old knight's delight,
　Therefore my poor heart is slain."

115

"What is thy name?" asked Robin Hood.
    "Come tell me without fail."
"By the faith of my body," then said the young man,
    "My name is Allan a Dale."

"What wilt thou give me?" said Robin Hood,
    "In ready gold or fee,
To help thee get thy true love again
    And deliver her unto thee?"

"I have no money," quoth the young man,
    "No ready gold nor fee;
But I will swear upon the book
    Thy true servant for to be."

"How many miles to thy true love?
    Come tell me without guile."
"By the faith of my body," then said the young man,
    "It is but five little mile."

Then Robin hasted over the plain;
    He stopped for nor wine nor bread,
Until he came unto the church
    Where Allan would have been wed.

"Now who art thou?" the bishop said.
    "I prithee tell unto me."
"I am a harper bold," quoth Robin Hood,
    "And the best in the North Countrie."

"O welcome, O welcome," the bishop he said.
    "That music best pleaseth me;"
"You shall have no music," quoth Robin Hood,
    "Till the bride and the bridegroom I see."

With that came in a wealthy knight,
    Which was both grave and old,
And after him a delicate lass,
    Did shine like the glittering gold.

"This is not a fit match," quoth Robin Hood,
    "That you do seem to make here,
For since we are come into the church,
    The bride shall choose her own dear."

Then Robin Hood put his horn to his mouth,
  And blew blasts two or three;
When four-and-twenty bowmen bold
  Came leaping over the lea.

And when they came into the churchyard,
  Marching all in a row,
The very first man was Allan a Dale,
  To give bold Robin his bow.

"This is thy true love," Robin he said,
  "Young Allan as I hear say;
And you shall be married at this same time,
  Before we depart away."

"That shall not be," the bishop he said,
  "For thy word shall not stand;
They shall be three times asked in the church,
  As the law is of our land."

Robin Hood pulled off the bishop's coat
  And put it on Little John.
"By the faith of my body," then Robin said,
  "This cloth doth make thee a man!"

When Little John went into the church,
  The people began to laugh;
He asked all the questions seven times,
  Lest three times should not be enough.

"Now who gives this maid?" asked Little John.
  Quoth Robin Hood, "That do I,
And he that takes her from Allan a Dale,
  Full dearly he shall pay."

And thus having end of this merry wedding,
  The bride looked like a queen;
And they all returned to the merry greenwood,
  Amongst the leaves so green.

Robin Hood and the Widow's Sons

There are twelve months in all the year,
　　As I hear many men say,
But the merriest month in all the year
　　Is the merry month of May.

Now Robin Hood is to Nottingham gone,
　　With a link a down and a day,
And there he met a simple widow,
　　Was weeping on the way.

"What news? what news, thou simple widow?
　　What news hast thou for me?"
Said she, "There's my three sons in Nottingham town
　　To-day condemned to die."

"Oh, what have they done?" said Robin Hood,
　　"I pray thee tell to me."
"Oh, it is for killing the king's fallow deer,
　　That they are condemned to die."

"Dost thou not mind, old woman," he said,
　　"How thou madest me sup and dine?
By the truth of my body," quoth bold Robin Hood,
　　"You could not tell it in better time."

Now Robin Hood is to Nottingham gone,
　　With a link a down and a day,
And there he met with a simple old beggar,
　　Was walking along the highway.

"What news? what news, thou simple old man?
　　What news, I do thee pray?"
Said he, "Three squires in Nottingham town
　　Are condemned to die this day."

"Come change thy apparel with me, old man,
　　Come change thy apparel for mine;
Here are forty shillings in good silver,
　　Go drink it in beer or wine."

"O, thine apparel is good," he said,
　　"And mine is ragged and torn;
Wherever you go, wherever you ride,
　　Laugh not an old man to scorn."

"Come change thy apparel with me, old fellow,
　　Come change thy apparel with mine;
Here are twenty pieces of good broad gold,
　　Go feast thy brethren with wine."

Then he put on the old man's cloak,
　　Was patched black, blue and red;
He thought it no shame all the day long,
　　To wear the bags of bread.

Then he put on the old man's breeches,
   Was patched from leg to side:
"By the truth of my body," bold Robin did say,
   "This man loved little pride."

Then he put on the old man's hose,
   Were patched from knee to wrist:
"By the truth of my body," said bold Robin Hood,
   "I'd laugh if I had any list."[1]

Then he put on the old man's shoes,
   Were patched both beneath and aboon;[2]
Then Robin Hood swore a solemn oath,
   "It's good habit that makes a man."

Now Robin Hood is to Nottingham gone,
   With a link a down and a down,
And there he met with the proud sheriff,
   Was walking along the town.

"A boon, a boon," says jolly Robin,
   "A boon I beg of thee;
That as for the death of these three squires,
   Their hangman I may be."

"Soon granted, soon granted," says Master Sheriff,
   "Soon granted unto thee;
And you shall have all their gay clothing,
   And all their white money."[3]

"O I will have none of their gay clothing,
   And none of their white money,
But I'll have three blasts on my bugle horn,
   That their souls to heaven may flee."

Then Robin Hood mounted the gallows so high,
   Where he blew both loud and shrill,
Till a hundred and ten of Robin Hood's men
   Came trooping over the hill.

"Whose men are these?" says Master Sheriff,
   "Whose men are these? Tell unto me."
"O they are mine, but none of thine,
   And are come for the squires all three."

They took the gallows from the slack,
   They set it up in the glen,
They hanged the proud sheriff on that,
   And released their own three men.

[1] List: desire   [2] Aboon: above   [3] White money: silver

*Riddle stories, in which a forfeit of money or even a life had to be paid
if the hero gave a wrong answer, or a great prize won by a shrewd reply,
have been popular since at least the seventh century. In* King John and the
Abbot of Canterbury, *a tale dating from Elizabethan times, we are kept in
amused suspense over the outcome.*

King John and the Abbot of Canterbury

An ancient story I'll tell you anon,
Of a notable prince, that was called King John;
He ruled over England with main and might,
But he did great wrong, and maintained little right.

And I'll tell you a story, a story so merry,
Concerning the Abbot of Canterbury;
How for his housekeeping and high renown,
They rode post to bring him to London town.

A hundred men, as the King heard say,
The Abbot kept in his house every day;
And fifty gold chains, without any doubt,
In velvet coats waited the Abbot about.

"How now, Father Abbot? I hear it of thee,
Thou keepest a far better house than me;
And for thy housekeeping and high renown,
I fear thou work'st treason against my crown."

"My liege," quoth the Abbot, "I would it were known,
I am spending nothing but what is my own;
And I trust your grace will not put me in fear,
For spending my own true-gotten gear."

"Yes, yes, Father Abbot, thy fault is high,
And now for the same thou needest must die;
And except thou canst answer me questions three,
Thy head struck off from thy body shall be.

"Now first," quoth the King, "as I sit here,
With my crown of gold on my head so fair,
Among all my liegemen of noble birth,
Thou must tell to one penny what I am worth.

120

"Secondly, tell me, beyond all doubt,
How quickly I may ride the whole world about;
And at the third question thou must not shrink,
But tell me here truly, what do I think?"

"O, these are deep questions for my shallow wit,
And I cannot answer your Grace as yet;
But if you will give me a fortnight's space,
I'll do my endeavor to answer your Grace."

"Now a fortnight's space to thee will I give,
And that is the longest thou hast to live;
For unless thou answer my questions three,
Thy life and thy lands are forfeit to me."

Away rode the Abbot all sad at this word;
He rode to Cambridge and Oxenford;
But never a doctor there was so wise,
That could by his learning an answer devise.

Then home rode the Abbot, with comfort so cold,
And he met his shepherd, a-going to fold:
'Now, good Lord Abbot, you are welcome home;
What news do you bring us from great King John?"

'Sad news, sad news, Shepherd, I must give;
That I have but three days more to live.
I must answer the King his questions three,
Or my head struck off from my body shall be.

'The first is to tell him, as he sits there,
With his crown of gold on his head so fair
Among all his liegemen of noble birth,
To within one penny, what he is worth.

'The second, to tell him, beyond all doubt,
How quickly he may ride this whole world about;
And at question the third, I must not shrink,
But tell him there truly, what does he think?"

'O, cheer up, my lord; did you never hear yet
That a fool may teach a wise man wit?
Lend me your serving-men, horse, and apparel,
And I'll ride to London to answer your quarrel.

121

"With your pardon, it oft has been told to me
   That I'm like your lordship as ever can be:
   And if you will but lend me your gown,
   There is none shall know us at London town."

"Now horses and serving-men thou shalt have,
   With sumptuous raiment gallant and brave;
   With crosier, and mitre, and rochet, and cope,
   Fit to draw near to our father, the pope."

"Now welcome, Sir Abbot," the King he did say,
"'Tis well thou'rt come back to keep the day;
   For if thou canst answer my questions three,
   Thy life and thy living both saved shall be.

"And first, as thou seest me sitting here,
   With my crown of gold on my head so fair,
   Among my liegemen of noble birth,
   Tell to one penny what I am worth."

"For thirty pence our Savior was sold
   Among the false Jews as I have been told;
   And twenty-nine is the worth of thee;
   For I think thou are one penny worse than he."

The King, he laughed, and swore by St. Bittle,
"I did not think I was worth so little!
   Now secondly tell me, beyond all doubt,
   How quickly I may ride this world about."

"You must rise with the sun, and ride with the same
   Until the next morning he riseth again;
   And then your Grace need never doubt
   But in twenty-four hours you'll ride it about."

The King he laughed, and swore by St. Jone,
"I did not think I could do it so soon!
   Now from question the third thou must not shrink
   But tell me truly, what do I think?"

"Yea, that I shall do, and make your Grace merry:
   You think I'm the Abbot of Canterbury.
   But I'm his poor shepherd, as plain you may see,
   That am come to beg pardon for him and for me."

The King he laughed, and swore by the mass,
"I'll make thee Lord Abbot this day in his place!"
"Now nay, my Liege, be not in such speed;
For alas! I can neither write nor read."

"Four nobles a week, then I'll give to thee,
For this merry jest thou has shown to me;
And tell the old Abbot, when thou gettest home,
Thou has brought a free pardon from good King John."

Get Up and Bar the Door, *an old, old joke with its origins in the Orient,
was turned by some unknown English balladeer into this merry account of
a stubborn man and his equally stubborn wife.*

Get Up and Bar the Door

It fell about the Martinmas time,
　　And a gay time it was then,
When our goodwife got puddings to make,
　　And she's boiled them in the pan.

The wind so cold blew south and north,
　　And blew into the floor;
Quoth our goodman to our goodwife,
　　"Get up and bar the door."

"My hand is in my household work,
　　Goodman, as ye may see;
And it will not be barred for a hundred years,
　　If it's to be barred by me!"

They made a pact between them both,
　　They made it firm and sure,
That whosoe'er should speak the first,
　　Should rise and bar the door.

Then by there came two gentlemen,
　　At twelve o'clock at night,
And they could see neither house nor hall,
　　Nor coal nor candlelight.

"Now whether is this a rich man's house,
　　Or whether is it a poor?"
But never a word would one of them speak,
　　For barring of the door.

The guests they ate the white puddings,
　　And then they ate the black;
Tho' much the goodwife thought to herself,
　　Yet never a word she spake.

Then said one stranger to the other,
　　"Here, man, take ye my knife;
Do ye take off the old man's beard,
　　And I'll kiss the goodwife."

"There's no hot water to scrape it off,
　　And what shall we do then?"
"Then why not use the pudding broth,
　　That boils into the pan?"

O up then started our goodman,
　　An angry man was he;
"Will ye kiss my wife before my eyes!
　　And with pudding broth scald me!"

Then up and started our goodwife,
Gave three skips on the floor:
"Goodman, you've spoken the very first word!
Get up and bar the door!"

True Thomas was an actual person, Thomas of Erceldoune, who lived in the thirteenth century, a seer who delivered his predictions under the Eildon tree. It was said that the Queen of Elfland fell in love with this poet-prophet and spirited him off to her enchanted realm. There have been many modern versions of this eerie ballad and some of the old phrases still stick to it, such as "harp and carp," which means to converse pleasantly; "lily leven" which means lovely lawn; and "even cloth," a fine fabric.

True Thomas

True Thomas lay on Huntlie bank;
   A marvel he did see;
For there he saw a lady bright,
   Come riding down by the Eildon tree.

Her skirt was of the grass-green silk,
   Her mantle of the velvet fine;
On every lock of her horse's mane,
   Hung fifty silver bells and nine.

True Thomas he pulled off his cap,
   And bowed low down on his knee;
"All hail, thou mighty Queen of Heaven!
   For thy peer on earth could never be."

"O no, O no, Thomas," she said,
   "That name does not belong to me;
I'm but the Queen of fair Elfland,
   That hither am come to visit thee.

124

"Harp and carp, Thomas," she said,
  "Harp and carp along with me;
And if ye dare to kiss my lips,
  Sure of your body I will be!"

"Betide me weal, betide me woe,
  That threat shall never frighten me!"
Then he has kissed her on the lips,
  All underneath the Eildon tree.

"Now ye must go with me," she said,
  "True Thomas, ye must go with me;
And ye must serve me seven years,
  Through weal or woe as may chance to be."

She's mounted on her milk-white steed,
  She's taken True Thomas up behind;
And aye, whene'er her bridle rang,
  The steed flew swifter than the wind.

O they rode on, and farther on,
  The steed flew swifter than the wind;
Until they reached a desert wide,
  And living land was left behind.

"Light down, light down now, Thomas," she said,
  "And lean your head upon my knee;
Light down, and rest a little space,
  And I will show you marvels three.

"O see ye not yon narrow road,
  So thick beset with thorns and briers?
That is the Path of Wickedness,
  Though after it but few enquires.

"And see ye not yon broad, broad road,
  That stretches o'er the lily leven?
That is the Path of Wickedness,
  Though some call it the Road to Heaven.

"And see ye not yon bonny road,
  That winds about the green hillside?
That is the way to fair Elfland,
  Where you and I this night must bide.

"But, Thomas, ye shall hold your tongue,
  Whatever ye may hear or see;
For if ye speak word in Elfin-land,
  Ye'll ne'er win back to your own countree!"

O they rode on, and farther on;
  They waded through rivers above the knee,
And they saw neither sun nor moon,
  But they heard the roaring of a sea.

It was mirk, mirk night; there was no star-light;
  They waded through red blood to the knee;
For all the blood that's shed on earth,
  Runs through the springs o' that countree.

At last they came to a garden green,
  And she pulled an apple from on high—
"Take this for thy wages, True Thomas;
  It will give thee the tongue that can never lie!"

"My tongue is my own," True Thomas he said,
  "A goodly gift ye would give to me!
I neither could dare to buy or sell
  At fair or tryst where I may be.

"I could neither speak to prince or peer,
  Nor ask of grace from fair ladye."
"Now hold thy peace!" the lady said,
  "For as I say, so must it be."

He has gotten a coat of the even cloth,
  And a pair of shoes of the velvet green;
And till seven years were gone and past,
  True Thomas on earth was never seen.

John Keats was one of the many poets who were fascinated by the old ballads. More than three hundred years after True Thomas *became popular, it suggested to Keats the basis for a haunting ballad. Keats, however, changed the prophecying poet into a wandering knight and, instead of the enamored* Queen of Elfland, *the enchantress is a cruel "faery's child," known by her other victims as* La Belle Dame Sans Merci—The Beautiful Lady Without Mercy. *In both poems, a mortal is bewitched by an immortal.*

La Belle Dame Sans Merci

"Oh, what can ail thee, knight-at-arms,
    Alone and palely loitering?
The sedge has withered from the lake,
    And no birds sing.

"Oh, what can ail thee, knight-at-arms,
    So haggard and so woebegone?
The squirrel's granary is full,
    And the harvest's done.

"I see a lily on thy brow,
    With anguish moist and fever dew;
And on thy cheeks a fading rose
    Fast withereth, too."

I met a lady in the meads,
    Full beautiful—a faëry's child;
Her hair was long, her foot was light,
    And her eyes were wild.

I made a garland for her head,
    And bracelets too, and fragrant zone;
She looked at me as she did love,
    And made sweet moan.

I set her on my pacing steed,
    And nothing else saw, all day long.
For sidelong would she bend, and sing
    A faëry's song.

She found me roots of relish sweet,
    And honey wild, and manna dew;
And sure in language strange she said,
    "I love thee true."

She took me to her elfin grot,
    And there she wept, and sighed full sore;
And there I shut her wild, wild eyes
    With kisses four.

And there she lullèd me asleep,
    And there I dreamed, ah, woe betide!
The latest dream I ever dreamt
    On the cold hill's side.

I saw pale kings, and princes, too,
    Pale warriors, death-pale were they all;
They cried, "La Belle Dame Sans Merci
    Hath thee in thrall!"

I saw their starved lips in the gloom
  With horrid warning gapèd wide—
And I awoke, and found me here,
  On the cold hill's side.

And this is why I sojourn here,
  Alone and palely loitering,
Though the sedge is withered from the lake,
  And no birds sing.

JOHN KEATS

Even in our modern machine age, themes of sorcery, the enchantments of a mysterious and beautiful woman still continue to fascinate the poet. The Irish William Butler Yeats, who died in 1939, sings of a silver fish magically transformed into a "glimmering girl," whose vanished loveliness casts a spell over the entire life of Aengus. This poem, written in Yeats's most musical mood, ends with two lines as exquisite and haunting as a heart-touching tune.

The Song of Wandering Aengus

I went out to the hazel wood,
Because a fire was in my head,
And cut and peeled a hazel wand,
And hooked a berry to a thread,
And when white moths were on the wing,
And moth-like stars were flickering out,
I dropped the berry in a stream
And caught a little silver trout.

When I had laid it on the floor
I went to blow the fire a-flame,
But something rustled on the floor,
And someone called me by my name:
It had become a glimmering girl
With apple blossoms in her hair
Who called me by my name and ran
And faded through the brightening air.

Though I am old with wandering
Through hollow lands and hilly lands,
I will find out where she has gone,
And kiss her lips and take her hands;
And walk among long dappled grass,
And pluck till time and times are done,
The silver apples of the moon,
The golden apples of the sun.

WILLIAM BUTLER YEATS

The poetry of our own time has developed a manner totally different from the ballad-singing of a Keats or a Yeats. It has a rhythm and even a language of its own. The gripping episode in The Fish *is sharpened by the stark, uncompromising pictures presented: the skin of the old fish hanging in strips "like ancient wall-paper," the flat eyes "backed and packed with tarnished tinfoil," the grim hooks "grown firmly in his mouth." Dispensing with rhyme, Elizabeth Bishop packs her short lines with feeling, startling us by their precision and moving us by their compassion.*

The Fish

I caught a tremendous fish
and held him beside the boat,
half out of water, with my hook
fast in a corner of his mouth.
He didn't fight.
He hadn't fought at all.
He hung a grunting weight
battered and venerable
and homely. Here and there
his brown skin hung in strips
like ancient wall-paper:
shapes like full-blown roses
stained and lost through age.
He was speckled with barnacles,
fine rosettes of lime,
and infested
with tiny white sea-lice,
and underneath two or three
rags of green weed hung down.
While his gills were breathing in
the terrible oxygen
—the frightening gills
fresh and crisp with blood
that can cut so badly—
I thought of the coarse white flesh
packed in like feathers,
the big bones and the little bones,
the dramatic reds and blacks
of his shiny entrails,
and the pink swim-bladder
like a big peony.

I looked into his eyes
which were far larger than mine
but shallower, and yellowed,
the irises backed and packed
with tarnished tinfoil
seen through the lenses
of old scratched isinglass.
They shifted a little, but not
to return my stare.
—It was more like the tipping
of an object toward the light.
I admired his sullen face,
the mechanism of his jaw,
and then I saw
that from his lower lip
—if you could call it a lip—
grim, wet, and weapon-like,
hung five old pieces of fish-line,
or four and a wire leader
with the swivel still attached,
with all their five big hooks
grown firmly in his mouth.
A green line, frayed at the end
where he broke it, two heavier lines,
and a fine black thread
still crimped from the strain and snap
when it broke and he got away.
Like medals with their ribbons
frayed and wavering,
a five-haired beard of wisdom
trailing from his aching jaw.

128

I stared and stared
and victory filled up
the little rented boat,
from the pool of bilge
where oil had spread a rainbow
around the rusted engine
to the bailer rusted orange,
the sun-cracked thwarts,
the oarlocks on their strings,
the gunnels—until everything
was rainbow, rainbow, rainbow!
And I let the fish go.

ELIZABETH BISHOP

The Highwayman *is probably the most popular story-poem of the last half-century. Written in the traditional, romantic manner, it is a headlong heroic tale which can never lose its appeal.*

The Highwayman

Part One

The wind was a torrent of darkness among the gusty trees,
The moon was a ghostly galleon tossed upon cloudy seas,
The road was a ribbon of moonlight over the purple moor,
And the highwayman came riding—
       Riding—riding—
The highwayman came riding, up to the old inn-door.

He'd a French cocked-hat on his forehead, a bunch of lace at his chin,
A coat of the claret velvet, and breeches of brown doeskin:
They fitted with never a wrinkle; his boots were up to the thigh!
And he rode with a jewelled twinkle,
       His pistol butts a-twinkle,
His rapier hilt a-twinkle, under the jewelled sky.

Over the cobbles he clattered and clashed in the dark inn-yard,
And he tapped with his whip on the shutters, but all was locked and barred:
He whistled a tune to the window; and who should be waiting there
But the landlord's black-eyed daughter,
       Bess, the landlord's daughter,
Plaiting a dark red love-knot into her long black hair.

And dark in the dark old inn-yard a stable-wicket creaked
Where Tim, the ostler, listened; his face was white and peaked,
His eyes were hollows of madness, his hair like moldy hay;
But he loved the landlord's daughter,
       The landlord's red-lipped daughter:
Dumb as a dog he listened, and he heard the robber say—

One kiss, my bonny sweetheart, I'm after a prize tonight,
But I shall be back with the yellow gold before the morning light.
Yet if they press me sharply, and harry me through the day,
Then look for me by moonlight,
       Watch for me by moonlight:
I'll come to thee by moonlight, though Hell should bar the way."

He rose upright in the stirrups, he scarce could reach her hand;
But she loosened her hair i' the casement! His face burnt like a brand
As the black cascade of perfume came tumbling over his breast;
And he kissed its waves in the moonlight,
         (Oh, sweet black waves in the moonlight)
Then he tugged at his reins in the moonlight, and galloped away to the West.

Part Two

He did not come in the dawning; he did not come at noon;
And out of the tawny sunset, before the rise o' the moon,
When the road was a gypsy's ribbon, looping the purple moor,
A red-coat troop came marching—
         Marching—marching—
King George's men came marching, up to the old inn-door.

They said no word to the landlord, they drank his ale instead;
But they gagged his daughter and bound her to the foot of her narrow bed.
Two of them knelt at her casement, with muskets at the side!
There was death at every window;
         And Hell at one dark window;
For Bess could see, through her casement, the road that *he* would ride.

They had tied her up to attention, with many a sniggering jest:
They had bound a musket beside her, with the barrel beneath her breast!
"Now keep good watch!" and they kissed her.
         She heard the dead man say—
Look for me by moonlight;
         Watch for me by moonlight;
I'll come to thee by moonlight, though Hell should bar the way!

She twisted her hands behind her; but all the knots held good!
She writhed her hands till her fingers were wet with sweat or blood!
They stretched and strained in the darkness, and the hours crawled by like
     years;
Till, now, on the stroke of midnight,
         Cold, on the stroke of midnight,
The tip of one finger touched it! The trigger at least was hers!

The tip of one finger touched it; she strove no more for the rest!
Up, she stood up to attention, with the barrel beneath her breast,
She would not risk their hearing: she would not strive again;
For the road lay bare in the moonlight,
         Blank and bare in the moonlight;
And the blood of her veins in the moonlight throbbed to her Love's refrain.

Tlot-tlot, tlot-tlot! Had they heard it? The horse-hoofs ringing clear—
Tlot-tlot, tlot-tlot, in the distance? Were they deaf that they did not hear?
Down the ribbon of moonlight, over the brow of the hill,
The highwayman came riding,
            Riding, riding!
The red-coats looked to their priming! She stood up straight and still!

Tlot-tlot, in the frosty silence! *Tlot-tlot* in the echoing night!
Nearer he came and nearer! Her face was like a light!
Her eyes grew wide for a moment; she drew one last deep breath,
Then her finger moved in the moonlight,
            Her musket shattered the moonlight,
Shattered her breast in the moonlight and warned him—with her death.

He turned; he spurred him westward; he did not know who stood
Bowed with her head o'er the musket, drenched with her own red blood!
Not till the dawn he heard it, and slowly blanched to hear
How Bess, the landlord's daughter,
            The landlord's black-eyed daughter,
Had watched for her Love in the moonlight; and died in the darkness there.

Back, he spurred like a madman, shrieking a curse to the sky,
With the white road smoking behind him, and his rapier brandished high!
Blood-red were his spurs i' the golden noon; wine-red was his velvet coat;
When they shot him down on the highway,
            Down like a dog on the highway,
And he lay in his blood on the highway, with the bunch of lace at his throat.

                *   *   *   *   *

And still of a winter's night, they say, when the wind is in the trees,
When the moon is a ghostly galleon tossed upon cloudy seas,
When the road is a ribbon of moonlight over the purple moor,
A highwayman comes riding—
            Riding—riding—
A highwayman comes riding, up to the old inn-door.

Over the cobbles he clatters and clangs in the dark inn-yard;
And he taps with his whip on the shutters, but all is locked and barred:
He whistles a tune to the window, and who should be waiting there
But the landlord's black-eyed daughter,
            Bess, the landlord's daughter,
Plaiting a dark red love-knot into her long black hair.

ALFRED NOYES

133

Lochinvar, written in the romantic manner of the early nineteenth century, was as popular in its day as The Highwayman *is in ours. It is the work of Sir Walter Scott who wrote* Ivanhoe *and some thirty other novels; it is part of the Scottish saga,* Marmion.

Lochinvar

Oh, young Lochinvar is come out of the West,—
Through all the wide Border his steed was the best,
And save his good broadsword he weapons had none,—
He rode all unarm'd and he rode all alone.
So faithful in love, and so dauntless in war,
There never was knight like the young Lochinvar.

He stay'd not for brake, and he stopp'd not for stone,
He swam the Eske river where ford there was none,
But ere he alighted at Netherby gate,
The bride had consented, the gallant came late;
For a laggard in love and a dastard in war
Was to wed the fair Ellen of brave Lochinvar.

So boldly he enter'd the Netherby hall,
'Mong bridesmen and kinsmen and brothers and all.
Then spoke the bride's father, his hand on his sword
(For the poor craven bridegroom said never a word),
"Oh, come ye in peace here, or come ye in war,
Or to dance at our bridal, young Lord Lochinvar?"

"I long woo'd your daughter,—my suit you denied;
Love swells like the Solway, but ebbs like its tide;
And now am I come, with this lost love of mine
To lead but one measure, drink one cup of wine.
There are maidens in Scotland more lovely, by far,
That would gladly be bride to the young Lochinvar."

The bride kissed the goblet, the knight took it up,
He quaff'd off the wine and he threw down the cup.
She look'd down to blush, and she look'd up to sigh,
With a smile on her lips and a tear in her eye.
He took her soft hand ere her mother could bar:
"Now tread we a measure," said young Lochinvar.

So stately his form, and so lovely her face,
That never a hall such a galliard[1] did grace,
While her mother did fret, and her father did fume,
And the bridegroom stood dangling his bonnet and plume,
And the bridesmaids whisper'd, "'Twere better by far
To have match'd our fair cousin with young Lochinvar."

One touch to her hand, and one word in her ear,
When they reach'd the hall-door, and the charger stood near;
So light to the croup the fair lady he swung,
So light to the saddle before her he sprung!
"She is won! we are gone, over bank, bush, and scaur;[2]
They'll have fleet steeds that follow," quoth young Lochinvar.

There was mounting 'mong Graemes of the Netherby clan;
Forsters, Fenwicks, and Musgraves, they rode and they ran;
There was racing and chasing on Cannobie Lee,
But the lost bride of Netherby ne'er did they see.
So daring in love, and so dauntless in war,
Have ye e'er heard of gallant like young Lochinvar?

[1] Galliard: a lively dance
[2] Scaur: a cliff

SIR WALTER SCOTT

Like the ancient ballads which it imitates, Shameful Death *begins in the very thick of the story. No words are wasted in introduction, background or scenery; we are plunged into the heart of a tragic situation. Swiftly we learn of the cowardly way in which a hero was waylaid by the betraying "recreants" and slain by them and their henchmen. Even before we can recover from our horror, we learn that justice has been done: the speaker, although now seventy years old, has avenged his brother's death.*

Shameful Death

There were four of us about that bed;
   The mass-priest knelt at the side,
I and his mother stood at the head,
   Over his feet lay the bride;
We were quite sure that he was dead,
   Though his eyes were open wide.

He did not die in the night,
   He did not die in the day,
But in the morning twilight
   His spirit passed away,
When neither sun nor moon was bright,
   And the trees were merely gray.

He was not slain with the sword,
   Knight's ax, or the knightly spear,
Yet spoke he never a word
   After he came in here;
I cut away the cord
   From the neck of my brother dear.

He did not strike one blow,
   For the recreants came behind,
In a place where the hornbeams grow,
   A path right hard to find,
For the hornbeam boughs swing so
   That the twilight makes it blind.

They lighted a great torch then,
   When his arms were pinioned fast
Sir John the knight of the Fen,
   Sir Guy of the Dolorous Blast,
With knights threescore and ten,
   Hung brave Lord Hugh at last.

I am three score and ten,
   And my hair is all turned gray,
But I met Sir John of the Fen
   Long ago on a summer day,
And am glad to think of the moment when
   I took his life away.

I am threescore and ten
   And my strength is mostly passed,
But long ago I and my men
   When the sky was overcast,
And the smoke rolled over the reeds of the fen,
   Slew Guy of the Dolorous Blast.

And now, all knights of you,
I pray you pray for Sir Hugh,
A good knight and a true,
And for Alice, his wife, pray too.

WILLIAM MORRIS

Folklore is full of myths about mischievous spirits: tricksy elves, teasing gnomes and mocking spirits. But there is also the sinister side of legendry in which loveliness is a mask for evil. The Greeks and Romans believed that certain sea-nymphs, called sirens, had the power of hypnotizing sailors with their seductive songs and luring them to destruction, as related in the great epic poem, The Odyssey. *The belief persisted for centuries. In Germany the siren was called the Loreley, and the great German lyric poet, Heinrich Heine, made her the subject of one of his most famous poems.*

The Loreley

I cannot tell why this imagined
 Despair has fallen on me;
The ghost of an ancient legend
 That will not let me be:

The air is cool, and twilight
 Flows down the quiet Rhine;
A mountain alone in the high light
 Still holds the lingering shine.

The last peak rosily gleaming
 Reveals, enthroned in air,
A maiden, lost in dreaming,
 Who combs her golden hair.

Combing her hair with a golden
 Comb in her rocky bower,
She sings the tune of an olden
 Song that has magical power.

The boatman has heard; it has bound him
 In the throes of a strange, wild love;
Blind to the reefs that surround him,
 He sees but the vision above.

And lo, hungry waters are springing—
 The boat and the boatman are gone . . . .
Then silence. And this, with her singing,
 The Loreley has done.

HEINRICH HEINE
Translated by LOUIS UNTERMEYER

Beth Gêlert is a tense version of the ever-appealing story about a dog's devotion to his owner. The poem is placed in medieval times when game was hunted by spearsmen with packs of hounds and "brachs," dogs that hunt entirely by scent.

Beth Gêlert

The spearmen heard the bugle sound,
  And cheerily smiled the morn;
And many a brach, and many a hound
  Obeyed Llewellyn's horn.

And still he blew a louder blast,
  And gave a lustier cheer,
"Come, Gêlert, come, wert never last
  Llewellyn's horn to hear.

"O where does faithful Gêlert roam
  The flower of all his race;
So true, so brave—a lamb at home,
  A lion in the chase?"

In sooth, he was a peerless hound,
  The gift of royal John;
But now no Gêlert could be found,
  And all the chase rode on.

That day Llewellyn little loved
  The chase of hart and hare;
And scant and small the booty proved,
  For Gêlert was not there.

Unpleased, Llewellyn homeward hied,
  When, near the portal seat,
His truant Gêlert he espied
  Bounding his lord to greet.

But when he gained the castle-door,
  Aghast the chieftain stood;
The hound all o'er was smeared with gore;
  His lips, his fangs, ran blood.

Llewellyn gazed with fierce surprise;
  Unused such looks to meet,
His favorite checked his joyful guise,
  And crouched, and licked his feet.

Onward, in haste, Llewellyn passed,
  And on went Gêlert too;
And still, where'er his eyes he cast,
  Fresh blood-gouts shocked his view.

O'erturned his infant's bed he found,
  With blood-stained covert rent;
And all around the walls and ground
  With recent blood besprent.

He called his child—no voice replied—
  He searched with terror wild;
Blood, blood he found on every side,
  But nowhere found his child.

"Hell-hound! my child's by thee devoured,"
  The frantic father cried;
And to the hilt his vengeful sword
  He plunged in Gêlert's side.

Aroused by Gêlert's dying yell,
  Some slumberer wakened nigh;
What words the parent's joy could tell
  To hear his infant's cry!

Concealed beneath a tumbled heap
  His hurried search had missed,
All glowing from his rosy sleep
  The cherub boy he kissed.

No hurt had he, nor harm, nor dread,
  But, the same couch beneath,
Lay a gaunt wolf, all torn and dead,
  Tremendous still in death.

Ah, what was then Llewellyn's pain!
  For now the truth was clear;
His gallant hound the wolf had slain
  To save Llewellyn's heir.

WILLIAM ROBERT SPENCER

Phoebe Cary and her sister Alice supported themselves entirely by their writing in a day when few American women had careers. Alice was a journalist who wrote prose and verse; Phoebe wrote nothing but poetry. Deeply religious, she devoted herself mainly to hymns and moral poems like A Legend of the Northland.

A Legend of the Northland

Away, away in the Northland,
   Where the hours of the day are few,
And the nights are so long in winter
   That they cannot sleep them through;

Where they harness the swift reindeer
   To the sledges, when it snows;
And the children look like bear's cubs
   In their funny, furry clothes:

They tell them a curious story—
   I don't believe 'tis true;
And yet you may learn a lesson
   If I tell the tale to you.

Once, when the good Saint Peter
   Lived in the world below,
And walked about it, preaching,
   Just as he did, you know,

He came to the door of a cottage,
   In traveling round the earth,
Where a little woman was making cakes,
   And baking them on the hearth;

And being faint with fasting,
   For the day was almost done,
He asked her, from her store of cakes,
   To give him a single one.

So she made a very little cake,
   But as it baking lay,
She looked at it, and thought it seemed
   Too large to give away.

Therefore she kneaded another,
   And still a smaller one;
But it looked, when she turned it over,
   As large as the first had done.

Then she took a tiny scrap of dough,
   And rolled and rolled it flat;
And baked it thin as a wafer—
   But she couldn't part with that.

For she said, "My cakes that seem too small
   When I eat of them myself
Are yet too large to give away."
   So she put them on the shelf.

Then good Saint Peter grew angry,
   For he was hungry and faint;
And surely such a woman
   Was enough to provoke a saint.

And he said, "You are far too selfish
   To dwell in a human form,
To have both food and shelter,
   And fire to keep you warm.

"Now, you shall build as the birds do,
  And shall get your scanty food
By boring, and boring, and boring,
  All day in the hard, dry wood."

Then up she went through the chimney,
  Never speaking a word,
And out of the top flew a woodpecker,
  For she was changed to a bird.

She had had a scarlet cap on her head,
  And that was left the same;
But all the rest of her clothes were burned
  Black as a coal in the flame.

And every country schoolboy
  Has seen her in the wood,
Where she lives in the trees till this very day,
  Boring and boring for food.

PHOEBE CARY

A buccaneer is a sea robber, and the word suggests a pirate full of reckless dash and deviltry. But the buccaneer of this poem is old and tired and at the end of his roving days. The only pleasure left to him is remembering and recounting his past adventures.

The Last Buccaneer

Oh England is a pleasant place for them that's rich and high,
But England is a cruel place for such poor folks as I;
And such a port for mariners I ne'er shall see again
As the pleasant Isle of Avès, beside the Spanish Main.

There were forty craft in Avès that were both swift and stout,
All furnished well with small arms and cannons round about;
And a thousand men in Avès made laws so fair and free,
To choose their valiant captains and obey them loyally.

Thence we sailed against the Spaniard with his hoards of plate and gold,
Which he wrung with cruel tortures from Indian folk of old;
Likewise the merchant captains, with hearts as hard as stone,
Who flog men and keel-haul them, and starve them to the bone.

Oh, the palms grew high in Avès, and fruits that shone like gold,
And the colibris[1] and parrots they were gorgeous to behold;
And the negro maids to Avès from bondage fast did flee.
To welcome gallant sailors, a-sweeping in from sea.

Oh, sweet it was in Avès to hear the landward breeze,
A-swing with good tobacco in a net between the trees,
With a negro lass to fan you, while you listened to the roar
Of the breakers on the reef outside, that never touched the shore.

[1] Colibris: tropical hummingbirds

140

But Scripture saith, an ending to all fine things must be;
So the King's ships sailed on Avès, and quite put down were we.
All day we fought like bull-dogs, but they burst the booms at night;
And I fled in a piragua,[2] sore wounded, from the fight.

Nine days I floated starving, and a negro lass beside,
Till for all I tried to cheer her, the poor young thing she died;
But as I lay a-gasping, a Bristol sail came by,
And brought me home to England here, to beg until I die.

And now I'm old and going—I'm sure I can't tell where;
One comfort is, this world's so hard, I can't be worse off there:
If I might but be a sea dove, I'd fly across the main
To the pleasant Isle of Aves, to look at it once again.

CHARLES KINGSLEY

*Not all of the marvelous judgments of Solomon are found in the Bible.
His clever solution of the riddle of the true and false flowers comes from
the Talmud, a book of Jewish law and legend.*

Solomon and the Bees

When Solomon was reigning in his glory,
Unto his throne the Queen of Sheba came
(So in the Talmud you may read the story),
Drawn by the magic of the monarch's fame,
To see the splendors of his court, and bring
Some fitting tribute to the mighty king.

[2] **Piragua:** a boat made by hollowing out a large log

Nor this alone; much had her Highness heard
What flowers of learning graced the royal speech;
What gems of wisdom dropped with every word;
What wholesome lessons he was wont to teach
In pleasing proverbs; and she wished, in sooth,
To know if rumor spoke the simple truth.

And straight she held before the monarch's view,
In either hand, a radiant wreath of flowers;
The one, bedecked with every charming hue,
Was newly culled from nature's choicest bowers;
The other, no less fair in every part,
Was the rare product of divinest art.

"Which is the true, and which the false?" she said.
Great Solomon was silent. All-amazed,
Each wondering courtier shook his puzzled head,
While at the garlands long the monarch gazed,
As one who sees a miracle, and fain,
For very rapture, ne'er would speak again.

While thus he pondered, presently he sees,
Hard by the casement,—so the story goes—
A little band of busy, bustling bees,
Hunting for honey in a withered rose.
The monarch smiled, and raised his royal head;
"Open the window!"—that was all he said.

The window opened at the king's command;
Within the room the eager insects flew,
And sought the flowers in Sheba's dexter[1] hand!
And so the king and all the courtiers knew
That wreath was nature's; and the baffled queen
Returned to tell the wonders she had seen.

My story teaches (every tale should bear
A fitting moral) that the wise may find,
In trifles light as atoms in the air,
Some useful lesson to enrich the mind,
Some truth designed to profit or to please—
As Israel's king learned wisdom from the bees!

JOHN GODFREY SAXE

[1] Dexter: right

142

George Gordon, Lord Byron, was a daring horseman, a tireless swimmer, a reckless gallant, and a fiery rebel who met his death fighting for freedom in Greece. He loved rather theatrical writing and frequently took legendary events for his subjects.

The basis for The Destruction of Sennacherib *is in the Old Testament, in the Second Book of Kings. Sennacherib was an Assyrian king who besieged Jerusalem. Before he could destroy it, "the angel of Jehovah went forth and smote in the camp of the Assyrians a hundred four-score and five thousand," and the army of Sennacherib was annihilated. Ashur was the war god of the Assyrians; therefore, Byron refers to the wives of the slain warriors as the "widows of Ashur." Baal was one of the chief heathen gods.*

The Destruction of Sennacherib

The Assyrian came down like the wolf on the fold,
And his cohorts were gleaming in purple and gold;
And the sheen of their spears was like stars on the sea,
When the blue wave rolls nightly on deep Galilee.

Like the leaves of the forest when summer is green,
That host with their banners at sunset were seen:
Like the leaves of the forest when autumn hath blown,
That host on the morrow laid withered and strown.

For the Angel of Death spread his wings on the blast,
And breathed in the face of the foe as he passed;
And the eyes of the sleepers waxed deadly and chill,
And their hearts but once heaved, and forever grew still!

And there lay the steed with his nostril all wide,
But through it there rolled not the breath of his pride:
And the foam of his gasping lay white on the turf,
And cold as the spray of the rock-beating surf.

And there lay the rider distorted and pale,
With the dew on his brow, and the rust on his mail;
And the tents were all silent, the banners alone,
The lances unlifted, the trumpet unblown.

And the widows of Ashur are loud in their wail,
And the idols are broke in the temple of Baal;
And the might of the Gentile, unsmote by the sword,
Hath melted like snow in the glance of the Lord!

GEORGE GORDON, LORD BYRON

143

The story in which one baby is substituted for another is an old one and has been used by many writers in a variety of ways. W. S. Gilbert made it the comic basis of General John, which you will find on page 202. Tennyson took the situation seriously and gave it the tone of an antique ballad.

Lady Clare

Lord Ronald courted Lady Clare,
    I trow they did not part in scorn;
Lord Ronald, her cousin, courted her,
    And they will wed the morrow morn.

"He does not love me for my birth,
    Nor for my lands so broad and fair;
He loves me for my own true worth,
    And that is well," said Lady Clare.

In there came old Alice the nurse,
    Said, "Who was this that went from thee?"
"It was my cousin," said Lady Clare,
    "To-morrow he weds with me."

"O God be thanked!" said Alice the nurse,
    "That all comes round so just and fair:
Lord Ronald is heir of all your lands,
    And you are not the Lady Clare."

"Are ye out of your mind, my nurse, my nurse?"
    Said Lady Clare, "that ye speak so wild?"
"As God's above!" said Alice the nurse,
    "I speak the truth: you are my child.

"The old Earl's daughter died at my breast;
    I speak the truth, as I live by bread!
I buried her like my own sweet child,
    And put my child in her stead."

"Falsely, falsely have ye done,
    O mother," she said, "if this be true,
To keep the best man under the sun
    So many years from his due."

"Nay now, my child," said Alice the nurse,
    "But keep the secret for your life,
And all you have will be Lord Ronald's,
    When you are man and wife."

"If I'm a beggar born," she said,
    "I will speak out, for I dare not lie.
Pull off, pull off, the brooch of gold,
    And fling that diamond necklace by."

"Nay now, my child," said Alice the nurse,
    "But keep the secret all ye can."
She said, "Not so, but I will know
    If there be any faith in man."

"Nay now, what faith?" said Alice the nurse,
    "The man will cleave unto his right."
"And he shall have it," the lady replied,
    "Though I should die to-night."

"Yet give one kiss to your mother dear;
    Alas, my child, I sinned for thee."
"O mother, mother, mother," she said,
    "So strange it seems to me.

"Yet here's a kiss for my mother dear,
    My mother dear, if this be so;
And lay your hand upon my head,
    And bless me, mother, ere I go."

She clad herself in a russet gown,
    She was no longer Lady Clare:
She went by dale, and she went by down,
    With a single rose in her hair.

Down stept Lord Ronald from his tower:
  "O Lady Clare, you shame your worth!
Why come you drest like a village maid,
  That are the flower of the earth?"

"If I come drest like a village maid,
  I am but as my fortunes are:
I am a beggar born," she said,
  "And not the Lady Clare."

"Play me no tricks," said Lord Ronald,
  "For I am yours in word and in deed.
Play me no tricks," said Lord Ronald,
  "Your riddle is hard to read."

O and proudly stood she up!
  Her heart within her did not fail:
She looked into Lord Ronald's eyes,
  And told him all her nurse's tale.

He laughed a laugh of merry scorn:
  He turned, and kissed her where she stood,
"If you are not the heiress born,
  And I," said he, "the next in blood—

"If you are not the heiress born,
  And I," said he, "the lawful heir,
We two will wed to-morrow morn,
  And you shall still be Lady Clare."

ALFRED, LORD TENNYSON

145

Blenheim is a Bavarian village on the banks of the Danube. In 1704 it was the scene of a bloody encounter in which the French and Bavarian troops fought the Austrian and English armies who were under the command of the Duke of Marlborough and Prince Eugene.

The following poem is not about the battle itself but about an old Bavarian peasant and his two grandchildren. One of the children discovers a soldier's skull in the field, and Old Kaspar tries to tell the children what the battle was about. But he no longer remembers—if he ever knew— why it was fought. To the children war seems wasteful and wicked, and when one of them asks what good came of it in the end, Old Kaspar cannot answer. He can only stupidly repeat the false words of history that it was a "famous victory!"

The Battle of Blenheim

It was a summer evening;
  Old Kaspar's work was done,
And he before his cottage door
  Was sitting in the sun;
And by him sported on the green
His little grandchild Wilhelmine.

She saw her brother Peterkin
  Roll something large and round,
Which he beside the rivulet
  In playing there had found.
He came to ask what he had found,
That was so large, and smooth, and round.

Old Kaspar took it from the boy,
  Who stood expectant by;
And then the old man shook his head,
  And with a natural sigh,
"'Tis some poor fellow's skull," said he,
"Who fell in the great victory.

"I find them in the garden,
  For there's many here about;
And often, when I go to plow,
  The plowshare turns them out;
For many thousand men," said he,
"Were slain in that great victory."

"Now tell us what 'twas all about,"
    Young Peterkin, he cries;
And little Wilhelmine looks up
    With wonder-waiting eyes;
"Now tell us all about the war,
And what they fought each other for."

"It was the English," Kaspar cried,
    "Who put the French to rout;
But what they fought each other for,
    I could not well make out;
But everybody said," quoth he,
"That 'twas a famous victory.

"My father lived at Blenheim then,
    Yon little stream hard by;
They burnt his dwelling to the ground,
    And he was forced to fly;
So with his wife and child he fled,
Nor had he where to rest his head.

"With fire and sword the country round
    Was wasted far and wide,
And many a childing mother then,
    And new-born baby, died;
But things like that, you know, must be
At every famous victory.

"They say it was a shocking sight
    After the field was won;
For many thousand bodies here
    Lay rotting in the sun;
But things like that, you know, must be
After a famous victory.

"Great praise the Duke of Marlboro' won,
    And our good Prince Eugene."
"Why, 'twas a very wicked thing!"
    Said little Wilhelmine.
"Nay, nay, my little girl," quoth he;
"It was a famous victory.

"And everybody praised the Duke
    Who this great fight did win."
"But what good came of it at last?"
    Quoth little Peterkin.
"Why, that I cannot tell," said he;
"But 'twas a famous victory."

ROBERT SOUTHEY

147

Although a purely imaginary episode, Incident of the French Camp *is supposed to have taken place in 1809 when Napoleon attacked the city of Ratisbon. The speaker is one of Napoleon's aides. He sets the stage and presents the characters: the Emperor and a young messenger, both of whom live deathlessly in the climax of the last verse.*

In a few lines, Robert Browning sketches a sharply delineated picture of Napoleon. We see him in his characteristic posture, with sunk head, his neck thrust out, his "legs wide, arms locked behind." We also see the battle-ground with the cannon smoke beyond, and little details, such as the two-pointed flags flapping in the breeze, like the wings (or "vans") of a bird.

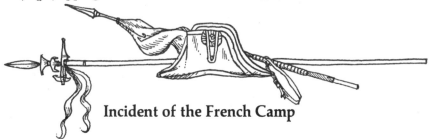

Incident of the French Camp

You know, we French stormed Ratisbon.
    A mile or so away,
On a little mound, Napoleon
    Stood on our storming-day;
With neck out-thrust, you fancy how,
    Legs wide, arms locked behind,
As if to balance the prone brow
    Oppressive with its mind.

Just as perhaps he mused "My plans
    That soar, to earth may fall,
Let once my army-leader Lannes
    Waver at yonder wall"—
Out 'twixt the battery smokes there flew
    A rider, bound on bound
Full-galloping; nor bridle drew
    Until he reached the mound.

Then off there flung in smiling joy,
    And held himself erect
By just his horse's mane, a boy:
    You hardly could suspect—
(So tight he kept his lips compressed,
    Scarce any blood came through)
You looked twice ere you saw his breast
    Was all but shot in two.

"Well," cried he, "Emperor, by God's grace
    We've got you Ratisbon!
The Marshal's in the market-place,
    And you'll be there anon
To see your flag-bird flap his vans
    Where I, to heart's desire,
Perched him!" The chief's eye flashed; his plans
    Soared up again like fire.

The chief's eye flashed; but presently
    Softened itself, as sheathes
A film the mother-eagle's eye
    When her bruised eaglet breathes;
"You're wounded!" "Nay," the soldier's pride
    Touched to the quick, he said:
"I'm killed, Sire!" And, his chief beside,
    Smiling, the boy fell dead.

ROBERT BROWNING

There is no real historical foundation for Browning's How They Brought the Good News from Ghent to Aix. The action is supposed to take place in the early seventeenth century when some of the Dutch states, under the leadership of William of Orange, banded together against the tyrannical power of Philip II of Spain. The story is only half told; the other half must be imagined. Three men hasten to bring good tidings from Ghent to Aix, a ride of about ninety miles, but only one of them—the speaker on his sturdy mount, Roland—arrives at his destination after riding from midnight to midday. The news must be delivered at once. But we are not told what the news is. Perhaps the enemy has been defeated and the defenders of the besieged town of Aix are saved. Perhaps a new alliance has been made which will turn the tide of battle. It is not the words, but the breathless rhythm—the hurry of the headlong lines, the steady beat of the hoofs, the forward lurch of the horses—which make it plain that this ride is a matter of life and death.

How They Brought the Good News from Ghent to Aix

I sprang to the stirrup, and Joris, and he;
I galloped, Dirck galloped, we galloped all three;
"Good speed!" cried the watch, as the gate bolts undrew,
"Speed!" echoed the wall to us galloping through;
Behind shut the postern, the lights sank to rest,
And into the midnight we galloped abreast.

Not a word to each other; we kept the great pace
Neck by neck, stride by stride, never changing our place;
I turned in my saddle and made its girths tight,
Then shortened each stirrup, and set the pique right,
Rebuckled the cheek-strap, chained slacker the bit,
Nor galloped less steadily Roland a whit.

149

'Twas moonset at starting; but while we drew near
Lokeren, the cocks crew and twilight dawned clear;
At Boom, a great yellow star came out to see;
At Düffeld, 'twas morning as plain as could be;
And from Mecheln church-steeple we heard the half-chime,
So, Joris broke silence with, "Yet there is time!"

At Aershot, up leaped of a sudden the sun,
And against him the cattle stood black every one,
To stare thro' the mist at us galloping past,
And I saw my stout galloper Roland at last,
With resolute shoulders, each butting away
The haze, as some bluff river headland its spray:

And his low head and crest, just one sharp ear bent back
For my voice, and the other pricked out on his track;
And one eye's black intelligence,—ever that glance
O'er its white edge at me, his own master askance!
And the thick heavy spume-flakes which aye and anon
His fierce lips shook upwards in galloping on.

By Hasselt, Dirck groaned; and cried Joris, "Stay spur!
Your Roos galloped bravely, the fault's not in her,
We'll remember at Aix"—for one heard the quick wheeze
Of her chest, saw the stretched neck and staggering knees,
And sunk tail, and horrible heave of the flank,
As down on her haunches she shuddered and sank.

So, we were left galloping, Joris and I,
Past Looz and past Tongres, no cloud in the sky;
The broad sun above laughed a pitiless laugh,
'Neath our feet broke the brittle bright stubble like chaff;
Till over by Dalhem a dome-spire sprang white,
And "Gallop," gasped Joris, "for Aix is in sight!"

"How they'll greet us!"—and all in a moment his roan
Rolled neck and croup over, lay dead as a stone;
And there was my Roland to bear the whole weight
Of the news which alone could save Aix from her fate,
With his nostrils like pits full of blood to the brim,
And with circles of red for his eye-sockets' rim.

Then I cast loose my buffcoat, each holster let fall,
Shook off both my jack-boots, let go belt and all,
Stood up in the stirrup, leaned, patted his ear,
Called my Roland his pet-name, my horse without peer;
Clapped my hands, laughed and sang, any noise, bad or good,
Till at length into Aix Roland galloped and stood.

And all I remember is—friends flocking round
As I sat with his head 'twixt my knees on the ground;
And no voice but was praising this Roland of mine,
As I poured down his throat our last measure of wine,
Which (the burgesses voted by common consent)
Was no more than his due who brought good news from Ghent.

ROBERT BROWNING

151

There is a Persian story about a miserly person who, as punishment for his meanness, was spirited away by the wind. The seed of this slender idea was planted in Robert Browning's imagination and blossomed into the richly colored The Pied Piper of Hamelin. Every picture in the poem is as graphic as an old print, while the story itself holds us spellbound.

Suddenly, the poem turns into a fable and ends with a moral about what can happen when people do not keep their promises. The "Willy" of the last stanza is the boy for whom the poem was written. He was the son of Browning's good friend, the well-known actor, William Macready.

The Pied Piper of Hamelin

Hamelin Town's in Brunswick,
y famous Hanover city;
  The river Weser, deep and wide,
  Washes its wall on the southern side;
  A pleasanter spot you never spied;
ut, when begins my ditty,
  Almost five hundred years ago,
  To see the townsfolk suffer so
rom vermin was a pity.

    Rats!
hey fought the dogs, and kill'd the cats,
  And bit the babies in the cradles,
nd ate the cheeses out of the vats,
  And lick'd the soup from the cook's own ladles,
lit open the kegs of salted sprats,
Iade nests inside men's Sunday hats,
nd even spoil'd the women's chats,
    By drowning their speaking
    With shrieking and squeaking
ı fifty different sharps and flats.

t last the people in a body
  To the Town Hall came flocking:
'Tis clear," cried they, "our Mayor's a noddy;
  And as for our Corporation—shocking
o think we buy gowns lined with ermine
ır dolts that can't or won't determine
'hat's best to rid us of our vermin!
ıu hope, because you're old and obese,
ɔ find in the furry civic robe ease?
ıuse up, sirs! Give your brains a racking
ɔ find the remedy we're lacking,
r, sure as fate, we'll send you packing!"
t this the Mayor and Corporation
ιaked with a mighty consternation.

ı hour they sate in counsel,
  At length the Mayor broke silence:
ɪr a guilder I'd my ermine gown sell;
  I wish I were a mile hence!
s easy to bid one rack one's brain—

I'm sure my poor head aches again,
I've scratch'd it so, and all in vain.
Oh for a trap, a trap, a trap!"
Just as he said this, what should hap
At the chamber-door but a gentle tap?
"Bless us!" cried the Mayor, "what's that?"
(With the Corporation as he sat,
Looking little though wondrous fat;
Nor brighter was his eye, nor moister
Than a too long-open'd oyster,
Save when at noon his paunch grew mutinous
For a plate of turtle, green and glutinous)
"Only a scraping of shoes on the mat?
Anything like the sound of a rat
Makes my heart go pit-a-pat!"

"Come in!"—the Mayor cried, looking bigger:
And in did come the strangest figure!
His queer long coat from heel to head
Was half of yellow and half of red;
And he himself was tall and thin,
With sharp blue eyes, each like a pin,
And light loose hair, yet swarthy skin,
No tuft on cheek nor beard on chin,
But lips where smiles went out and in—
There was no guessing his kith and kin!
And nobody could enough admire
The tall man and his quaint attire:
Quoth one: "It's as if my great-grandsire,
Starting up at the Trump of Doom's tone,
Had walk'd this way from his painted
                              tombstone!"
He advanced to the council-table:
And, "Please your honors," said he, "I'm able,
By means of a secret charm, to draw
All creatures living beneath the sun,
That creep, or swim, or fly, or run,
After me so as you never saw!
And I chiefly use my charm
On creatures that do people harm,
The mole, and toad, and newt, and viper;
And people call me the Pied Piper."

153

(And here they noticed round his neck
A scarf of red and yellow stripe,
To match with his coat of the selfsame check;
And at the scarf's end hung a pipe;
And his fingers, they noticed, were ever straying
As if impatient to be playing
Upon this pipe, as low it dangled
Over his vesture so old-fangled.)
"Yet," said he, "poor piper as I am,
In Tartary I freed the Cham,
Last June, from his huge swarm of gnats;
I eased in Asia the Nizam
Of a monstrous brood of vampire bats;
And, as for what your brain bewilders—
If I can rid your town of rats,
Will you give me a thousand guilders?"
"One? Fifty thousand!" was the exclamation
Of the astonish'd Mayor and Corporation.

Into the street the Piper stept,
    Smiling first a little smile,
As if he knew what magic slept
    In his quiet pipe the while;
Then, like a musical adept,
To blow the pipe his lips he wrinkled,
And green and blue his sharp eyes twinkled,
Like a candle-flame where salt is sprinkled;
And ere three shrill notes the pipe had utter'd,
You heard as if an army mutter'd;

And the muttering grew to a grumbling;
And the grumbling grew to a mighty rumbling;
And out of the houses the rats came tumbling.
Great rats, small rats, lean rats, brawny rats,
Brown rats, black rats, gray rats, tawny rats,
Grave old plodders, gay young friskers,
    Fathers, mothers, uncles, cousins,
Cocking tails and pricking whiskers,
    Families by tens and dozens,
Brothers, sisters, husbands, wives—
Follow'd the Piper for their lives.
From street to street he piped advancing,
And step for step they follow'd dancing,
Until they came to the river Weser,
Wherein all plunged and perish'd,
Save one who, stout as Julius Caesar,
Swam across and lived to carry
(As the manuscript he cherish'd)
To Rat-land home his commentary,
Which was, "At the first shrill notes of the pipe
I heard a sound as of scraping tripe,
And putting apples, wondrous ripe,
Into a cider press's gripe:
And a moving away of pickle-tub boards,
And a leaving ajar of conserve-cupboards,
And a drawing the corks of train-oil flasks,
And a breaking the hoops of butter-casks;
And it seemed as if a voice
(Sweeter far than by harp or by psaltery
Is breathed) call'd out, O rats, rejoice!
The world is grown to one vast dry-saltery!
So munch on, crunch on, take your nuncheon,
Breakfast, supper, dinner, luncheon!
And just as a bulky sugar-puncheon,
All ready staved, like a great sun shone
Glorious scarce an inch before me,
Just as methought it said, Come, bore me!
I found the Weser rolling o'er me."

You should have heard the Hamelin people
Ringing the bells till they rock'd the steeple;
"Go," cried the Mayor, "and get long poles!
Poke out the nests and block up the holes!
Consult with carpenters and builders,
And leave in our town not even a trace
Of the rats!"—when suddenly up the face
Of the Piper perk'd in the market-place,
With a, "First, if you please, my thousand guilders!"

A thousand guilders! The Mayor look'd blue;
So did the Corporation too.
For council dinners made rare havoc
With Claret, Moselle, Vin-de-Grave, Hock;
And half the money would replenish
Their cellar's biggest butt with Rhenish.
To pay this sum to a wandering fellow
With a gypsy coat of red and yellow!
"Beside," quoth the Mayor, with a knowing wink,
"Our business was done at the river's brink;
We saw with our eyes the vermin sink,
And what's dead can't come to life, I think.
So, friend, we're not the folks to shrink
From the duty of giving you something for drink,

And a matter of money to put in your poke;
But, as for the guilders, what we spoke
Of them, as you very well know, was in joke.
Beside, our losses have made us thrifty;
A thousand guilders! Come, take fifty!"

The Piper's face fell and he cried,
"No trifling! I can't wait! beside,
I've promised to visit by dinner-time
Bagdad, and accept the prime
Of the Head Cook's pottage, all he's rich in,
For having left, in the Caliph's kitchen,
Of a nest of scorpions no survivor—

With him I proved no bargain-driver.
With you, don't think I'll bate a stiver!
And folks who put me in a passion
May find me pipe to another fashion."

"How?" cried the Mayor, "d'ye think I'll brook
Being worse treated than a cook?
Insulted by a lazy ribald
With idle pipe and vesture piebald?
You threaten us, fellow? Do your worst,
Blow your pipe there till you burst!"

Once more he stept into the street;
    And to his lips again
Laid his long pipe of smooth straight cane;
    And ere he blew three notes (such sweet
Soft notes as yet musician's cunning
    Never gave the enraptured air)
There was a rustling that seem'd like a bustling
Of merry crowds justling at pitching and hustling,
Small feet were pattering, wooden shoes clattering,
Little hands clapping, and little tongues chattering,
And, like fowls in a farm-yard when barley is scattering,
Out came the children running.
All the little boys and girls,
With rosy cheeks and flaxen curls,
And sparkling eyes and teeth like pearls,
Tripping and skipping, ran merrily after
The wonderful music with shouting and laughter.

156

The Mayor was dumb, and the Council stood
As if they were changed into blocks of wood,
Unable to move a step, or cry
To the children merrily skipping by—
And could only follow with the eye
That joyous crowd at the Piper's back.
But how the Mayor was on the rack,
And the wretched Council's bosoms beat,
As the Piper turn'd from the High Street
To where the Weser roll'd its waters
Right in the way of their sons and daughters!
However, he turned from south to west,
And to Koppelberg Hill his steps address'd,
And after him the children press'd;
Great was the joy in every breast.

"He never can cross that mighty top!
 He's forced to let the piping drop,
 And we shall see our children stop!"
When, lo, as they reach'd the mountain's side,
A wondrous portal open'd wide,
As if a cavern was suddenly hollow'd;
And the Piper advanced and the children follow'd,
And when all were in to the very last,
The door in the mountain-side shut fast.
Did I say all? No! one was lame,
And could not dance the whole of the way,
And in after years, if you would blame
His sadness, he was used to say,
"It's dull in our town since my playmates left!
 I can't forget that I'm bereft
 Of all the pleasant sights they see,
 Which the Piper also promised me,
 For he led us, he said, to a joyous land,
 Joining the town and just at hand,
 Where waters gush'd and fruit trees grew,
 And flowers put forth a fairer hue,
 And everything was strange and new;
 The sparrows were brighter than peacocks here,
 And the dogs outran our fallow deer,
 And honey-bees had lost their stings,
 And horses were born with eagles' wings;
 And just as I became assured
 My lame foot would be speedily cured,
 The music stopp'd, and I stood still,
 And found myself outside the Hill,
 Left alone against my will,
 To go now limping as before,
 And never hear of that country more!"

Alas, alas for Hamelin!
     There came into many a burgher's pate
     A text which says that Heaven's Gate
     Opes to the rich at as easy rate
As the needle's eye takes a camel in!

The Mayor sent east, west, north, and south
To offer the Piper by word of mouth,
    Wherever it was men's lot to find him,
Silver and gold to his heart's content,
If he'd only return the way he went,
    And bring the children behind him.
But when they saw 'twas a lost endeavor,
And Piper and dancers were gone forever,
They made a decree that lawyers never
    Should think their records dated duly
If, after the day of the month and year,
These words did not as well appear:
"And so long after what happen'd here
    On the twenty-second of July,
Thirteen hundred and Seventy-six;"
And the better in memory to fix
The place of the children's last retreat,
They call'd it the Pied Piper's Street,
Where any one playing on pipe or tabor
Was sure for the future to lose his labor.
Nor suffer'd they hostelry or tavern
    To shock with mirth a street so solemn,
But opposite the place of the cavern
    They wrote the story on a column,
And on the great church-window painted
The same, to make the world acquainted
How their children were stolen away,
And there it stands to this very day.
And I must not omit to say
That in Transylvania there's a tribe
Of alien people that ascribe
The outlandish ways and dress
On which their neighbors lay such stress,
To their fathers and mothers having risen
Out of some subterranean prison,
Into which they were trepann'd
Long time ago in a mighty band
Out of Hamelin town in Brunswick land,
But how or why, they don't understand.

So, Willy, let you and me be wipers
Of scores out with all men—especially pipers;
And, whether they pipe us free, from rats or from mice,
If we've promised them aught, let us keep our promise.

ROBERT BROWNING

158

Casabianca was supposed to have happened just as the poet tells it. Historians have given it a date and a place: August 1, 1798, the Battle of the Nile between Napoleon's French forces and the British fleet under the command of Admiral Nelson. The first line of the poem has become so familiar that countless parodies of it have been circulated.

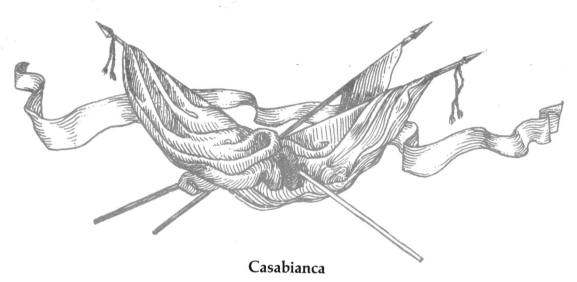

Casabianca

The boy stood on the burning deck
    Whence all but he had fled;
The flame that lit the battle's wreck
    Shone round him o'er the dead.

The flames rolled on. He would not go
    Without his father's word;
That father faint in death below,
    His voice no longer heard.

He called aloud: "Say, father, say
    If yet my task is done!"
He knew not that the chieftain lay
    Unconscious of his son.

"Speak, father!" once again he cried,
    "If I may yet be gone!"
And but the booming shots replied,
    And fast the flames rolled on.

Upon his brow he felt their breath,
    And in his waving hair,

And looked from that lone post of death
    In still yet brave despair;

And shouted but once more aloud,
    "My father! must I stay?"
While o'er him fast through sail and shroud,
    The wreathing fires made way.

They wrapt the ship in splendor wild,
    They caught the flag on high,
And streamed above the gallant child
    Like banners in the sky.

Then came a burst of thunder-sound—
    The boy—oh! where was he?
Ask of the winds that far around
    With fragments strewed the sea,

With mast, and helm, and pennon fair,
    That well had borne their part.
But the noblest thing that perished there
    Was that young faithful heart.

FELICIA HEMANS

159

Reading a story in which evil seems to triumph, we derive a particular satisfaction when, at the end, the villain gets his just deserts. Sir Ralph was such a villain, and The Inchcape Rock *brings him to the end he deserves.*

The Inchcape Rock

No stir in the air, no stir in the sea—
The ship was as still as she could be;
Her sails from heaven received no motion;
Her keel was steady in the ocean.

Without either sign or sound of their shock,
The waves flowed over the Inchcape rock;
So little they rose, so little they fell,
They did not move the Inchcape bell.

The holy Abbot of Aberbrothok
Had placed that bell on the Inchcape rock;
On a buoy in the storm it floated and swung
And over the waves it warning rung.

When the rock was hid by the surges' swell,
The mariners heard the warning bell;
And then they knew the perilous rock,
And blessed the Abbot of Aberbrothok.

The sun in heaven was shining gay—
All things were joyful on that day;
The sea-birds screamed as they wheeled around,
And there was joyance in their sound.

The buoy of the Inchcape bell was seen,
A darker speck on the ocean green;
Sir Ralph, the rover, walked his deck,
And he fixed his eyes on the darker speck.

His eye was on the bell and float:
Quoth he, "My men, put out the boat;
And row me to the Inchcape rock,
And I'll plague the priest of Aberbrothok."

The boat is lowered, the boatmen row,
And to the Inchcape rock they go;
Sir Ralph bent over from the boat,
And cut the warning bell from the float.

Down sank the bell with a gurgling sound;
The bubbles rose, and burst around.
Quoth Sir Ralph,
  "The next who comes to the rock
Will not bless the Abbot of Aberbrothok."

Sir Ralph, the rover, sailed away—
He scoured the seas for many a day;
And now, grown rich with plundered store,
He steers his course to Scotland's shore.

So thick a haze o'erspreads the sky
They cannot see the sun on high;
The wind hath blown a gale all day;
At evening it hath died away.

On the deck the rover takes his stand;
So dark it is they see no land.
Quoth Sir Ralph, "It will be lighter soon,
For there is the dawn of the rising moon."

"Canst hear," said one, "the breakers roar?
For yonder, methinks, should be the shore.
Now where we are I cannot tell,
But I wish we could hear the Inchcape bell."

They hear no sound; the swell is strong;
Though the wind hath fallen,
    they drift along;
Till the vessel strikes with a shivering shock—
O Christ! it is the Inchcape rock!

Sir Ralph, the rover, tore his hair;
He cursed himself in his despair.
The waves rush in on every side;
The ship is sinking beneath the tide.

But ever in his dying fear
One dreadful sound he seemed to hear—
A sound as if with the Inchcape bell
The Devil below was ringing his knell.

ROBERT SOUTHEY

161

It was believed by the ancients that the god of fields and gardens was a wild creature, half-man, half-goat, called Pan. There seemed to be something frightening about his occasional appearances to mortals—the word "panic" comes from his name. Yet he was a laughing demigod and supposedly the inventor of one of the first musical instruments: a pipe which he made from river reeds—the pipe of Pan. Elizabeth Barrett Browning, the wife of Robert Browning, has made the creation of the pipe the center of her poem, catching not only the restorative magic of the music but the careless side of Pan who "scattered ban" (destruction) as he went his way.

A Musical Instrument

What was he doing, the great god Pan,
    Down in the reeds by the river?
Spreading ruin and scattering ban,
Splashing and paddling with hoofs of a goat,
And breaking the golden lilies afloat
    With the dragon-fly on the river.

He tore out a reed, the great god Pan,
    From the deep cool bed of the river;
The limpid waters turbidly ran,
And the broken lilies a-dying lay,
And the dragon-fly had fled away,
    Ere he brought it out of the river.

He cut it short, did the great god Pan,
    (How tall it stood in the river!)
Then drew the pith, like the heart of a man,
Steadily from the outside ring,
And notched the poor dry empty thing
    In holes, as he sat by the river.

"This is the way," laughed the great god Pan
    (Laughed while he sat by the river),
"The only way, since gods began
    To make sweet music, they could succeed."
Then, dropping his mouth to a hole in the reed,
    He blew in power by the river.

Sweet, sweet, sweet, O Pan!
    Piercing sweet by the river!
Blinding sweet, O great god Pan!
The sun on the hill forgot to die,
And the lilies revived, and the dragon-fly
    Came back to dream on the river.

Yet half a beast is the great god Pan,
    To laugh as he sits by the river,
Making a poet out of a man.
The true gods sigh for the cost and pain—
For the reed which grows nevermore again
    As a reed with the reeds in the river.

ELIZABETH BARRETT BROWNING

Edgar Allan Poe, who wrote The Murders in the Rue Morgue *and* The Gold Bug, *was the father of the murder mystery and detective story. He also created tales of grotesque and imaginative horror, such as* The Tell-Tale Heart. *Many of his poems weave together the chilling quality of his fiction with a sad and echoing melodiousness.*

Annabel Lee

It was many and many a year ago,
    In a kingdom by the sea,
That a maiden there lived whom you may know
    By the name of Annabel Lee;
And this maiden she lived with no other thought
    Than to love and be loved by me.

I was a child and *she* was a child,
    In this kingdom by the sea,
But we loved with a love that was more than love,
    I and my Annabel Lee;
With a love that the winged seraphs of heaven
    Coveted her and me.

And this was the reason that, long ago,
    In this kingdom by the sea,
A wind blew out of a cloud, chilling
    My beautiful Annabel Lee;
So that her highborn kinsmen came
    And bore her away from me,
To shut her up in a sepulchre
    In this kingdom by the sea.

The angels, not half so happy in heaven,
    Went envying her and me;
Yes! that was the reason (as all men know,
    In this kingdom by the sea)
That the wind came out of the cloud by night,
    Chilling and killing my Annabel Lee.

But our love it was stronger by far than the love
    Of those who were older than we,
    Of many far wiser than we;
And neither the angels in heaven above,
    Nor the demons down under the sea,
Can ever dissever my soul from the soul
    Of the beautiful Annabel Lee:

163

For the moon never beams, without bringing me dreams
    Of the beautiful Annabel Lee;
And the stars never rise, but I see the bright eyes
    Of the beautiful Annabel Lee;
And so, all the night-tide, I lie down by the side
Of my darling—my darling—my life and my bride,
    In her sepulchre there by the sea,
    In her tomb by the sounding sea.

EDGAR ALLAN POE

So odd and fanciful is the idea behind The Dumb Soldier *that, although nothing really happens in the poem, something happens in the reader—if only to his imagination.*

The Dumb Soldier

When the grass was closely mown,
Walking on the lawn alone,
In the turf a hole I found,
And hid a soldier underground.

Spring and daisies came apace;
Grasses hide my hiding place;
Grasses run like a green sea
O'er the lawn up to my knee.

Under grass alone he lies,
Looking up with leaden eyes,
Scarlet coat and pointed gun,
To the stars and to the sun.

When the grass is ripe like grain,
When the scythe is stoned again,
When the lawn is shaven clear,
Then my hole shall reappear.

I shall find him, never fear,
I shall find my grenadier;
But for all that's gone and come,
I shall find my soldier dumb.

He has lived, a little thing,
In the grassy woods of spring;
Done, if he could tell me true,
Just as I should like to do.

He has seen the starry hours
And the springing of the flowers;
And the fairy things that pass
In the forests of the grass.

In the silence he has heard
Talking bee and ladybird,
And the butterfly has flown
O'er him as he lay alone.

Not a word will he disclose,
Not a word of all he knows.
I must lay him on the shelf,
And make up the tale myself.

ROBERT LOUIS STEVENSON

Nathalia Crane was nine years old in 1922 when she sent some verses to a New York newspaper. The editor was glad to print them; he had no idea that they were written by a little girl. She was ten and a half when her first volume, The Janitor's Boy and Other Poems, *was published and created a sensation. It was followed by several other books, all of which showed a maturity of thought as well as a youthful fancy.*

The Janitor's Boy

Oh I'm in love with the janitor's boy,
   And the janitor's boy loves me;
He's going to hunt for a desert isle
   In our geography.

A desert isle with spicy trees
   Somewhere near Sheepshead Bay;
A right nice place, just fit for two
   Where we can live alway.

Oh I'm in love with the janitor's boy,
   He's busy as he can be;
And down in the cellar he's making a raft
   Out of an old settee.

He'll carry me off, I know that he will,
   For his hair is exceedingly red;
And the only thing that occurs to me
   Is to dutifully shiver in bed.

The day that we sail, I shall leave this brief note,
   For my parents I hate to annoy:
I have flown away to an isle in the bay
   With the janitor's red-haired boy."

NATHALIA CRANE

165

*All story-poems aren't meant to be taken seriously. The next one cer-
tainly is not. It requires that you believe in a girl who owned a pet dragon
and—of all things—a dragon named Custard. Even if you suspect that
the tale isn't true, you will find Custard the most amusing—and most
amazing—dragon you ever met.*

The Tale of Custard the Dragon

Belinda lived in a little white house,
With a little black kitten and a little gray mouse,
And a little yellow dog and a little red wagon,
And a realio, trulio, little pet dragon.

Now the name of the little black kitten was Ink,
And the little gray mouse, she called her Blink,
And the little yellow dog was sharp as Mustard,
But the dragon was a coward, and she called him Custard.

Custard the dragon had big sharp teeth,
And spikes on top of him and scales underneath,
Mouth like a fireplace, chimney for a nose,
And realio, trulio daggers on his toes.

Belinda was as brave as a barrel-full of bears,
And Ink and Blink chased lions down the stairs,
Mustard was as brave as a tiger in a rage,
But Custard cried for a nice safe cage.

Belinda tickled him, she tickled him unmerciful,
Ink, Blink and Mustard, they rudely called him Percival,
They all sat laughing in the little red wagon
At the realio, trulio, cowardly dragon.

Belinda giggled till she shook the house,
And Blink said *Weeek!,* which is giggling for a mouse,
Ink and Mustard rudely asked his age,
When Custard cried for a nice safe cage.

166

Suddenly, suddenly they heard a nasty sound,
And Mustard growled, and they all looked around.
Meowch! cried Ink, and Ooh! cried Belinda,
For there was a pirate, climbing in the winda.

Pistol in his left hand, pistol in his right,
And he held in his teeth a cutlass bright;
His beard was black, one leg was wood.
It was clear that the pirate meant no good.

Belinda paled, and she cried Help! Help!
But Mustard fled with a terrified yelp,
Ink trickled down to the bottom of the household,
And little mouse Blink strategically mouseholed.

But up jumped Custard, snorting like an engine,
Clashed his tail like irons in a dungeon,
With a clatter and a clank and a jangling squirm
He went at the pirate like a robin at a worm.

The pirate gaped at Belinda's dragon,
And gulped some grog from his pocket flagon,
He fired two bullets, but they didn't hit,
And Custard gobbled him, every bit.

Belinda embraced him, Mustard licked him;
No one mourned for his pirate victim.
Ink and Blink in glee did gyrate
Around the dragon that ate the pyrate.

Belinda still lives in her little white house,
With her little black kitten and her little gray mouse,
And her little yellow dog and her little red wagon,
And her realio, trulio, little pet dragon.

Belinda is as brave as a barrel full of bears,
And Ink and Blink chase lions down the stairs,
Mustard is as brave as a tiger in a rage,
But Custard keeps crying for a nice safe cage.

OGDEN NASH

167

The Black Forest in Germany is a vast stretch of dark woods that once seemed enchanted. In it, a grown man felt suddenly transformed. He seemed to be a boy who imagined himself the hero of a fairy tale in which there were pixies, gnomes, loreleys, and kobolds. He waited, half-eagerly, half-fearfully, for something to happen. He waited...and waited...

Disenchanted

Here in the German
  Fairy forest;
And here I turn in,
  I, the poorest
Son of an aging
  Humble widow.
The light is fading;
  Every shadow
Conceals a kobold,
  A gnome's dark eye,
Or even some troubled
  Loreley.
A ruined castle
  Invites me to prowl;
Its only vassal
  A frightened owl
(Most likely a princess
  Under a spell)—
And what light dances
  Behind that wall?
Perhaps great riches
  Are hidden there,
Perhaps a witch's
  Magic snare.

I walk up boldly,
  Though my breath falters;
But no one holds me,
  Nothing alters
Except the dying

Phosphorescence,
Where the rocks lie in
  Broken crescents.
These rocks are haunted,
  Everyone says,
And here the enchanted
  Dragon obeys
Only the youngest
  Son of a widow,
Who waits the longest,
  Fearing no shadow
Of any uncommon
  Phantom in metal,

But dares to summon
  The Thing to battle.
I've said my vespers,
  I've tightened my gloves;
The forest whispers
  And chuckles and moves.
Darker and closer
  The stillness surges.
Not even the ghost of
  A rabbit emerges.
I rattle my weapons,
  I call and I call
But nothing happens,
  Nothing at all.

  Nothing at all.

LOUIS UNTERMEYER

168

The One Answer, *half-story, half-song, has been sung for over a century. People continue to relish it for its coy humor, and especially for its trick ending.*

The One Answer

On yonder hill there stands a creature,
　　Who she is I do not know.
I'll go ask her hand in marriage,
　　And she'll answer yes or no.
"O, no, John; no, John; no, John, no!

"My father was a Spanish captain,
　　Went to sea a year ago;
First he kissed me, then he left me,
　　Bade me always answer no.
So no, John; no, John; no, John, no."

Madam, in your face is beauty;
　　On your lips red roses grow.
Will you take me for your husband?
　　Madam, answer yes or no.
"O, no, John; no, John; no, John, no."

Madam, since you are so cruel,
　　And since you do scorn me so,
If I may not be your husband,
　　Madam, will you let me go?
"O, no, John; no, John; no, John, no."

Hark! I hear the church-bells ringing;
　　Will you come and be my wife?
Or, dear madam, have you settled
　　To live single all your life?
"O, no, John; no, John; no, John, no!"

The next three poems, The Frogs Who Wanted a King, The Fox and the Grapes, *and* The Enchanted Shirt, *are fables. The originals of the first two were written over two thousand years ago by Aesop. The third is by John Hay, a major in the United States Army, a poet, secretary to Abraham Lincoln and later, Secretary of State. Fables are stories which, even when playful—as these three are—point a moral which adorns the tale.*

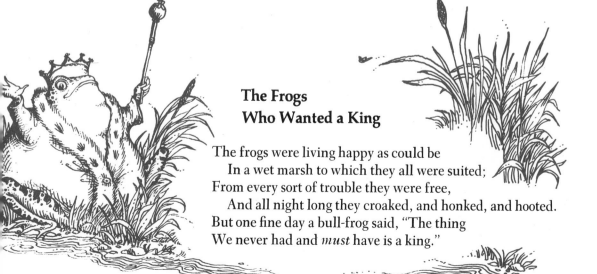

The Frogs Who Wanted a King

The frogs were living happy as could be
　　In a wet marsh to which they all were suited;
From every sort of trouble they were free,
　　And all night long they croaked, and honked, and hooted.
But one fine day a bull-frog said, "The thing
We never had and *must* have is a king."

So all the frogs immediately prayed;
   "Great Jove," they chorused from their swampy border,
"Send us a king and he will be obeyed,
   A king to bring a rule of Law and Order."
Jove heard and chuckled. That night in the bog
There fell a large and most impressive Log.

The swamp was silent; nothing breathed. At first
   The badly frightened frogs did never *once* stir;
But gradually some neared and even durst
   To touch, aye, even dance upon, the monster.
Whereat they croaked again, "Great Jove, oh hear!
Send us a *living* king, a king to fear!"

Once more Jove smiled, and sent them down a Stork.
   "Long live—!" they croaked. But ere they framed the sentence,
The Stork bent down and, scorning knife or fork,
   Swallowed them all, with no time for repentance!

The moral's this: No matter what your lot,
It might be worse. Be glad with what you've got.

JOSEPH LAUREN

The Fox and the Grapes

One summer's day a fox was passing through
A vineyard; faint he was and hungry, too.
When suddenly his keen eye chanced to fall
Upon a bunch of grapes above the wall.
"Ha! Just the thing!" he said. "Who could resist it!"
He eyed the purple cluster—jumped—and missed it.
"Ahem!" he coughed. "I'll take more careful aim,"
And sprang again. Results were much the same,
Although his leaps were desperate and high.
At length he paused to wipe a tearful eye,
And shrug a shoulder. "I am not so dry,
And lunch is bound to come within the hour ...
Besides," he said, "I'm sure those grapes are sour."

The moral is: We seem to want the peach
That always dangles just beyond our reach.
Yet, like the fox, we must not be upset
When sometimes things are just too hard to get.

JOSEPH LAUREN

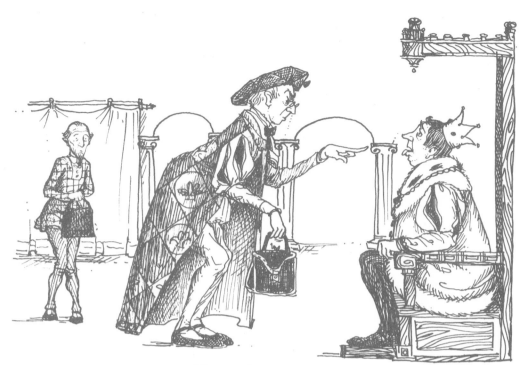

The Enchanted Shirt

The King was sick. His cheek was red,
 And his eye was clear and bright;
He ate and drank with a kingly zest,
 And peacefully snored at night.

But he said he was sick, and a king should know,
 And doctors came by the score.
They did not cure him. He cut off their heads,
 And sent to the schools for more.

At last two famous doctors came,
 And one was as poor as a rat,—
He had passed his life in studious toil,
 And never found time to grow fat.

The other had never looked in a book;
 His patients gave him no trouble:
If they recovered, they paid him well;
 If they died, their heirs paid double.

Together they looked at the royal tongue,
 As the King on his couch reclined;
In succession they thumped his august chest,
 But no trace of disease could find.

The old sage said, "You're as sound as a nut."
 "Hang him up," roared the King in a gale—
In a ten-knot gale of royal rage!
 The other leech grew a shade pale;

But he pensively rubbed his sagacious nose,
 And thus his prescription ran—
The King will be well, if he sleeps one night
 In the Shirt of a Happy Man.

Wide o'er the realm the couriers rode,
 And fast their horses ran,
And many they saw, and to many they spoke,
 But they found no Happy Man.

They found poor men who would fain be rich,
 And rich who thought they were poor;
And men who twisted their waist in stays,
 And women that shorthose wore.

They saw two men by the roadside sit,
 And both bemoaned their lot;
For one had buried his wife, he said,
 And the other one had not.

171

At last they came to a village gate,
    A beggar lay whistling there;
He whistled, and sang, and laughed, and rolled
    On the grass in the soft June air.

The weary courtiers paused and looked
    At the scamp so blithe and gay;
And one of them said, "Heaven save you, friend!
    You seem to be happy to-day."

"Oh yes, fair sirs," the rascal laughed,
    And his voice rang free and glad;
"An idle man has so much to do
    That he never has time to be sad."

"This is our man," the courier said;
    "Our luck has led us aright.
I will give you a hundred ducats, friend,
    For the loan of your shirt to-night."

The merry blackguard lay back on the grass,
    And laughed till his face was black;
"I would do it, God wot," and he roared with the fun,
    "But I haven't a shirt to my back."

             ✳   ✳   ✳   ✳

Each day to the King the reports came in
    Of his unsuccessful spies,
And the sad panorama of human woes
    Passed daily under his eyes.

And he grew ashamed of his useless life,
    And his maladies hatched in gloom;
He opened his windows and let the air
    Of the free heaven into his room.

And out he went in the world, and toiled
    In his own appointed way;
And the people blessed him, the land was glad,
    And the King was well and gay.

JOHN HAY

_About one hundred and fifty years ago, a grave was found in Massachu-
setts which contained bones and a few pieces of rusted armor. Some people
believed that the skeleton was that of a Viking warrior, one of the seafarers
from Scandinavia who, it has been claimed, discovered the New World
long before Columbus. It was thought that the Norsemen even established
a settlement in New England; there is a ruin in Rhode Island supposed to
be the remains of a stone tower erected by them. Around these few frag-
mentary facts, Longfellow built this stirring and briskly rhymed tale of one
of those fierce, or Berserk, adventurers._

The Skeleton in Armor

"Speak! speak! thou fearful guest!
Who, with thy hollow breast
Still in rude armor drest,
   Comest to daunt me!
Wrapt not in Eastern balms,
But with thy fleshless palms
Stretched, as if asking alms,
   Why dost thou haunt me?"

Then, from those cavernous eyes
Pale flashes seemed to rise,
As when the Northern skies
   Gleam in December;
And, like the water's flow
Under December's snow,
Came a dull voice of woe
   From the heart's chamber.

"I was a Viking old!
My deeds, though manifold,
No Skald in song has told,
   No Saga taught thee!
Take heed, that in thy verse
Thou dost the tale rehearse,
Else dread a dead man's curse;
   For this I sought thee.

"Far in the Northern Land,
By the wild Baltic's strand,
I, with my childish hand,
   Tamed the gerfalcon;[1]

And, with my skates fast-bound,
Skimmed the half-frozen Sound,
That the poor whimpering hound
   Trembled to walk on.

"Oft to his frozen lair
Tracked I the grisly bear,
While from my path the hare
   Fled like a shadow;
Oft through the forest dark
Followed the were-wolf's bark,
Until the soaring lark
   Sang from the meadow.

But when I older grew,
Joining a corsair's crew,
O'er the dark sea I flew
   With the marauders.
Wild was the life we led;
Many the souls that sped,
Many the hearts that bled
   By our stern orders.

"Many a wassail-bout
Wore the long winter out;
Often our midnight shout
   Set the cocks crowing,
As we the Berserk's tale
Measured in cups of ale,
Draining the oaken pail,
   Filled to o'erflowing.

173

"Once as I told in glee
   Tales of the stormy sea,
   Soft eyes did gaze on me,
      Burning yet tender;
   And as the white stars shine
   On the dark Norway pine,
   On that dark heart of mine
      Fell their soft splendor.

"I wooed the blue-eyed maid,
   Yielding, yet half afraid,
   And in the forest's shade
      Our vows were plighted.
   Under its loosened vest
   Fluttered her little breast,
   Like birds within their nest
      By the hawk frighted.

"Bright in her father's hall
   Shields gleamed upon the wall,
   Loud sang the minstrels all,
      Chanting his glory;
   When of old Hildebrand
   I asked his daughter's hand,
   Mute did the minstrels stand
      To hear my story.

"While the brown ale he quaffed,
   Loud then the champion laughed,
   And as the wind-gusts waft
      The sea-foam brightly,
   So the loud laugh of scorn,
   Out of those lips unshorn,
   From the deep drinking-horn
      Blew the foam lightly.

"She was a Prince's child,
   I but a Viking wild,
   And though she blushed and smiled,
      I was discarded!
   Should not the dove so white
   Follow the sea-mew's flight,
   Why did they leave that night
      Her nest unguarded?

"Scarce had I put to sea,
   Bearing the maid with me,—
   Fairest of all was she
      Among the Norsemen!—
   When on the white sea-strand,
   Waving his armèd hand,
   Saw we old Hildebrand,
      With twenty horsemen.

"Then launched they to the blast,
   Bent like a reed each mast,
   Yet we were gaining fast,
      When the wind failed us;
   And with a sudden flaw
   Came round the gusty Skaw,
   So that our foe we saw
      Laugh as he hailed us.

"And as to catch the gale
   Round veered the flapping sail,
   'Death!' was the helmsman's hail,
      'Death without quarter!'
   Mid-ships with iron keel
   Struck with her ribs of steel;
   Down her black hulk did reel
      Through the black water!

"As with his wings aslant,
   Sails the fierce cormorant,
   Seeking some rocky haunt,
      With his prey laden—
   So toward the open main,
   Beating to sea again,
   Through the wild hurricane,
      Bore I the maiden.

"Three weeks we westward bore,
   And when the storm was o'er,
   Cloud-like we saw the shore
      Stretching to leeward;
   There for my lady's bower
   Built I the lofty tower,
   Which to this very hour,
      Stands looking seaward.

"There lived we many years;
    Time dried the maiden's tears;
    She had forgot her fears,
        She was a mother;
    Death closed her mild blue eyes,
    Under the tower she lies;
    Ne'er shall the sun arise
        On such another!

"Still grew my bosom then,
    Still as a stagnant fen!
    Hateful to me were men,
        The sunlight hateful!
    In the vast forest here,
    Clad in my warlike gear,
    Fell I upon my spear,
        Oh, death was grateful!

"Thus, seamed with many scars,
    Bursting these prison bars,
    Up to its native stars
        My soul ascended!
    There from the flowing bowl
    Deep drinks the warrior's soul,
    Skoal![2] to the Northland! *Skoal!*"
        Thus the tale ended.

HENRY WADSWORTH LONGFELLOW

[1] Gerfalcon: a large wild hawk
[2] *Skoal!*: Health! a Scandinavian toast

Some of America's most famous poems have celebrated events which can never be forgotten. It is difficult to think of the growth of the country without them; they are the milestones of our history.

On August 5, 1620, a company of about one hundred men, women, and children sailed from England on the little "Mayflower" to find a land where they could worship as they pleased. Nine weeks after leaving Plymouth—on November 19, to be exact—the Pilgrims brought their ship to the "stern and rock-bound coast" and anchored in Cape Cod Harbor. It is interesting that Landing of the Pilgrim Fathers, *this most typical of American poems, was written by an Englishwoman, Felicia Hemans.*

Landing of the Pilgrim Fathers

The breaking waves dashed high,
  On a stern and rock-bound coast,
And the woods against a stormy sky,
  Their giant branches tossed;

And the heavy night hung dark,
  The hills and waters o'er,
When a band of exiles moored their bark
  On the wild New England shore.

Not as the conqueror comes,
  They, the true-hearted came;
Not with the roll of the stirring drums,
  And the trumpet that sings of fame;

Not as the flying come,
  In silence and in fear;—
They shook the depths of the desert gloom
  With their hymns of lofty cheer.

Amidst the storm they sang,
  And the stars heard, and the sea;
And the sounding aisles of the dim woods rang
  To the anthem of the free.

The ocean eagle soared
  From his nest by the white wave's foam;
And the rocking pines of the forest roared—
  This was their welcome home.

There were men with hoary hair
  Amidst that pilgrim band:
Why had they come to wither there,
  Away from their childhood's land?

There was a woman's fearless eye,
  Lit by her deep love's truth;
There was manhood's brow serenely high,
  And the fiery heart of youth.

What sought they thus afar?
  Bright jewels of the mine?
The wealth of seas, the spoils of war?
  They sought a faith's pure shrine!

Aye, call it holy ground,
  The soil where first they trod;
They have left unstained what there they found—
  Freedom to worship God.

FELICIA HEMAN

In the spring of 1607, another group of English colonists settled in James-town, Virginia. Captain John Smith was the leader of this band. In December 1607 he was taken prisoner and brought to the tent of Powhatan, chief of the tribes of the Atlantic Coast. Powhatan sentenced Smith to die, but the chieftain's daughter Pocahontas pleaded for him so touchingly that his life was spared.

It would be romantic to relate that the grateful John Smith married Pocahontas. But such was not the case. Instead, the Indian princess married John Rolfe, a Jamestown planter. In 1616 Pocahontas was taken to Eng-land and was presented at the Court. In England she led a life of fashion and had one son, Thomas Rolfe, whose descendants still live in Virginia.

Pocahontas

Wearied arm and broken sword
  Wage in vain the desperate fight;
Round him press a countless horde,
  He is but a single knight.
Hark! a cry of triumph shrill
  Through the wilderness resounds,
  As, with twenty bleeding wounds,
Sinks the warrior, fighting still.

Now they heap the funeral pyre,
  And the torch of death they light;
Ah! 'tis hard to die by fire!
  Who will shield the captive knight?
Round the stake with fiendish cry
  Wheel and dance the savage crowd,
  Cold the victim's mien and proud,
And his breast is bared to die.

Who will shield the fearless heart?
  Who avert the murderous blade?
From the throng with sudden start
  See, there springs an Indian maid.
Quick she stands before the knight;
  "Loose the chain, unbind the ring!
  I am daughter of the king,
And I claim the Indian right!"

Dauntlessly aside she flings
  Lifted axe and thirsty knife,
Fondly to his heart she clings,
  And her bosom guards his life!
In the woods of Powhatan,
  Still 't is told by Indian fires
  How a daughter of their sires
Saved a captive Englishman.

WILLIAM MAKEPEACE THACKERAY

177

On June 17, 1775, three thousand veteran English troops were ordered to scatter the American farmers, blacksmiths, and shopkeepers who were defending Boston. Under the command of General Howe the red-coats advanced up Bunker Hill, but were met by so shattering a volley of musket-fire that they were forced to withdraw. Reforming their lines, the British again attacked the hill and were again repulsed. At the third attempt to dislodge the Americans... But listen to the way Oliver Wendell Holmes tells the story through the lips of a grandmother who witnessed the entire battle from the tower of a church in Boston.

Grandmother's Story of Bunker Hill Battle

Tis like stirring living embers when, at eighty, one remembers
All the aching and the quakings of "the times that tried men's souls";
When I talk of "Whig" and "Tory," when I tell the "Rebel" story,
To you the words are ashes, but to me they're burning coals.

I had heard the muskets' rattle of the April running battle;
Lord Percy's hunted soldiers, I can see their red coats still;
But a deadly chill comes o'er me, as the day looms up before me,
When a thousand men lay bleeding on the slopes of Bunker's Hill.

'Twas a peaceful summer's morning, when the first thing gave us warning
Was the booming of the cannon from the river and the shore:
"Child," says grandma, "what's the matter, what is all this noise and clatter?
Have those scalping Indian devils come to murder us once more?"

Poor old soul! my sides were shaking in the midst of all my quaking,
To hear her talk of Indians when the guns began to roar;
She had seen the burning village, and the slaughter and the pillage,
When the Mohawks killed her father with their bullets through his door.

Then I said, "Now, dear old granny, don't you fret and worry any,
For I'll soon come back and tell you whether this is work or play;
There can't be mischief in it, so I won't be gone a minute"—
For a minute then I started. I was gone the livelong day!

No time for bodice-lacing or for looking-glass grimacing;
Down my hair went as I hurried, tumbling half-way to my heels;
God forbid your ever knowing, when there's blood around her flowing,
How the lonely, helpless daughter of a quiet household feels!

In the street I heard a thumping; and I knew it was the stumping
Of the Corporal, our old neighbor, on that wooden leg he wore,
With a knot of women round him,—it was lucky I had found him,
So I followed with the others, and the Corporal marched before.

They were making for the steeple,—the old soldier and his people;
The pigeons circled round us as we climbed the creaking stair.
Just across the narrow river—oh, so close it made me shiver!—
Stood a fortress on the hill-top that but yesterday was bare.

Not slow our eyes to find it; well we knew who stood behind it,
Though the earthwork hid them from us, and the stubborn walls were dumb:
Here were sister, wife, and mother, looking wild upon each other,
And their lips were white with terror as they said, THE HOUR HAS COME!

The morning slowly wasted, not a morsel had we tasted,
And our heads were almost splitting with the cannons' deafening thrill,
When a figure tall and stately round the rampart strode sedately;
It was PRESCOTT, one since told me; he commanded on the hill.

179

Every woman's heart grew bigger when we saw his manly figure,
With the banyan buckled round it, standing up so straight and tall;
Like a gentleman of leisure who is strolling out for pleasure,
Through the storm of shells and cannon-shot he walked around the wall.

At eleven the streets were swarming, for the redcoats' ranks were forming;
At noon in marching order they were moving to the piers;
How the bayonets gleamed and glistened, as we looked far down, and listened
To the trampling and the drum-beat of the belted grenadiers!

At length the men have started, with a cheer (it seemed faint-hearted),
In their scarlet regimentals, with their knapsacks on their backs,
And the reddening, rippling water, as after a sea-fight's slaughter,
Round the barges gliding onward blushed like blood along their tracks.

So they crossed to the other border, and again they formed in order;
And the boats came back for soldiers, came for soldiers, soldiers still:
The time seemed everlasting to us women faint and fasting,—
At last they're moving, marching, marching proudly up the hill.

We can see the bright steel glancing all along the lines advancing,—
Now the front rank fires a volley,—they have thrown away their shot;
For behind their earthwork lying, all the balls above them flying,
Our people need not hurry; so they wait and answer not.

Then the Corporal, our old cripple (he would swear sometimes and tipple),—
He had heard the bullets whistle (in the old French war) before,—
Calls out in words of jeering, just as if they all were hearing,—
And his wooden leg thumps fiercely on the dusty belfry floor:—

"Oh! fire away, ye villains, and earn King George's shillin's,
But ye'll waste a ton of powder afore a 'rebel' falls;
You may bang the dirt and welcome, they're as safe as Dan'l Malcolm
Ten foot beneath the gravestone that you've splintered with your balls!"

In the hush of expectation, in the awe and trepidation
Of the dread approaching moment, we are well-nigh breathless all;
Though the rotten bars are failing on the rickety belfry railing,
We are crowding up against them like the waves against a wall.

Just a glimpse (the air is clearer), they are nearer,—nearer,—nearer,
When a flash,—a curling smoke-wreath,—then a crash,—the steeple shakes,
The deadly truce is ended; the tempest's shroud is rended;
Like a morning mist it gathered, like a thunder-cloud it breaks!

O the sight our eyes discover as the blue-black smoke blows over!
The red-coats stretched in windrows as a mower rakes his hay;
Here a scarlet heap is lying, there a headlong crowd is flying
Like a billow that has broken and is shivered into spray.

Then we cried, "The troops are routed! they are beat,—it can't be doubted!
God be thanked, the fight is over!"—Ah! the grim old soldier's smile!
"Tell us, tell us why you look so?" (we could hardly speak, we shook so),—
"Are they beaten? *Are* they beaten? ARE they beaten?"—"Wait a while."

O the trembling and the terror! For too late we saw our error:
They are baffled, not defeated; we have driven them back in vain.
And the columns that were scattered, round the colors that were tattered,
Toward the sullen silent fortress turn their belted breasts again.

All at once, as we are gazing, lo the roofs of Charlestown blazing!
They have fired the harmless village; in an hour it will be down!
The Lord in heaven confound them, rain his fire and brimstone round them,—
The robbing, murdering red-coats, that would burn a peaceful town!

They are marching, stern and solemn; we can see each massive column
As they near the naked earth-mound with the slanting walls so steep.
Have our soldiers got faint-hearted, and in noiseless haste departed?
Are they panic-struck and helpless? Are they palsied or asleep?

Now! the walls they're almost under! scarce a rod the foes asunder!
Not a firelock flashed against them! up the earthwork they will swarm!
But the words have scarce been spoken, when the ominous calm is broken,
And a bellowing crash has emptied all the vengeance of the storm!

So again, with murderous slaughter, pelted backwards to the water,
Fly Pigot's running heroes and the frightened braves of Howe;
And we shout, "At last they're done for, it's their barges they have run for:
They are beaten, beaten, beaten; and the battle's over now!"

And we looked, poor timid creatures, on the rough old soldier's features,
Our lips afraid to question, but he knew what we would ask:
"Not sure," he said; "keep quiet,—once more, I guess, they'll try it,—
Here's damnation to the cut-throats!"—then he handed me his flask,

Saying, "Gal, you're looking shaky; have a drop of old Jamaiky;
I'm afeard there'll be more trouble afore the job is done";
So I took one scorching swallow; dreadful faint I felt and hollow,
Standing there from early morning when the firing was begun.

All through those hours of trial I had watched a calm clock dial,
As the hands kept creeping, creeping,—they were creeping round to four,
When the old man said, "They're forming with their bayonets fixed for storming;
It's the death-grip that's a-coming—they will try the works once more."

With brazen trumpets blaring, the flames behind them glaring,
The deadly wall before them in close array they come;
Still onward, upward toiling, like a dragon's fold uncoiling,
Like the rattlesnake's shrill warning the reverberating drum!

Over heaps all torn and gory—Shall I tell the fearful story,
How they surged above the breastwork, as a sea breaks over a deck;
How driven, yet scarce defeated, our wornout men retreated,
With their powder-horns all emptied, like the swimmers from a wreck.

It has all been told and painted; as for me, they say I fainted,
And the wooden-legged old Corporal stumped with me down the stair:
When I woke from dreams affrighted the evening lamps were lighted,—
On the floor a youth was lying; his bleeding breast was bare.

And I heard through all the flurry, "Send for WARREN! hurry! hurry!
Tell him here's a soldier bleeding, and he'll come and dress his wound."
Ah, we knew not till the morrow told its tale of death and sorrow,
How the starlight found him stiffened on the dark and bloody ground.

Who the youth was, what his name was, where the place from which he came was,
Who had brought him from the battle, and had left him at our door,
He could not speak to tell us; but 'twas one of our brave fellows,
As the homespun plainly showed us which the dying soldier wore.

For they all thought he was dying, as they gathered round him crying,—
And they said, "Oh, how they'll miss him!" and, "What *will* his mother do?"
Then, his eyelids just unclosing like a child's that has been dozing,
He faintly murmured, "Mother!"—and—I saw his eyes were blue.

"Why, grandma, how you're winking!" Ah, my child, it sets me thinking
Of a story not like this one. Well, he somehow lived along;
So we came to know each other, and I nursed him like a—mother,
Till at last he stood before me, tall, and rosy-cheeked, and strong.

And we sometimes walked together in the pleasant summer weather,—
"Please to tell us what his name was?" Just your own, my little dear.
There's his picture Copley painted. We became so well acquainted,
That—in short, that's why I'm grandma, and you children all are here!

OLIVER WENDELL HOLMES

It was during the battle of Monmouth (June 28, 1778) in the Revolutionary War, that Washington, almost beaten, started to pursue the British army. One of the men firing a big brass cannon was killed by a bullet just as his wife, Molly Pitcher, was bringing him a pail of water. Without pausing a moment, Molly seized the ramrod, loaded and fired the gun time and again. Next morning, covered with dirt and blood, she was greeted by Washington, who made her a sergeant on the spot.

Molly Pitcher

'Twas hurry and scurry at Monmouth town,
    For Lee was beating a wild retreat;
The British were riding the Yankees down,
    And panic was pressing on flying feet.

Galloping down like a hurricane
    Washington rode with his sword swung high,
Mighty as he of the Trojan plain
    Fired by a courage from the sky.

"Halt, and stand to your guns!" he cried.
    And a bombardier made swift reply.
Wheeling his cannon into the tide,
    He fell 'neath the shot of a foeman nigh.

Molly Pitcher sprang to his side,
    Fired as she saw her husband do.
Telling the king in his stubborn pride
    Women like men to their homes are true.

Washington rode from the bloody fray
    Up to the gun that a woman manned.
"Molly Pitcher, you saved the day,"
    He said, as he gave her a hero's hand.

He named her sergeant with manly praise,
    While her war-brown face was wet with tears—
A woman has ever a woman's ways,
    And the army was wild with cheers.

                    KATE BROWNLEE SHERWOOD

183

In the spring of 1775, the British General Gage resolved to make an example of the American patriots, Samuel Adams and John Hancock, by arresting them and sending them to England, where they would be tried for treason. He learned they were in Lexington, and decided to trap them. The scheme was kept under cover; but Paul Revere got wind of it, realized what was involved, and determined to spread the alarm and rouse the countryside.

Longfellow's immortal poem tells most of the story. It even hints at the sequel: how Hancock and Adams were warned in time, how the minutemen of the village sprang to arms and confronted the much greater British force. There they "gave them ball for ball . . . only pausing to fire and load." Thus the Revolutionary War began with "a cry of defiance and not of fear . . . and a word that shall echo forevermore!"

Paul Revere's Ride

Listen, my children, and you shall hear
Of the midnight ride of Paul Revere,
On the eighteenth of April, in Seventy-five;
Hardly a man is now alive
Who remembers that famous day and year.

He said to his friend, "If the British march
By land or sea from the town to-night,
Hang a lantern aloft in the belfry arch
Of the North Church tower as a signal light,—
One, if by land, and two, if by sea;
And I on the opposite shore will be
Ready to ride and spread the alarm
Through every Middlesex village and farm,
For the country folk to be up and to arm."
Then he said "Good-night," and with muffled oar
Silently row'd to the Charlestown shore,
Just as the moon rose over the bay,
Where swinging wide at her moorings lay
The Somerset, British man-of-war;
A phantom ship, with each mast and spar
Across the moon like a prison bar,
And a huge black hulk, that was magnified
By its own reflection in the tide.

Meanwhile his friend, through alley and street,
Wanders and watches with eager ears,
Till in the silence around him he hears
The master of men at the barrack-door,
The sound of arms, and the tramp of feet,
And the measured tread of the grenadiers
Marching down to their boats on the shore.
Then he climb'd the tower of the Old North Church,
By the wooden stairs, with stealthy tread,
To the belfry-chamber overhead,
And started the pigeons from their perch
On the sombre rafters, that round him made
Masses of moving shapes of shade,—
By the trembling ladder, steep and tall,
To the highest window in the wall,
Where he paused to listen and look down
A moment on the roofs of the town,
And the moonlight flowing over all.

Beneath, in the churchyard, lay the dead,
In their night-encampment on the hill,
Wrapp'd in silence so deep and still
That he could hear, like a sentinel's tread,
The watchful night-wind, as it went
Creeping along from tent to tent,
And seeming to whisper, "All is well!"
A moment only he feels the spell
Of the place and the hour, and the secret dread
Of the lonely belfry and the dead;
For suddenly all his thoughts are bent
On a shadowy something far away,
Where the river widens to meet the bay,
A line of black that bends and floats
On the rising tide like a bridge of boats.

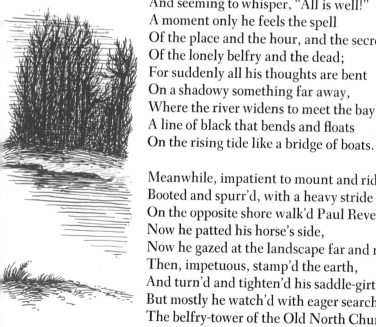

Meanwhile, impatient to mount and ride,
Booted and spurr'd, with a heavy stride
On the opposite shore walk'd Paul Revere.
Now he patted his horse's side,
Now he gazed at the landscape far and near,
Then, impetuous, stamp'd the earth,
And turn'd and tighten'd his saddle-girth;
But mostly he watch'd with eager search
The belfry-tower of the Old North Church,
As it rose above the graves on the hill,

Lonely and spectral and sombre and still.
And lo! as he looks, on the belfry's height
A glimmer, and then a gleam of light!
He springs to the saddle, the bridle he turns,
But lingers and gazes, till full on his sight
A second lamp in the belfry burns.

A hurry of hoofs in a village street,
A shape in the moonlight, a bulk in the dark,
And beneath, from the pebbles, in passing, a spark
Struck out by a steed flying fearless and fleet:
That was all; and yet, through the gloom and the light,
The fate of a nation was riding that night;
And the spark struck out by that steed in his flight
Kindled the land into flame with its heat.

He had left the village and mounted the steep,
And beneath him, tranquil and broad and deep,
Is the Mystic, meeting the ocean tides,
And under the alders that skirts its edge,
Now soft on the sand, now loud on the ledge,
Is heard the tramp of his steed as he rides.

It was twelve by the village clock
When he crossed the bridge into Medford town.
He heard the crowing of the cock,
And the barking of the farmer's dog,
And felt the damp of the river fog,
That rises after the sun goes down.

It was one by the village clock
When he galloped into Lexington.
He saw the gilded weathercock
Swim in the moonlight as he pass'd,
And the meeting-house windows, blank and bare,
Gaze at him with a spectral glare,
As if they already stood aghast
At the bloody work they would look upon.

It was two by the village clock
When he came to the bridge in Concord town.
He heard the bleating of the flock,
And the twitter of birds among the trees,
And felt the breath of the morning breeze
Blowing over the meadows brown.

And one was safe and asleep in his bed
Who at the bridge would be first to fall,
Who that day would be lying dead,
Pierced by a British musket-ball.

You know the rest; in the books you have read,
How the British regulars fired and fled,—
How the farmers gave them ball for ball,
From behind each fence and farmyard wall,
Chasing the red-coats down the lane,
Then crossing the fields to emerge again
Under the trees at the turn of the road,
And only pausing to fire and load.

So through the night rode Paul Revere,
And so through the night went his cry of alarm
To every Middlesex village and farm,—
A cry of defiance, and not of fear,
A voice in the darkness, a knock at the door,
And a word that shall echo for evermore!
For, borne on the night-wind of the past,
Through all our history, to the last,
In the hour of darkness, and peril, and need,
The people will waken and listen to hear
The hurrying hoof-beats of that steed,
And the midnight message of Paul Revere.

HENRY WADSWORTH LONGFELLOW

The Little Black-Eyed Rebel *is as much truth as it is poetry. The "rebel" of the story was a Philadelphia girl by the name of Mary Redmond. When the British soldiers occupied her city, she helped her country's cause in many ways. Chiefly she got important news through the enemy lines by delivering smuggled letters that contained hidden information. Beloved by the Continental Army, Mary Redmond is one of the little-known heroines of American history.*

The Little Black-Eyed Rebel

A boy drove into the city, his wagon loaded down
With food to feed the people of the British-governed town;
And the little black-eyed rebel, so innocent and sly,
Was watching for his coming from the corner of her eye.

His face looked broad and honest, his hands were brown and tough,
The clothes he wore upon him were homespun, coarse and rough;
But one there was who watched him, who long time lingered nigh,
And cast at him sweet glances from the corner of her eye.

He drove up to the market, he waited in the line;
His apples and potatoes were fresh and fair and fine;
But long and long he waited, and no one came to buy,
Save the black-eyed rebel, watching from the corner of her eye.

188

"Now who will buy my apples?" he shouted, long and loud;
And "Who wants my potatoes?" he repeated to the crowd;
But from all the people round him came no word of a reply,
Save the black-eyed rebel, answering from the corner of her eye.

For she knew that 'neath the lining of the coat he wore that day,
Were long letters from the husbands and the fathers far away,
Who were fighting for the freedom that they meant to gain or die;
And a tear like silver glistened in the corner of her eye.

But the treasures—how to get them? crept the question through her mind,
Since keen enemies were watching for what prizes they might find;
And she paused a while and pondered, with a pretty little sigh;
Then resolve crept through her features, and a shrewdness fired her eye.

So she resolutely walked up to the wagon old and red;
"May I have a dozen apples for a kiss?" she sweetly said.
And the brown face flushed to scarlet, for the boy was somewhat shy,
And he saw her laughing at him from the corner of her eye.

"You may have them all for nothing, and more, if you want," said he.
"I will have them, my good fellow, but I'll pay for them," said she;
And she clambered on the wagon, minding not who all were by,
With a laugh of reckless romping in the corner of her eye.

Clinging round his brawny neck, she clasped her fingers white and small,
And then whispered, "Quick! the letters! thrust them underneath my shawl!
Carry back again *this* package, and be sure that you are spry!"
And she sweetly smiled upon him from the corner of her eye.

Loud the motley crowd were laughing at the strange, ungirlish freak,
And the boy was scared and panting, and so dashed he could not speak;
And, "Miss, *I* have good apples," a bolder lad did cry;
But she answered, "No, I thank you," from the corner of her eye.

With the news of loved ones absent to the dear friends they would greet,
Searching them who hungered for them, swift she glided through the street.
"There is nothing worth the doing that it does not pay to try,"
Thought the little black-eyed rebel, with a twinkle in her eye.

WILL CARLETON

189

During the Civil War the country was bitterly divided. There were many Union supporters living in the southern states and many Confederate sympathizers living in the north. Stories circulated about women so staunch in their convictions that they flaunted their allegiance in the face of their enemies. John Greenleaf Whittier combined several of these incidents and created a composite heroine. He called her Barbara Frietchie.

Barbara Frietchie

Up from the meadows rich with corn,
Clear in the cool September morn,

The clustered spires of Frederick stand
Green-walled by the hills of Maryland.

Round about them orchards sweep,
Apple and peach tree fruited deep,

Fair as the garden of the Lord
To the eyes of the famished rebel horde,

On that pleasant morn of the early fall
When Lee marched over the mountain wall;

Over the mountains winding down,
Horse and foot, into Frederick town.

Forty flags with their silver stars,
Forty flags with their crimson bars,

Flapped in the morning wind: the sun
Of noon looked down, and saw not one.

Up rose old Barbara Frietchie then,
Bowed with her fourscore years and ten;

Bravest of all in Frederick town,
She took up the flag the men hauled down;

In her attic window the staff she set,
To show that one heart was loyal yet.

Up the street came the rebel tread,
Stonewall Jackson riding ahead.

Under his slouched hat left and right
He glanced; the old flag met his sight.

"Halt!"—the dust-brown ranks stood fast,
"Fire!"—out blazed the rifle-blast.

It shivered the window, pane and sash;
It rent the banner with seam and gash.

Quick as it fell, from the broken staff
Dame Barbara snatched the silken scarf.

She leaned far out on the window-sill,
And shook it forth with a royal will.

"Shoot, if you must, this old gray head,
But spare your country's flag," she said.

A shade of sadness, a blush of shame,
Over the face of the leader came;

The nobler nature within him stirred
To life at that woman's deed and word;

"Who touches a hair of yon gray head
Dies like a dog! March on!" he said.

All day long through Frederick street
Sounded the tread of marching feet:

All day long that free flag tossed
Over the heads of the rebel host.

Ever its torn folds rose and fell
On the loyal winds that loved it well;

And through the hill-gaps sunset light
Shone over it with a warm good-night.

Barbara Frietchie's work is o'er,
And the Rebel rides on his raids no more.

Honor to her! and let a tear
Fall, for her sake, on Stonewall's bier.

Over Barbara Frietchie's grave,
Flag of Freedom and Union, wave!

Peace and order and beauty draw
Round thy symbol of light and law;

And ever the stars above look down
On thy stars below in Frederick town!

JOHN GREENLEAF WHITTIER

Kentucky Belle, *which centers about a farmer's wife and her thorough-bred horse, is a Civil War story that takes place far from the battlefield. Not defiant like* Barbara Frietchie, *the heroine of this poem has divided loyalties which lead her to a touching and tremendous act of sacrifice.*

Kentucky Belle

Summer of 'sixty-three, sir, and Conrad was gone away—
Gone to the country town, sir, to sell our first load of hay.
We lived in the log house yonder, poor as ever you've seen;
Röschen there was a baby, and I was only nineteen.

Conrad, he took the oxen, but he left Kentucky Belle;
How much we thought of Kentuck, I couldn't begin to tell—
Came from the Bluegrass country; my father gave her to me
When I rode north with Conrad, away from the Tennessee.

Conrad lived in Ohio—a German he is, you know—
The house stood in broad cornfields, stretching on, row after row;
The old folks made me welcome; they were kind as kind could be;
But I kept longing, longing, for the hills of the Tennessee.

O, for a sight of water, the shadowed slope of a hill!
Clouds that hang on the summit, a wind that never is still!
But the level land went stretching away to meet the sky—
Never a rise, from north to south, to rest the weary eye!

From east to west, no river to shine out under the moon,
Nothing to make a shadow in the yellow afternoon;
Only the breathless sunshine, as I looked out, all forlorn,
Only the "rustle, rustle," as I walked among the corn.

When I felt sick with pining we didn't wait any more,
But moved away from the cornlands out to this river shore—
The Tuscarawas it's called, sir—off there's a hill, you see—
And now I've grown to like it next best to the Tennessee.

I was at work that morning. Someone came riding like mad
Over the bridge and up the road—Farmer Rouf's little lad.
Bareback he rode; he had no hat, he hardly stopped to say,
"Morgan's men are coming, Frau, they're galloping on this way.

"I'm sent to warn the neighbors. He isn't a mile behind;
He sweeps up all the horses—every horse that he can find;
Morgan, Morgan the raider, and Morgan's terrible men,
With bowie knives and pistols, are galloping up the glen."

192

The lad rode down the valley, and I stood still at the door—
The baby laughed and prattled, playing with spools on the floor;
Kentuck was out in the pasture; Conrad, my man, was gone;
Near, near Morgan's men were galloping, galloping on!

Sudden I picked up baby and ran to the pasture bar:
"Kentuck!" I called; "Kentucky!" She knew me ever so far!
I led her down the gully that turns off there to the right,
And tied her to the bushes; her head was just out of sight.

As I ran back to the log house at once there came a sound—
The ring of hoofs, galloping hoofs, trembling over the ground,
Coming into the turnpike out from the White-Woman Glen—
Morgan, Morgan the raider, and Morgan's terrible men.

As near they drew and nearer my heart beat fast in alarm;
But still I stood in the doorway, with baby on my arm.
They came; they passed; with spur and whip in haste they sped along;
Morgan, Morgan the raider, and his band six hundred strong.

Weary they looked and jaded, riding through night and through day;
Pushing on east to the river, many long miles away,
To the border strip where Virginia runs up into the west,
And for the Upper Ohio before they could stop to rest.

On like the wind they hurried, and Morgan rode in advance;
Bright were his eyes like live coals, as he gave me a sideways glance;
And I was just breathing freely, after my choking pain,
When the last one of the troopers suddenly drew his rein.

Frightened I was to death, sir; I scarce dared look in his face,
As he asked for a drink of water and glanced around the place;
I gave him a cup, and he smiled—'twas only a boy, you see,
Faint and worn, with his blue eyes; and he'd sailed on the Tennessee.

Only sixteen he was, sir—a fond mother's only son—
Off and away with Morgan before his life had begun!
The damp drops stood on his temples; drawn was the boyish mouth;
And I thought me of the mother waiting down in the South!

O, plucky was he to the backbone and clear grit through and through;
Boasted and bragged like a trooper; but the big words wouldn't do;
The boy was dying, sir, dying, as plain as plain could be,
Worn out by his ride with Morgan up from the Tennessee.

But, when I told the laddie that I too was from the South,
Water came in his dim eyes and quivers around his mouth.
"Do you know the Bluegrass country?" he wistful began to say,
Then swayed like a willow sapling and fainted dead away.

I had him into the log house, and worked and brought him to;
I fed him and coaxed him, as I thought his mother'd do;
And, when the lad got better, and the noise in his head was gone,
Morgan's men were miles away, galloping, galloping on.

"O, I must go," he muttered; "I must be up and away!
Morgan, Morgan is waiting for me! O, what will Morgan say?"
But I heard a sound of tramping and kept him back from the door—
The ringing sound of horses' hoofs that I had heard before.

194

And on, on came the soldiers—the Michigan cavalry—
And fast they rode, and black they looked galloping rapidly;
They had followed hard on Morgan's track; they had followed day and night;
But of Morgan and Morgan's raiders they had never caught a sight.

And rich Ohio sat startled through all those summer days,
For strange, wild men were galloping over her broad highways;
Now here, now there, now seen, now gone, now north, now east, now west,
Through river valleys and corn-land farms, sweeping away her best.

A bold ride and a long ride! But they were taken at last.
They almost reached the river by galloping hard and fast;
But the boys in blue were upon them ere ever they gained the ford,
And Morgan, Morgan the raider, laid down his terrible sword.

Well, I kept the boy till evening—kept him against his will—
But he was too weak to follow, and sat there pale and still;
When it was cool and dusky—you'll wonder to hear me tell—
But I stole down to that gully and brought up Kentucky Belle.

I kissed the star on her forehead—my pretty, gentle lass—
But I knew that she'd be happy back in the old Bluegrass;
A suit of clothes of Conrad's, with all the money I had,
And Kentuck, pretty Kentuck, I gave to the worn-out lad.

I guided him to the southward as well as I knew how;
The boy rode off with many thanks, and many a backward bow;
And then the glow it faded, and my heart began to swell,
As down the glen away she went, my lost Kentucky Belle!

When Conrad came in the evening the moon was shining high;
Baby and I were both crying—I couldn't tell him why—
But a battered suit of rebel gray was hanging on the wall,
And a thin old horse with drooping head stood in Kentucky's stall.

Well, he was kind, and never once said a hard word to me;
He knew I couldn't help it—'twas all for the Tennessee;
But, after the war was over, just think what came to pass—
A letter, sir; and the two were safe back in the old Bluegrass.

The lad had got across the border, riding Kentucky Belle;
And Kentuck she was thriving, and fat, and hearty, and well;
He cared for her, and kept her, nor touched her with whip or spur:
Ah! we've had many horses, but never a horse like her!

CONSTANCE FENIMORE WOOLSON

Tall tales are as natural an expression of the American spirit as its sky-scrapers. Our country is big, and our talk tries to match its bigness. Much of the talk, full of wildness and fantasy, is humorous in its very exaggeration. Carl Sandburg, typically American as poet and biographer of Abraham Lincoln, has garnered a full crop of yarns, folk-sayings, and whimsical lore, and crammed them into a hugely entertaining passage which comes from his panoramic poem, The People, Yes.

Yarns

They have yarns
   Of a skyscraper so tall
     they had to put hinges
      On the two top stories
       so to let the moon go by,
   Of one corn crop in Missouri when the roots
     Went so deep and drew off so much water
      The Mississippi riverbed that year was dry,
   Of pancakes so thin
     they had only one side,
   Of " a fog so thick
     we shingled the barn
      and six feet out on the fog,"
   Of Pecos Pete straddling a cyclone
     in Texas and riding it to the west coast
      where "it rained out under him,"
   Of the man who drove a swarm of bees
     across the Rocky Mountains and the Desert
      "and didn't lose a bee."
   Of a mountain railroad curve
     where the engineer in his cab can touch the caboose
     and spit in the conductor's eye,

Of the boy who climbed a cornstalk
     growing so fast he would have starved to dea
      if they hadn't shot biscuits up to him,
Of the old man's whiskers:
   "When the wind was with him
     his whiskers arrived a day before he did,"
Of the hen laying a square egg
   and cackling, "Ouch!" and of hens laying eg
   with the dates printed on them,
Of the ship captain's shadow:
   it froze to the deck
     one cold winter night,
Of mutineers on that same ship
   put to chipping rust
     with rubber hammers,
Of the sheep-counter
   who was fast and accurate:
     "I just count their feet and divide by four

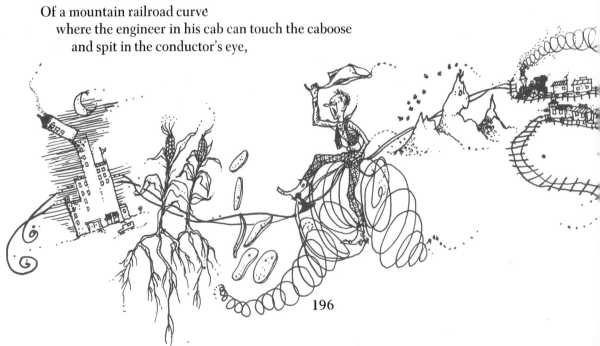

Of the man so tall
   he must climb a ladder
      to shave himself,

Of the runt so teeny-weeny
   it takes two men and a boy
      to see him,
Of mosquitoes:
   one can kill a dog,
      two of them a man,
Of a cyclone that sucked cookstoves
   out of the kitchen, up the chimney flue,
      and on to the next town,
Of the same cyclone picking up wagon-tracks
   in Nebraska and dropping them
      over in the Dakotas,
Of the hook-and-eye snake
   unlocking itself into forty pieces, each piece two inches long,
      then in nine seconds flat snapping itself together again,
Of the watch swallowed by the cow:
   when they butchered her a year later the watch was running
      and had the correct time,
Of horned snakes, hoop snakes that roll themselves
   where they want to go, and rattlesnakes
      carrying bells instead of rattles on their tails,
Of the herd of cattle in California
   getting lost in a giant redwood tree
      that had been hollowed out,
Of the man who killed a snake
   by putting its tail in its mouth
      so it swallowed itself,
Of railroad trains whizzing along
   so fast they reached the station
      before the whistle,
Of pigs so thin
   the farmer had to tie knots
      in their tails
         to keep them from crawling
            through the cracks in their pens,
Of Paul Bunyan's big blue ox, Babe,
   measuring between the eyes
      forty-two ax-handles and a plug
         of Star tobacco exactly,
Of John Henry's hammer
   and the curve of its swing
      and his singing of it
         as "a rainbow round my shoulder." They have yarns...

CARL SANDBURG

197

Little Breeches is the story of a miracle. It is no less miraculous for being about ordinary farming people and being told in a homely accent.

Little Breeches

I don't go much on religion,
 I never ain't had no show;
But I've got a middlin' tight grip, sir,
 On the handful o' things I know.
I don't pan out on the prophets
 An' free-will, an' that sort of thing—
But I b'lieve in God an' the angels,
 Ever sence one night last spring.

I come to town with some turnips,
 An' my little Gabe come along—
No four-year-old in the country
 Could beat him for pretty an' strong,
Peart an' chipper an' sassy.
 Always ready to swear and fight,—
And I'd l'arnt him to chaw terbacker,
 Jest to keep his milk-teeth white.

The snow come down like a blanket
 As I passed by Taggart's store;
I went in for a jug of molasses
 An' left the team at the door.
They scared at something an' started—
 I heard one little squall,
An' hell-to-split over the prairie
 Went team, Little Breeches an' all.

Hell-to-split over the prairie!
 I was almost froze with skeer;
But we rousted up some torches,
 An' s'arched for 'em far an' near.
At last we struck horse an' wagon,
 Snowed under a soft white mound,
Upsot, dead beat—but of little Gabe
 No hide nor hair was found.

And here all hope soured on me,
 Of my feller-critter's aid—
I jest flopped down on my marrow-bones
 Crotch-deep in the snow, an' prayed....
By this, the torches wuz played out,
 An' me an' Isrul Parr
Went off for some wood to a sheepfold
 That he said wuz somewhar thar.

We found it at last, an' a little shed
 Where they shut up the lambs at night.
We looked in an' seen them huddled thar,
 So warm an' sleepy an' white;
An' thar sot Little Breeches an' chirped,
 As peart as ever you see,
"I wants a chaw of terbacky,
 An' that's what's the matter of me."

How did he git thar? Angels.
 He could never have walked in that storm.
They jest scooped down an' toted him
 To whar it was safe an' warm.
An' I think that savin' a little child,
 An' bringin' him to his own,
Is a derned sight better business
 Than loafin' around The Throne.

JOHN HAY

198

LAUGHTER
HOLDING BOTH HIS SIDES

Most poetry, like life, is serious, real and earnest. But much of it is full of fun. Even the most serious poets enjoyed moments of comic relief. Shakespeare had his clowns. John Milton, the Puritan poet, who wrote on the most solemn and sublime subjects, relished the spirit of Mirth and wrote happily about Mirth's joyous companions:

> Jest and youthful Jollity,
> Quips and Cranks and wanton Wiles,
> Nods and Becks and Wreathed Smiles....
> Sport, that wrinkled Care derides,
> And Laughter holding both his sides.

Laughter has its instructive as well as its carefree side. Some of the poems in this section mingle wisdom with wit. Some of them, like the first poem, have a "moral" half-hidden in the merriment.

199

The Blind Men and the Elephant

It was six men of Hindostan,
To learning much inclined,
Who went to see the elephant,
(Though all of them were blind);
That each by observation
Might satisfy his mind.

The first approached the elephant,
And happening to fall
Against his broad and sturdy side,
At once began to bawl,
"Bless me, it seems the elephant
Is very like a wall."

The second, feeling of his tusk,
Cried, "Ho! what have we here
So very round and smooth and sharp?
To me 'tis mighty clear
This wonder of an elephant
Is very like a spear."

The third approached the animal,
And happening to take
The squirming trunk within his hands,
Then boldly up and spake;
"I see," quoth he, "the elephant
Is very like a snake."

The fourth stretched out his eager hand
And felt about the knee,
"What most this mighty beast is like
Is mighty plain," quoth he;
"'Tis clear enough the elephant
Is very like a tree."

The fifth who chanced to touch the ear
Said, "Even the blindest man
Can tell what this resembles most;
Deny the fact who can,
This marvel of an elephant
Is very like a fan."

The sixth no sooner had begun
About the beast to grope
Than, seizing on the swinging tail
That fell within his scope,
"I see," cried he, "the elephant
Is very like a rope."

And so these men of Hindostan
Disputed loud and long,
Each of his own opinion
Exceeding stiff and strong,
Though each was partly in the right,
And all were in the wrong!

JOHN GODFREY SAXE

The Owl-Critic does not point a moral directly But, like The Blind Men and the Elephant, *it pokes fun at people who are sure that they know everything. There are people who, in common with the young man in the poem, are blind even though they can see.*

The Owl-Critic

"Who stuffed that white owl?" No one spoke in the shop,
The barber was busy, and he couldn't stop;
The customers, waiting their turns, were all reading
The "Daily," the "Herald," the "Post," little heeding
The young man who blurted out such a blunt question;
Not one raised a head, or even made a suggestion;
And the barber kept on shaving.

200

"Don't you see, Mr. Brown,"
 Cried the youth, with a frown,
"How wrong the whole thing is,
 How preposterous each wing is,
 How flattened the head is, how jammed down the neck is—
 In short, the whole owl, what an ignorant wreck 't is!
 I make no apology;
 I've learned owl-eology.
 I've passed days and nights in a hundred collections,
 And cannot be blinded to any deflections
 Arising from unskilful fingers that fail
 To stuff a bird right, from his beak to his tail.
 Mister Brown! Mister Brown!
 Do take that bird down,
 Or you'll soon be the laughing-stock all over town!"
    And the barber kept on shaving.

"I've *studied* owls,
 And other night-fowls,
 And I tell you
 What I know to be true;
 An owl cannot roost
 With his limbs so unloosed;
 No owl in this world
 Ever had his claws curled,
 Ever had his legs slanted,
 Ever had his bill canted,
 Ever had his neck screwed
 Into that attitude.
 He can't *do* it, because
 'Tis against all bird-laws.
 Anatomy teaches,
 Ornithology preaches,
 An owl has a toe
 That *can't* turn out so!
 I've made the white owl my study for years,
 And to see such a job almost moves me to tears!
 Mr. Brown, I'm amazed
 You should be so gone crazed
 As to put up a bird
 In that posture absurd!
 To *look* at that owl really brings on a dizziness.
 The man who stuffed *him* don't half know his business!"
    And the barber kept on shaving.

201

"Examine those eyes.
I'm filled with surprise
Taxidermists should pass
Off on you such poor glass;
So unnatural they seem
They'd make Audubon scream,
And John Burroughs laugh
To encounter such chaff.
Do take that bird down;
Have him stuffed again, Brown!"
   And the barber kept on shaving.

"With some sawdust and bark
I could stuff in the dark
An owl better than that.
I could make an old hat
Look more like an owl
Than that horrid fowl,
Stuck up there so stiff like a side of coarse leather.
In fact, about *him* there's not one natural feather."

Just then, with a wink and a sly normal lurch,
The owl, very gravely, got down from his perch,
Walked around, and regarded his fault-finding critic
(Who thought he was stuffed) with a glance analytic,
And then fairly hooted, as if he should say:
"Your learning's at fault *this* time, anyway;
Don't waste it again on a live bird, I pray.
I'm an owl; you're another. Sir Critic, good day!"
   And the barber kept on shaving.

JAMES THOMAS FIELDS

The names of Gilbert and Sullivan are immortally paired as the creators of The Mikado, Iolanthe, Pirates of Penzance, *and some half-dozen more of the most cherished comic operas of all time. Prior to 1870, when William Schwenck Gilbert met the composer, Arthur Sullivan, and their historic collaboration began, Gilbert had had a career as a journalist, and had written and illustrated a book of hilarious verses,* The Bab Ballads. *Later, when Gilbert needed a typically absurd plot for an opera, he would dip into* The Bab Ballads *and borrow one of his own stories. Thus General John was extracted and converted into the diverting* H.M.S. Pinafore.

General John

The bravest names for fire and flames
   And all that mortal durst,
Were GENERAL JOHN and PRIVATE JAMES,
   Of the Sixty-seventy-first.

GENERAL JOHN was a soldier tried,
   A chief of warlike dons;
A haughty stride and a withering pride
   Were MAJOR-GENERAL JOHN'S.

A sneer would play on his martial phiz,
   Superior birth to show;
"Pish!" was a favourite word of his,
   And he often said "Ho! ho!"

FULL-PRIVATE JAMES described might be,
   As a man of a mournful mind;
No characteristic trait had he
   Of any distinctive kind.

202

From the ranks, one day, cried PRIVATE JAMES,
  "Oh! MAJOR-GENERAL JOHN,
I've doubts of our respective names,
  My mournful mind upon.

A glimmering thought occurs to me
  (Its source I can't unearth),
But I've a kind of a notion we
  Were cruelly changed at birth.

I've a strange idea that each other's names
  We've each of us here got on.
Such things have been," said PRIVATE JAMES.
  "They have!" sneered GENERAL JOHN.

My GENERAL JOHN, I swear upon
  My oath I think 'tis so—"
"Pish!" proudly sneered his GENERAL JOHN,
  And he also said "Ho! ho!"

"My GENERAL JOHN! my GENERAL JOHN!
  My GENERAL JOHN!" quoth he,
"This aristocratical sneer upon
  Your face I blush to see!

"No truly great or generous cove
  Deserving of them names,
Would sneer at a fixed idea that's drove
  In the mind of a PRIVATE JAMES!"

Said GENERAL JOHN, "Upon your claims
  No need your breath to waste;
If this is a joke, FULL-PRIVATE JAMES,
  It's a joke of doubtful taste.

"But, being a man of doubtless worth,
  If you feel certain quite
That we were probably changed at birth,
  I'll venture to say you're right."

So GENERAL JOHN as PRIVATE JAMES
  Fell in, parade upon;
And PRIVATE JAMES, by change of names,
  Was MAJOR-GENERAL JOHN.

W. S. GILBERT

The Yarn of the "Nancy Bell" *is also one of* The Bab Ballads *and is probably the most outrageous of all Gilbert's wild fancies. It is an incredible combination of the grisly and the uproarious. When it was first submitted for publication, the editor thought it was too bloodthirsty and "cannibalistic," but it offended no one because no one could take it seriously. It has become Gilbert's most quoted poem.*

The Yarn of the "Nancy Bell"

'Twas on the shores that round our coast
  From Deal to Ramsgate span,
That I found alone, on a piece of stone,
  An elderly naval man.

His hair was weedy, his beard was long,
  And weedy and long was he;
And I heard this wight on the shore recite
  In a singular minor key:

"Oh, I am a cook and a captain bold,
  And the mate of the Nancy brig,
And a bo'sun tight, and a midshipmite,
  And the crew of the captain's gig."

And he shook his fists and he tore his hair,
  Till I really felt afraid,
For I couldn't help thinking the man had been drinking,
  And so I simply said:

"O elderly man, it's little I know
    Of the duties of men of the sea,
And I'll eat my hand if I understand
    How ever you can be

"At once a cook and a captain bold,
    And the mate of the Nancy brig,
And a bo'sun tight, and a midshipmite,
    And the crew of the captain's gig!"

Then he gave a hitch to his trousers, which
    Is a trick all seamen larn,
And having got rid of a thumping quid,
    He spun this painful yarn:

"For a month we'd neither wittles nor drink
    Till a-hungry we did feel,
So we draw'd a lot, and, accordin', shot
    The captain for our meal.

"The next lot fell to the Nancy's mate,
    And a delicate dish he made;
Then our appetite with the midshipmite
    We seven survivors stay'd.

"And then we murder'd the bo'sun tight,
    And he much resembled pig;
Then we wittled free, did the cook and me
    On the crew of the captain's gig.

"'Twas in the good ship Nancy Bell
    That we sail'd to the Indian sea,
And there on a reef we come to grief,
    Which has often occurr'd to me.

"And pretty nigh all o' the crew was drown'd
    (There was seventy-seven o' soul);
And only ten of the Nancy's men
    Said 'Here!' to the muster-roll.

"There was me, and the cook, and the captain bold,
    And the mate of the Nancy brig,
And the bo'sun tight and a midshipmite,
    And the crew of the captain's gig.

"Then only the cook and me was left,
    And the delicate question, 'Which
Of us two goes to the kettle?' arose,
    And we argued it out as sich.

"For I loved that cook as a brother I did,
　　And the cook he worshipp'd me;
　But we'd both be blow'd if we'd either be stow'd
　　In the other chap's hold, you see.

"'I'll be eat if you dines off me,' says Tom.
　　'Yes, that,' say I, 'you'll be.
　I'm boil'd if I die, my friend,' quoth I;
　　And 'Exactly so,' quoth he.

"Says he: 'Dear James, to murder me
　　Were a foolish thing to do,
　For don't you see that you can't cook *me,*
　　While I can—and will—cook *you?*'

"So he boils the water, and takes the salt
　　And the pepper in portions true
　(Which he never forgot), and some chopp'd shallot,
　　And some sage and parsley too.

"And I eat that cook in a week or less,
　　And as I eating be
　The last of his chops, why I almost drops,
　　For a wessel in sight I see.

"And I never larf, and I never smile,
　　And I never lark nor play;
　But I sit and croak, and a single joke
　　I have—which is to say:

"Oh, I am a cook and a captain bold,
　　And the mate of the Nancy brig,
　And a bo'sun tight, and a midshipmite,
　　And the crew of the captain's gig!"

W. S. Gilbert

"'Come here,' says he, with a proper pride,
　　Which his smiling features tell;
　''Twill soothing be if I let you see
　　How extremely nice you'll smell.'

"And he stirr'd it round and round and round,
　　And he sniff'd at the foaming froth;
　When I ups with his heels, and smothers his squeals
　　In the scum of the boiling broth.

Charles Lutwidge Dodgson was a nineteenth-century deacon, a university lecturer, and a famous mathematician. But when he wrote as "Lewis Carroll" he was anything but serious. He delighted in nonsense, and he particularly liked to burlesque over-serious poets. In a chapter of Alice's Adventures in Wonderland *Carroll makes fun of a poem by Robert Southey entitled* The Old Man's Comforts and How He Gained Them. *The Southey poem begins:*

"You are old, Father William," the young man cried,
    "The few locks which are left you are gray;
You are hale, Father William, a hearty old man,
    Now tell me the reason, I pray."

"In the days of my youth," Father William replied,
    "I remembered that youth would fly fast,
And abused not my health, and my vigor at first,
    That I never might need them at last."

Carroll took Southey's preachy Father William and turned him into an acrobatic, argumentative, and generally unforgettable old man.

Father William

"You are old, Father William," the young man said,
    "And your hair has become very white;
And yet you incessantly stand on your head—
    Do you think, at your age, it is right?"

"In my youth," Father William replied to his son,
    "I feared it might injure the brain;
But now that I'm perfectly sure I have none,
    Why, I do it again and again."

"You are old," said the youth, "as I mentioned before,
    And have grown most uncommonly fat;
Yet you turned a back somersault in at the door—
    Pray, what is the reason of that?"

"In my youth," said the sage, as he shook his gray locks,
    "I kept all my very limbs supple
By the use of this ointment—one shilling the box—
    Allow me to sell you a couple."

"You are old," said the youth, "and your jaws are too weak
  For anything tougher than suet;
Yet you finished the goose, with the bones and the beak—
  Pray, how did you manage to do it?"

"In my youth," said his father, "I took to the law,
  And argued each case with my wife;
And the muscular strength, which it gave to my jaw,
  Has lasted the rest of my life."

"You are old," said the youth, "one would hardly suppose
  That your eye was as steady as ever;
Yet you balanced an eel on the end of your nose—
  What made you so awfully clever?"

"I have answered three questions, and that is enough,"
  Said his father, "don't give yourself airs!
Do you think I can listen all day to such stuff?
  Be off, or I'll kick you down stairs!"

LEWIS CARROLL

Jabberwocky *is one of the greatest nonsense poems ever written, so we can't expect to find much meaning in it. Nevertheless, many people have found delight in the queer words, and even some meaning in them. Most of the strange syllables are "portmanteau" words—two different words jammed together, or two different ideas packed into one word, as into a suitcase or "portmanteau." For example, if you were to think of "fretful" and "fuming" and "furious" all at the same time, and then tried to say all three words at once, the result would be a "portmanteau" word exactly like "frumious."*

The sound of Jabberwocky *is so satisfying that you don't have to bother about the sense. But if you want to make sense out of it, the author is glad to give you some help. In the sixth chapter of* Through the Looking-Glass, *Humpty Dumpty tells Alice that he can explain all the poems that ever were invented—and a good many that haven't been invented yet. He begins by taking the first odd word in the first line. "Brillig" means four o'clock in the afternoon, for that is the time when you begin "broiling" things for dinner. Humpty Dumpty does not add that "brillig" is really a combination of "broiling" and "grilling." Also in the first line, those strange animals, the "toves" (which seem to be half "toads" and half "doves") are "slithy" because they are "lithe" and "slimy" and, although Humpty Dumpty neglects to mention it, also somewhat "sly." To "gyre" is to go round and round like a gyroscope, and to "gimble" is to make holes like a gimlet. The "wabe," Alice discovers, is the grass plot around a sun-dial because it goes a long way before it and a long way behind it. "Mimsy" is a mixture of "flimsy" and "miserable," while "mome" is short for "from home." "Whiffling" is a combination of "whistling" and "sniffling."*

Now see what you can do with the others.

Jabberwocky

'Twas brillig, and the slithy toves
    Did gyre and gimble in the wabe;
All mimsy were the borogoves,
    And the mome raths outgrabe.

"Beware the Jabberwock, my son!
    The jaws that bite, the claws that catch!
Beware the Jubjub bird, and shun
    The frumious Bandersnatch!"

He took his vorpal sword in hand:
    Long time the manxome foe he sought—

So rested he by the Tumtum tree,
    And stood awhile in thought.

And as in uffish thought he stood,
    The Jabberwock, with eyes of flame,
Came whiffling through the tulgey wood,
    And burbled as it came!

One, two! One, two! And through and through
    The vorpal blade went snicker-snack!
He left it dead, and with its head
    He went galumphing back.

"And hast thou slain the Jabberwock?
  Come to my arms, my beamish boy!
O frabjous day! Callooh! Callay!"
  He chortled in his joy.

'Twas brillig, and the slithy toves
  Did gyre and gimble in the wabe;
All mimsy were the borogoves,
  And the mome raths outgrabe.

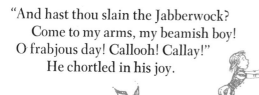

LEWIS CARROLL

Although Humpty Dumpty is an authority on "portmanteau" words and "Jabberwocky" talk, his own poem is written in the simplest and straightest English. Yet it makes no more sense than Jabberwocky. Perhaps even less.

Humpty Dumpty's Recitation

In winter, when the fields are white,
I sing this song for your delight—

In spring, when woods are getting green,
I'll try and tell you what I mean.

In summer, when the days are long,
Perhaps you'll understand the song:

In autumn, when the leaves are brown
Take pen and ink, and write it down.

I sent a message to the fish:
I told them "This is what I wish."

The little fishes of the sea
They sent an answer back to me.

The little fishes' answer was
"We cannot do it, Sir, because—"

I sent to them again to say
"It will be better to obey."

The fishes answered with a grin,
Why, what a temper you are in!"

I told them once, I told them twice:
They would not listen to advice.

I took a kettle large and new,
Fit for the deed I had to do.

My heart went hop, my heart went thump;
I filled the kettle at the pump.

Then some one came to me and said
"The little fishes are in bed."

I said to him, I said it plain,
"Then you must wake them up again."

I said it very loud and clear;
I went and shouted in his ear.

But he was very stiff and proud;
He said "You needn't shout so loud!"

And he was very proud and stiff;
He said "I'd go and wake them, if—"

I took a corkscrew from the shelf:
I went to wake them up myself.

And when I found the door was locked,
I pulled and pushed and kicked and knocked.

And when I found the door was shut,
I tried to turn the handle, but—

LEWIS CARROLL

209

The White Knight, one of Carroll's most appealingly foolish characters, wanders Through the Looking Glass *in a dazed way, falling off his horse regularly and inventing all manner of improbable, impractical, and unprofitable things. His song, with its faint air of melancholy and its total daffiness, is just like him.*

The White Knight's Song

I'll tell thee everything I can:
　　There's little to relate.
I saw an agèd agèd man,
　　A-sitting on a gate.
"Who are you, agèd man?" I said.
　　"And how is it you live?"
And his answer trickled through my head,
　　Like water through a sieve.

He said "I look for butterflies
    That sleep among the wheat.
I make them into mutton-pies,
    And sell them in the street.
I sell them unto men," he said,
    "Who sail on stormy seas;
And that's the way I get my bread—
    A trifle, if you please."

But I was thinking of a plan
    To dye one's whiskers green,
And always use so large a fan
    That they could not be seen.
So, having no reply to give
    To what the old man said,
I cried "Come, tell me how you live!"
    And thumped him on the head.

His accents mild took up the tale:
    He said "I go my ways,
And when I find a mountain-rill,
    I set it in a blaze;
And thence they make a stuff they call
    Rowland's Macassar-Oil—
Yet twopence-halfpenny is all
    They give me for my toil."

But I was thinking of a way
    To feed oneself on batter,
And so go on from day to day
    Getting a little fatter.
I shook him well from side to side,
    Until his face was blue:
"Come, tell me how you live," I cried,
    "And what it is you do!"

He said "I hunt for haddocks' eyes
    Among the heather bright,
And work them into waistcoat-buttons
    In the silent night.
And these I do not sell for gold
    Or coin of silvery shine,
But for a copper halfpenny,
    And that will purchase nine.

I sometimes dig for buttered rolls,
    Or set limed twigs for crabs:
I sometimes search the grassy knolls
    For wheels of Hansom-cabs.
And that's the way" (he gave a wink)
    "By which I get my wealth—
And very gladly will I drink
    Your Honor's noble health."

I heard him then, for I had just
    Completed my design
To keep the Menai bridge from rust
    By boiling it in wine.
I thanked him much for telling me
    The way he got his wealth,
But chiefly for his wish that he
    Might drink my noble health.

And now, if e'er by chance I put
    My fingers into glue,
Or madly squeeze a right-hand foot
    Into a left-hand shoe,
Or if I drop upon my toe
    A very heavy weight,
I weep for it reminds me so
Of that old man I used to know—
Whose look was mild, whose speech was slow,
Whose hair was whiter than the snow,
Whose face was very like a crow,
With eyes, like cinders, all aglow,
Who seemed distracted with his woe,
Who rocked his body to and fro,
And muttered mumblingly and low,
As if his mouth were full of dough,
Who snorted like a buffalo—
That summer evening long ago,
    A-sitting on a gate.

LEWIS CARROLL

211

Practically everyone knows the nonsense rhymes of Edward Lear. But not everyone knows that when he lived, about a century ago, he was an artist whose paintings of birds were compared to Audubon's, whose landscape sketches were used as models by scientists, and who taught drawing to Queen Victoria. He wrote many verses about himself, including these:

"How pleasant to know Mr. Lear!"
    Who has written such volumes of stuff!
Some think him ill-tempered and queer,
    But a few think him pleasant enough.

His mind is concrete and fastidious,
    His nose is remarkably big;
His visage is more or less hideous,
    His beard it resembles a wig.

When he walks out in waterproof white,
    The children run after him so!
Calling out, "He's come out in his night
    Gown, that crazy old Englishman, oh!"

He weeps by the side of the ocean,
    He weeps on the top of the hill;
He purchases pancakes and lotion,
    And chocolate shrimps from the mill.

These facts, of course, are not true, but Lear thought they were more interesting than the matter-of-fact truth. This also applies to The Pobble Who Has No Toes, The Courtship of the Yonghy-Bonghy-Bo, *and all Lear's other queer but captivating rhymes.*

Humorous poetry takes the most unexpected turns. Sometimes the fun is in the meaning; sometimes the fun is in the mere sound. Words that make no particular sense can make a persistent music. When we see names like the Pobble, Yonghy-Bonghy-Bo, and the Runcible Cat, we cannot help but chuckle, for nonsense is bound to make us laugh.

The Pobble Who Has No Toes

The Pobble who has no toes
    Had once as many as we;
When they said, "Some day you may lose them all;"
    He replied, "Fish fiddle de-dee!"
And his Aunt Jobiska made him drink
Lavender water tinged with pink;
For she said, "The World in general knows
There's nothing so good for a Pobble's toes!"

212

The Pobble who has no toes,
   Swam across the Bristol Channel;
But before he set out he wrapped his nose
   In a piece of scarlet flannel.
For his Aunt Jobiska said, "No harm
Can come to his toes if his nose is warm;
And it's perfectly known that a Pobble's toes
Are safe—provided he minds his nose."

The Pobble swam fast and well,
   And when boats or ships came near him,
He tinkledy-binkledy-winkled a bell
   So that all the world could hear him.
And all the Sailors and Admirals cried,
When they saw him nearing the further side,—
'He has gone to fish, for his Aunt Jobiska's
Runcible Cat with crimson whiskers!'

But before he touched the shore,—
   The shore of the Bristol Channel,
A sea-green Porpoise carried away
   His wrapper of scarlet flannel.
And when he came to observe his feet,
Formerly garnished with toes so neat,
His face at once became forlorn
On perceiving that all his toes were gone!

And nobody ever knew,
   From that dark day to the present,
Whoso had taken the Pobble's toes,
   In a manner so far from pleasant.
Whether the shrimps or crawfish grey,
Or crafty Mermaids stole them away,
Nobody knew; and nobody knows
How the Pobble was robbed of his twice five toes!

The Pobble who has no toes
   Was placed in a friendly Bark,
And they rowed him back, and carried him up
   To his Aunt Jobiska's Park.
And she made him a feast, at his earnest wish,
Of eggs and buttercups fried with fish;
And she said, "It's a fact the whole world knows,
That Pobbles are happier without their toes."

EDWARD LEAR

The Courtship of the Yonghy-Bonghy-Bo

On the Coast of Coromandel
   Where the early pumpkins blow,
     In the middle of the woods
     Lived the Yonghy-Bonghy-Bo.
Two old chairs, and half a candle,
One old jug without a handle—
     These were all his worldly goods,
     In the middle of the woods,
     These were all his worldly goods,
   Of the Yonghy-Bonghy-Bo,
   Of the Yonghy-Bonghy Bo.

Once, among the Bong-trees walking
   Where the early pumpkins blow,
     To a little heap of stones
     Came the Yonghy-Bonghy-Bo.
There he heard a Lady talking,
To some milk-white Hens of Dorking—
     "'Tis the Lady Jingly Jones!
     On that little heap of stones
     Sits the Lady Jingly Jones!"
   Said the Yonghy-Bonghy-Bo,
   Said the Yonghy-Bonghy-Bo.

"Lady Jingly! Lady Jingly!
    Sitting where the pumpkins blow,
Will you come and be my wife?"
Said the Yonghy-Bonghy-Bo.
"I am tired of living singly—
On this coast so wild and shingly—
    I'm a-weary of my life;
    If you'll come and be my wife,
    Quite serene would be my life!"
  Said the Yonghy-Bonghy-Bo,
  Said the Yonghy-Bonghy-Bo.

"On this Coast of Coromandel
    Shrimps and watercresses grow,
        Prawns are plentiful and cheap,"
Said the Yonghy-Bonghy-Bo.
"You shall have my chairs and candle,
And my jug without a handle!
    Gaze upon the rolling deep
    (Fish is plentiful and cheap);
    As the sea, my love is deep!"
  Said the Yonghy-Bonghy-Bo,
  Said the Yonghy-Bonghy-Bo.

Lady Jingly answered sadly,
    And her tears began to flow—
        "Your proposal comes too late,
Mr. Yonghy-Bonghy-Bo!
I would be your wife most gladly!"
(Here she twirled her fingers madly)
    "But in England I've a mate!
    Yes! you've asked me far too late,
    For in England I've a mate,
  Mr. Yonghy-Bonghy-Bo!
  Mr. Yonghy-Bonghy-Bo!

"Mr. Jones (his name is Handel—
    Handel Jones, Esquire, & Co.)
        Dorking fowls delights to send,
    Mr. Yonghy-Bonghy-Bo!
Keep, oh, keep your chairs and candle,
And your jug without a handle—
    I can merely be your friend!
    Should my Jones more Dorkings send,
    I will give you three, my friend!
  Mr. Yonghy-Bonghy-Bo!
  Mr. Yonghy-Bonghy-Bo!

"Though you've such a tiny body,
    And your head so large doth grow—
        Though your hat may blow away,
    Mr. Yonghy-Bonghy-Bo!
Though you're such a Hoddy Doddy,
Yet I wish that I could modi-
    fy the words I needs must say!
    Will you please to go away
    That is all I have to say,
  Mr. Yonghy-Bonghy-Bo!
  Mr. Yonghy-Bonghy-Bo!"

Down the slippery slopes of Myrtle,
    Where the early pumpkins blow,
        To the calm and silent sea
    Fled the Yonghy-Bonghy-Bo.
There, beyond the Bay of Gurtle,
Lay a large and lively Turtle.
    "You're the Cove," he said, "for me;
    On your back beyond the sea,
    Turtle, you shall carry me!"
  Said the Yonghy-Bonghy-Bo,
  Said the Yonghy-Bonghy-Bo.

Through the silent-roaring ocean
　　Did the Turtle swiftly go;
　　　Holding fast upon his shell
Rode the Yonghy-Bonghy-Bo.
With a sad primeval motion
Towards the sunset isles of Boshen
　　Still the Turtle bore him well.
　　Holding fast upon his shell,
　　"Lady Jingly Jones, farewell!"
Sang the Yonghy-Bonghy-Bo.
Sang the Yonghy-Bonghy-Bo.

From the Coast of Coromandel
　　Did that Lady never go;
　　　On that heap of stones she mourns
For the Yonghy-Bonghy-Bo.
On that Coast of Coromandel,
In his jug without a handle
　　Still she weeps, and daily moans;
　　On that little heap of stones
　　To her Dorking Hens she moans,
For the Yonghy-Bonghy-Bo,
For the Yonghy-Bonghy-Bo.

EDWARD LEAR

The Table and the Chair

Said the Table to the Chair,
"You can hardly be aware
How I suffer from the heat
And from chilblains on my feet.
If we took a little walk,
We might have a little talk;
Pray let us take the air,"
Said the Table to the Chair.

Said the Chair unto the Table,
"Now, you know we are not able:
How foolishly you talk,
When you know we cannot walk!"
Said the Table with a sigh,
"It can do no harm to try.
I've as many legs as you;
Why can't we walk on two?"

So they both went slowly down,
And walked about the town
With a cheerful bumpy sound
As they toddled round and round;

And everybody cried,
As they hastened to their side,
"See! the Table and the Chair
Have come out to take the air!"

But in going down an alley
To a castle in a valley,
They completely lost their way,
And wandered all the day;
Till, to see them safely back,
They paid a Ducky-quack,
And a Beetle, and a Mouse,
Who took them to their house.

Then they whispered to each other,
"O delightful little brother,
What a lovely walk we've taken!
Let us dine on beans and bacon."
So the Ducky and the leetle
Browny-Mousy *and* the Beetle
Dined and danced upon their heads
Till they toddled to their beds.

EDWARD LEAR

Before he died in 1953, Hilaire Belloc had written about one hundred volumes on every possible subject—he even wrote a book entitled On Nothing. *Although he was famous for his biographies and essays, he took great pleasure in his comical* Cautionary Tales for Children. *Written in the style of a kindergarten Primer, the verses rise to mock-serious heights only to descend to a flat and obvious "lesson."*

George Who Played with a Dangerous Toy, and Suffered a Catastrophe of Considerable Dimensions

When George's Grandmamma was told
That George had been as good as Gold,
She Promised in the Afternoon
To buy him an *Immense* BALLOON.
And so she did; but when it came,
It got into the candle flame,
And being of a dangerous sort
Exploded with a Loud Report!
The Lights went out! The Windows broke!
The Room was filled with reeking smoke!
And in the darkness shrieks and yells
Were mingled with Electric Bells,
And falling masonry and groans,
And crunching, as of broken bones,
And dreadful shrieks, when, worst of all,
The House itself began to fall!
It tottered, shuddering to and fro,
Then crashed into the street below—
Which happened to be Savile Row.

When Help arrived, among the Dead
Were Cousin Mary, Little Fred,
The Footmen (both of them), the Groom,
The man that cleaned the Billiard-Room,
The Chaplain, and the Still-Room Maid.
And I am dreadfully afraid
That Monsieur Champignon, the Chef,
Will now be permanently deaf—
And both his Aides are much the same;
While George, who was in part to blame,
Received, you will regret to hear,
A nasty lump behind his ear.

The moral is that little Boys
Should not be given dangerous Toys.

HILAIRE BELLOC

216

Many years ago a song writer, weary of all the thumping ballads that celebrated triumphant hunters, wrote a hunting song about three men who could not hit anything and were not even sure of what they were pursuing. These droll and helpless fellows proved so captivating that many versions of their misadventures exist. This is one of the liveliest.

Three Jolly Huntsmen

Three jolly huntsmen,
I've heard people say,
Went hunting together
On St. David's Day.

All day they hunted,
And nothing could they find,
But a ship a-sailing,
A-sailing with the wind.

One said it was a ship,
The other he said, Nay;
The third said it was a house,
With the chimney blown away.

And all the night they hunted,
And nothing could they find
But the moon a-gliding,
A-gliding with the wind.

One said it was the moon,
The other he said, Nay;
The third said it was a cheese,
And half of it cut away.

And all the day they hunted,
And nothing did they find
But a hedgehog in a bramble-bush,
And that they left behind.

The first said it was a hedgehog,
The second he said, Nay;
The third said it was a pin cushion,
And the pins stuck in wrong way.

And all the night they hunted,
And nothing could they find
But a hare in a turnip-field,
And that they left behind.

The first said it was a hare,
The second he said, Nay;
The third said it was a calf,
And the cow had run away.

And all the day they hunted,
And nothing could they find
But an owl in a holly-tree,
And that they left behind.

One said it was an owl,
The second he said, Nay;
The third said 'twas an old man,
And his beard was growing gray.

217

At the beginning of the twentieth century, Guy Wetmore Carryl rewrote many of the jingles, fables, and fairy tales of our youth. One of the best of his books was called Mother Goose for Grown-Ups. *In it, he took the tales out of the nursery and embellished them with tricky twists and complicated rhymes. All of his poems, like the one on Simple Simon (the original of which you have met on page 104), end with an unexpected (and usually unnecessary) "moral" but with a very necessary pun.*

The Gastronomic Guile of Simple Simon

Conveniently near to where
   Young Simple Simon dwelt
There was to be a county fair,
   And Simple Simon felt
That to the fair he ought to go
In all his Sunday clothes, and so,
Determined to behold the show,
   He put them on and went.
(One-half his clothes was borrowed
   And the other half was lent.)

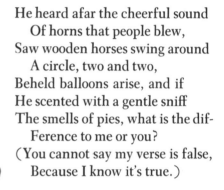

He heard afar the cheerful sound
   Of horns that people blew,
Saw wooden horses swing around
   A circle, two and two,
Beheld balloons arise, and if
He scented with a gentle sniff
The smells of pies, what is the dif-
   Ference to me or you?
(You cannot say my verse is false,
   Because I know it's true.)

As Simple Simon nearer came
   To these attractive smells,
Avoiding every little game
   Men played with walnut shells,
He felt a sudden longing rise.
The sparkle in his eager eyes
Betrayed the fact he yearned for pies:
   The eye the secret tells.
('Tis known the pie of county fairs
   All other pies excels.)

So when he saw upon the road,
   Some fifty feet away,
A pieman, Simple Simon strode
   Toward him, shouting: "Hey!
What kinds?" as lordly as a prince.
The pieman said: "I've pumpkin, quince,
Blueberry, lemon, peach, and mince."
   And, showing his array,
He added: "Won't you try one, sir?
   They're very nice to-day."

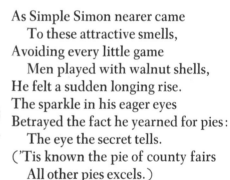

218

Now Simon's taste was most profuse,
  And so, by way of start,
He ate two cakes; a Charlotte Russe;
  Six buns; the better part
Of one big gingerbread; a pair
Of lady-fingers; an eclair;
And ten assorted pies; and there,
  His hand upon his heart,
He paused to choose between
  An apple dumpling and a tart.

Observing that upon his tray
  His goods were growing few,
The pieman cried: "I beg to say
  That patrons such as you
One does not meet in many a moon.
Pray, won't you try this macaroon?"
But soon suspicious, changed his tune,
  Continuing: "What is due
I beg respectfully to add's
  A dollar twenty-two."

Then Simple Simon put a curb
  Upon his appetite,
And turning with an air superb
  He suddenly took flight,
While o'er his shoulder this absurd
And really most offensive word
The trusting pieman shortly heard
  To soothe his bitter plight:
"Perhaps I should have said before
  Your wares are out of sight."

The MORAL is a simple one
  But still of consequence.
We've seen that Simon's sense of fun
  Was almost too intense:
Though blaming his deceitful guise,
We with the pieman sympathize,
The latter we must criticize
  Because he was so dense:
He might have known from what he ate
  That Simon had no cents!

GUY WETMORE CARRYL

Guy Wetmore Carryl, whose poem you have just read, had a father who was even more gifted than he was. Young Carryl was brought up on good books, some of them highly humorous, including Davy and the Goblin *and* The Admiral's Caravan, *charmingly nonsensical volumes written by his father, Charles Edward Carryl. You'll find the elder Carryl's poem about the camel on page 37. Here is another favorite in quite another style.*

The Walloping Window-Blind

A capital ship for an ocean trip
  Was *The Walloping Window-Blind;*
No gale that blew dismayed her crew
  Or troubled the captain's mind.

The man at the wheel was taught to feel
  Contempt for the wildest blow,
And it often appeared, when the weather had cleared,
  That he'd been in his bunk below.

The boatswain's mate was very sedate,
    Yet fond of amusement, too;
And he played hop-scotch with the starboard watch
    While the captain tickled the crew.
And the gunner we had was apparently mad,
    For he sat on the after-rail,
And fired salutes with the captain's boots,
    In the teeth of the booming gale.

The captain sat in a commodore's hat,
    And dined, in a royal way,
On toasted pigs and pickles and figs
    And gummery bread, each day.
But the cook was Dutch, and behaved as such;
    For the food that he gave the crew
Was a number of tons of hot-cross buns,
    Chopped up with sugar and glue.

And we all felt ill as mariners will,
    On a diet that's cheap and rude;
And we shivered and shook as we dipped the cook
    In a tub of his gluesome food.
Then nautical pride we laid aside,
    And we cast the vessel ashore
On the Gulliby Isles, where the Poohpooh smiles,
    And the Anagazanders roar.

Composed of sand was that favored land,
    And trimmed with cinnamon straws;
And pink and blue was the pleasing hue
    Of the Tickletoeteaser's claws.
And we sat on the edge of a sandy ledge
    And shot at the whistling bee;
And the Binnacle-bats wore water-proof hats
    As they danced in the sounding sea.

On rubagrub bark, from dawn to dark,
    We fed, till we all had grown
Uncommonly shrunk—when a Chinese junk
    Came by from the torriby zone.
She was stubby and square, but we didn't much car
    And we cheerily put to sea;
And we left the crew of the junk to chew
    The bark of the rubagrub tree.

CHARLES EDWARD CARR

Looking at the titles, you might think that The Common Cormorant, The Skippery Boo, The Chickamungus, *and* The Doze *should be in the section entitled "Creatures of Every Kind." But after the first glance you will realize that these are creatures of no kind at all. The skippery boo is a zoo in himself; the cormorant is certainly not a recognizable member of the animal kingdom; and the only place where the doze and the chickamungus exist is in a book entitled* Prefabulous Animiles.

The Skippery Boo

I went to bring,
    From the rippling spring,
One morning dry and damp,
    A brimming pail
    Of Adam's ale
For use about the camp;
    My happy frame
    Did well proclaim
A cheerful bent of mind,
    And I hummed a song,
    As I loped along,
Of the most enchanting kind.
    But my heart stood still,
    As I turned the hill,
And the spring came to my view,
    For drinking there
    Of the potion rare,
Was the terrible Skippery Boo.

He drank his fill
    From the flowing rill,
And shook his mighty mane,
    Then with his jaws
    And his hairy paws,
He ripped a tree in twain.
    With fear and dread
    To camp I sped,
For my trusty .30 bore,
    Then turned about
    With daring shout,
And sought the spring once more;
    But though my feet
    With speed were fleet,
As o'er the glade I flew,
    No sign was there
    On earth, in air,
Of the slippery Skippery Boo.

To left and right
    I strained my sight,
To find where he had gone,
    Among the pines
    I sought for signs,
But found not a single one.
    To East and West
    I turned my quest,
But all to no avail,
    No trace I found
    On gorse or ground,
Of his departing trail.
    And then aloft
    My gaze I doffed,
And there in the hazy blue,
    On the topmost spine
    Of the tallest pine,
Hung the fabulous Skippery Boo.

Oh, the Skippery Boo
Is a fanciful zoo:
A mermaid and a bat,
A grizzly hare
And a webfoot bear,
A goof and a bumble-cat.
He can fell an oak
With a single stroke,
Or shatter a mountain side,
Then lightly rise
To the azure skies,
And light as a zephyr ride.
My heart he fills
With terror's chills,
Oh, don't know what I'd do,
If some dark night,
In broad daylight,
I should meet a Skippery Boo.

A poison flows
From his warty toes,
And the grass where he shall tread,
Shall wilt and fade
At evening's shade,
And tomorrow shall be dead.
And who shall walk
Where he shall stalk,
O'er valley, hill or plain,
Shall die, 'tis said,
Of illness dread,
And a terrible dark-green pain.
So as you wade
This vale of shade,
And jog life's journey through,
At day, at night,
Be it dark or light,
Watch out for the Skippery Boo.

EARL L. NEWTON

The Chickamungus

All in the groves of dragon-fungus
Lives the mysterious Chickamungus.
The natives who inhabit there
Have never yet found out his lair;
And if by chance they did, no doubt
The Chickamungus would be out.
For he is seldom found at home;
He likes to rove, he likes to roam.
He never sleeps but what he snores,
He never barks but what he roars,
He never creeps but what he walks,
He never climbs but what he stalks,
He never trots but what he hobbles,
He never stands but what he wobbles,
He never runs but what he skims,
He never flies but what he swims,
At tom-tom time he romps and roves
Among the odorous dragon-groves.

He lives on half-grown formicoots
And other sorts of roots and shoots.
He has been seen at rest among
His multitudinivorous young;
And travellers returning late
Have heard him crying for his mate.
His tracks have been identified,
Straying a bit from side to side,
Across the desert plains of Quunce.
A native girl observed him once,
But could not say what she had seen,
So unobservant had she been.
Her evidence is inconclusive,
And so the beast remains elusive.
A naturalist who found his den
Was never after seen again.
Thus we must leave the Chickamungus
At large amidst the dragon-fungus.

JAMES REEVES

222

The Doze

Through Dangly Woods the aimless Doze
A-dripping and a-dribbling goes.
His company no beast enjoys.
He makes a sort of hopeless noise
Between a snuffle and a snort.
His hair is neither long nor short;
His tail gets caught on the briars and bushes,
As through the undergrowth he pushes.
His ears are big, but not much use.
He lives on blackberries and juice
And anything that he can get.
His feet are clumsy, wide and wet,
Slip-slopping through the bog and heather
All in the wild and weepy weather.
His young are many, and maltreat him;
But only hungry creatures eat him.
He pokes about in mossy holes,
Disturbing sleepless mice and moles,
And what he wants he never knows—
The damp, despised, and aimless Doze.

JAMES REEVES

The Common Cormorant

The common cormorant, or shag,
Lays eggs inside a paper bag.
The reason you will see, no doubt,
It is to keep the lightning out.
But what these unobservant birds
Have never noticed is that herds
Of wandering bears may come with buns
And steal the bags to hold the crumbs.

The next poem is about two girls, one of whom had a peculiar name, and both of whom lived on a peculiar diet. This, I may as well admit, is a somewhat baffling poem. It doesn't say much; it doesn't mean much; and yet I can't shake the rhythm out of my mind.

Isabel Jones & Curabel Lee

Isabel Jones & Curabel Lee
Lived on butter and bread and tea,
And as to that they would both agree:
Isabel, Curabel, Jones & Lee.

Isabel said: While prunes have stones
They aren't a promising food for Jones.
Curabel said: Well, as for me,
Tripe is a terrible thing for Lee.

There's not a dish or fowl or fish
For which we wish, said I. & C.
And that is why until we die
We'll eat no pie, nor beg nor buy
But butter and bread and a trace of tea.
(Signed) Isabel Jones & Curabel Lee.

DAVID McCORD

Those who are not familiar with Lear's nonsense read The Owl and the Pussy-Cat *and* Calico Pie *at their own risk. Once you have become acquainted with the meaningless music of the persistent refrains, it is impossible to get the words out of your mind.*

The Owl and the Pussy-Cat

The Owl and the Pussy-Cat went to sea
    In a beautiful pea-green boat:
They took some honey, and plenty of money
    Wrapped up in a five-pound note.
The Owl looked up to the stars above,
    And sang to a small guitar,
"O lovely Pussy, O Pussy, my love,
    What a beautiful Pussy you are,
        You are,
        You are!
What a beautiful Pussy you are!"

Pussy said to the Owl, "You elegant fowl,
    How charmingly sweet you sing!
Oh! let us be married; too long we have tarried:
    But what shall we do for a ring?"
They sailed away, for a year and a day,
    To the land where the bong-tree grows;
And there in a wood a Piggy-wig stood,
    With a ring at the end of his nose,
        His nose,
        His nose,
With a ring at the end of his nose.

"Dear Pig, are you willing to sell for one shilling
    Your ring?" Said the Piggy, "I will."
So they took it away, and were married next day
    By the turkey who lives on the hill.
They dined on mince and slices of quince,
    Which they ate with a runcible spoon;
And hand in hand, on the edge of the sand,
    They danced by the light of the moon,
        The moon,
        The moon,
They danced by the light of the moon.

EDWARD LEAR

Calico Pie

Calico Pie,
　The little Birds fly
Down to the calico tree,
　Their wings were blue,
　And they sang "Tilly-loo!"
　Till away they flew—
And they never came back to me!
　They never came back!
　They never came back!
They never came back to me!

Calico Jam,
　The little Fish swam
Over the syllabub sea,
　He took off his hat,
　To the Sole and the Sprat,
　And the Willeby-wat—
But he never came back to me!
　He never came back!
　He never came back!
He never came back to me!

Calico Ban,
　The little Mice ran,
To be ready in time for tea,
　Flippity flup,
　They drank it all up,
　And danced in the cup—
But they never came back to me!
　They never came back!
　They never came back!
They never came back to me!

Calico Drum,
　The Grasshoppers come,
The Butterfly, Beetle, and Bee,
　Over the ground,
　Around and round,
　With a hop and a bound—
But they never came back!
　They never came back!
　They never came back!
They never came back to me!

EDWARD LEAR

225

Here is a kind of game, a game that the author plays with himself. Edward Lear, the master of nonsense, tries to see how long he can go on making sense out of a poem built on a single rhyme.

The Akond of Swat

Who or why, or which, or *what,*
      Is the Akond of SWAT?

      Is he tall or short, or dark or fair?
      Does he sit on a stool or a sofa or chair,   or SQUAT,
               The Akond of Swat?

      Is he wise or foolish, young or old?
      Does he drink his soup and his coffee cold,   or HOT,
               The Akond of Swat?

Does he sing or whistle, jabber or talk,
And when riding abroad does he gallop or walk,   or TROT,
      The Akond of Swat?

Does he wear a turban, a fez, or a hat?
Does he sleep on a mattress, a bed, or a mat,   or a COT,
      The Akond of Swat?

      When he writes a copy in round-hand size,
      Does he cross his T's and finish his I's   with a DOT,
               The Akond of Swat?

      Can he write a letter concisely clear
      Without a speck or a smudge or smear   or BLOT,
               The Akond of Swat?

Do his people like him extremely well?
Or do they, whenever they can, rebel,   or PLOT,
      At the Akond of Swat?

If he catches them then, either old or young,
Does he have them chopped in pieces or hung,   or SHOT,
      The Akond of Swat?

      Do his people steal in the lanes or park?
      Or even at times, when days are dark,   GAROTTE?
               O the Akond of Swat?

      Does he study the wants of his own dominion?
      Or doesn't he care for public opinion   a JOT,
               The Akond of Swat?

To amuse his mind do his people show him
Pictures, or any one's last new poem,   or WHAT,
            For the Akond of Swat?

At night if he suddenly screams and wakes,
Do they bring him only a few small cakes,   or a LOT,
            For the Akond of Swat?

Does he live on turnips, tea, or tripe?
Does he like his shawl to be marked with a stripe,   or a DOT,
            The Akond of Swat?

Does he like to lie on his back in a boat
Like the lady who lived in that isle remote,   SHALLOT,
            The Akond of Swat?

Is he quiet, or always making a fuss?
Is his steward a Swiss or a Swede or a Russ,   or a SCOT,
            The Akond of Swat?

Does he like to sit by the calm blue wave?
Or to sleep and snore in a dark green cave,   or a GROT,
            The Akond of Swat?

Does he drink small beer from a silver jug?
Or a bowl? or a glass? or a cup? or a mug?   or a POT,
            The Akond of Swat?

Does he beat his wife with a gold-topped pipe,
When she lets the gooseberries grow too ripe,   or ROT,
            The Akond of Swat?

Does he wear a white tie when he dines with friends,
And tie it neat in a bow with ends,   or a KNOT,
            The Akond of Swat?

Does he like new cream, and hate mince-pies?
When he looks at the sun does he wink his eyes,   or NOT,
            The Akond of Swat?

Does he teach his subjects to roast and bake?
Does he sail about on an inland lake,   in a YACHT,
            The Akond of Swat?

Some one, or nobody, knows I wot
Who or which or why or what
            Is the Akond of Swat!

EDWARD LEAR

I Sometimes Think is one man's philosophy—sprinkled with puns.
Both the philosophy and the punning leave us somewhat in the air.

I Sometimes Think

I sometimes think I'd rather crow
And be a rooster than to roost
And be a crow. But I dunno.

A rooster he can roost also,
Which don't seem fair when crows can't crow.
Which may help some. Still I dunno.

Crows should be glad of one thing, though;
Nobody thinks of eating crow,

While roosters they are good enough
For anyone unless they're tough.

There are lots of tough old roosters though,
And anyway a crow can't crow,
So mebby roosters stand more show.
It looks that way. But I dunno.

At first glance Not So Impossible *seems full of impossible things. If you read the lines the way they are printed, they become a set of absurdities. No one has ever seen "a peacock with a fiery tail," or "a blazing comet drop down hail." But if you put a dash in each line after the noun, then everything will be clear and simple. The poem then divides itself like this: "I saw a peacock—with a fiery tail I saw a blazing comet"—and so on to the end: "Bigger than the moon and higher I saw the sun—at twelve o'clock at night I saw the man that saw this wondrous sight."*

Of course, if you prefer, you can read it just the way it is printed. It is much more fantastic . . . and much more fun.

Not So Impossible

I saw a peacock with a fiery tail
I saw a blazing comet drop down hail
I saw a cloud wrapped with ivy round
I saw an oak creep on along the ground
I saw a pismire[1] swallow up a whale
I saw the sea brim full of ale

I saw a Venice glass five fathoms deep
I saw a well full of men's tears that weep
I saw red eyes all of a flaming fire
I saw a house bigger than the moon and higher
I saw the sun at twelve o'clock at night
I saw the man that saw this wondrous sight.

[1] pismire: an ant

The title of the next poem contains the key to the riddle which lies in the verses themselves. With this hint, you will find that it is not too difficult to solve the puzzle.

Enigma on the Letter H

'Twas whispered in heaven, 'twas muttered in hell,
And echo caught faintly the sound as it fell;
On the confines of earth 'twas permitted to rest,
And the depths of the ocean its presence confessed;
'Twill be found in the sphere when 'tis riven asunder,
Be seen in the lightning, and heard in the thunder.
'Twas allotted to man with his earliest breath,
It assists at his birth and attends him in death,
Presides o'er his happiness, honor, and health,
Is the prop of his house and the end of his wealth,
In the heaps of the miser is hoarded with care,
But is sure to be lost in his prodigal heir.
It begins every hope, every wish it must bound,
It prays with the hermit, with monarchs is crowned;
Without it the soldier, the sailor, may roam,
But woe to the wretch who expels it from home.
In the whisper of conscience 'tis sure to be found,
Nor e'en in the whirlwind of passion is drowned;
'Twill soften the heart, but, though deaf to the ear,
It will make it acutely and instantly hear;
But, in short, let it rest like a delicate flower;
Oh, breathe on it softly, it dies in an hour.

CATHERINE FANSHAWE

Truth, it is said, is stranger than fiction. And it is frequently funnier. Here are two poems that depend for their humor on mere statement of simple and unarguable fact.

The Guinea-Pig

There was a little guinea-pig,
Who, being little, was not big;
He always walked upon his feet,
And never fasted when he eat.

When from a place he ran away,
He never at that place did stay;
When he ran, as I am told,
He ne'er stood still for young or old.

He often squeaked and sometimes vi'lent,
And when he squeaked he ne'er was silent;
Though ne'er instructed by a cat,
He knew a mouse was not a rat.

One day, as I am certified,
He took a whim and fairly died;
And, as I'm told by men of sense,
He never has been living since.

How To Know the Wild Animals

If ever you should go by chance
    To jungles in the East,
And if there should to you advance
    A large and tawny beast—
If he roars at you as you're dyin',
You'll know it is the Asian Lion.

If, when in India loafing round,
    A noble wild beast meets you,
With dark stripes on a yellow ground,
    Just notice if he eats you.
This simple rule may help you learn
The Bengal Tiger to discern.

When strolling forth, a beast you view
    Whose hide with spots is peppered;
As soon as it has leapt on you,

    You'll know it is the Leopard.
'Twill do no good to roar with pain,
    He'll only lep and lep again.

If you are sauntering round your yard,
    And meet a creature there
Who hugs you very, very hard,
    You'll know it is the Bear.
If you have any doubt, I guess
He'll give you just one more caress . . .

The true Chameleon is small—
    A lizard sort of thing;
He hasn't any ears at all
    And not a single wing.
If there is nothing on the tree
'Tis the Chameleon you see.

CAROLYN WELLS

*The next four jingles seem to carry things
just about as far as fun-making can take them.*

The Answers

"When did the world begin and how?"
  I asked a lamb, a goat, a cow:

"What's it all about and why?"
  I asked a hog as he went by:

"Where will the whole thing end, and when?"
  I asked a duck, a goose, a hen:

And I copied all the answers too,
A quack, a honk, an oink, a moo.

ROBERT CLAIRMONT

230

The Cats of Kilkenny

There were once two cats of Kilkenny,
Each thought there was one cat too many;
So they fought and they fit,
And they scratched and they bit,
Till, excepting their nails
And the tips of their tails,
Instead of two cats, there weren't any.

The Animal Fair

I went to the animal fair,
The birds and beasts were there.
The big baboon, by the light of the moon,
Was combing his auburn hair.
The monkey, he got drunk,
And sat on the elephant's trunk.
The elephant sneezed and fell on his knees,
And what became of the monk, the monk?

Poor Old Lady

Poor old lady, she swallowed a fly.
I don't know why she swallowed a fly.
Poor old lady, I think she'll die.

Poor old lady, she swallowed a spider.
It squirmed and wriggled and turned inside her.
She swallowed the spider to catch the fly.
I don't know why she swallowed a fly.
Poor old lady, I think she'll die.

Poor old lady, she swallowed a bird.
How absurd! She swallowed a bird.
She swallowed the bird to catch the spider,
She swallowed the spider to catch the fly,
I don't know why she swallowed a fly.
Poor old lady, I think she'll die.

Poor old lady, she swallowed a cat.
Think of that! She swallowed a cat.
She swallowed the cat to catch the bird.
She swallowed the bird to catch the spider,
She swallowed the spider to catch the fly,
I don't know why she swallowed a fly.
Poor old lady, I think she'll die.

Poor old lady, she swallowed a dog.
She went the whole hog when she swallowed the dog.
She swallowed the dog to catch the cat,
She swallowed the cat to catch the bird,
She swallowed the bird to catch the spider.
She swallowed the spider to catch the fly,
I don't know why she swallowed a fly.
Poor old lady, I think she'll die.

Poor old lady, she swallowed a cow.
I don't know how she swallowed the cow.
She swallowed the cow to catch the dog,
She swallowed the dog to catch the cat,
She swallowed the cat to catch the bird,
She swallowed the bird to catch the spider,
She swallowed the spider to catch the fly,
I don't know why she swallowed a fly.
Poor old lady, I think she'll die.

Poor old lady, she swallowed a horse.
She died, of course.

231

Once you accept the first absurdity of jests like A Tragic Story, *or the poem after it,* The Twins, *you are lost. The logic of the situation becomes more and more convincing with every line, although the conclusions are too ridiculous!*

A Tragic Story

There lived a sage in days of yore,
And he a handsome pigtail wore;
But wondered much, and sorrowed more,
    Because it hung behind him.

He mused upon this curious case,
And swore he'd change the pigtail's place,
And have it hanging at his face,
    Not dangling there behind him.

Says he, "The mystery I've found—
I'll turn me round,"—he turned him round;
    But still it hung behind him.

Then round and round, and out and in,
All day the puzzled sage did spin;
In vain—it mattered not a pin—
    The pigtail hung behind him.

And right, and left, and round about,
And up, and down, and in, and out
He turned; but still the pigtail stout
    Hung steadily behind him.

And though his efforts never slack,
And though he twist, and twirl, and tack,
Alas! still faithful to his back,
    The pigtail hangs behind him.

WILLIAM MAKEPEACE THACKERAY

The Twins

In form and feature, face and limb,
    I grew so like my brother,
That folks got taking me for him,
    And each for one another.
It puzzled all our kith and kin,
    It reached an awful pitch;
For one of us was born a twin,
    Yet not a soul knew which.

One day (to make the matter worse),
    Before our names were fixed,
As we were being washed by nurse
    We got completely mixed;
And thus, you see, by Fate's decree,
    (Or rather nurse's whim),
My brother John got christened *me,*
    And I got christened *him.*

This fatal likeness even dogged
    My footsteps when at school,
And I was always getting flogged,
    For John turned out a fool.
I put this question hopelessly
    To everyone I knew—
What *would* you do, if you were me,
    To prove that you were *you?*

Our close resemblance turned the tide
    Of my domestic life;
For somehow my intended bride
    Became my brother's wife.
In short, year after year the same
    Absurd mistakes went on;
And when I died—the neighbors came
    And buried brother John!

HENRY S. LEIGH

James Thomas Fields put into verse a humorous New England yarn, a tribute to the traditional skill of the sea captains from the island of Nantucket. When "the lead was sounded"—that is, a weight dropped over the side to determine the depth of the water—the experienced skipper was said to be able to tell from the taste of the soil it brought up, exactly where the ship was. This is about a practical joke that missed and proved the skipper could not be completely fooled.

The Alarmed Skipper

Many a long, long year ago,
Nantucket skippers had a plan
Of finding out, though "lying low,"
How near New York their schooners ran.

They greased the lead before it fell,
And then, by sounding through the night,
Knowing the soil that stuck, so well,
They always guessed their reckoning right.

A skipper gray, whose eyes were dim,
Could tell, by *tasting,* just the spot,
And so below he'd "dowse the glim"—
After, of course, his "something hot."

Snug in his berth, at eight o'clock,
This ancient skipper might be found;
No matter how his craft would rock,
He slept—for skippers' naps are sound!

The watch on deck would now and then
Run down and wake him, with the lead;
He'd up, and taste, and tell the men
How many miles they went ahead.

One night, 'twas Jonathan Marden's watch,
A curious wag—the peddler's son—
And so he mused (the wanton wretch),
"To-night I'll have a grain of fun.

233

"We're all a set of stupid fools
To think the skipper knows by *tasting*
What ground he's on—Nantucket schools
Don't teach such stuff, with all their basting!"

And so he took the well-greased lead
And rubbed it o'er a box of earth
That stood on deck—a parsnip-bed—
And then he sought the skipper's berth.

"Where are we now, sir? Please to taste."
The skipper yawned, put out his tongue,
Then ope'd his eyes in wondrous haste,
And then upon the floor he sprung!

The skipper stormed and tore his hair,
Thrust on his boots, and roared to Marden,
"Nantucket's sunk; and here we are
Right over old Marm Hackett's garden!"

JAMES THOMAS FIELDS

GOOD THINGS

IN SMALL PACKAGES

There is an old Latin phrase, multum in parvo, *which tells us that there is "much in little." There is also an English proverb that good things come in small packages. This is particularly true of poetry. Perhaps the smallest of all poetic forms are those tight-packed, quick-thrusting verses we call epigrams and epitaphs.*

The poet is often inspired, but he is also human; he has his angry as well as his uplifted moods. In his less lofty moments he is likely to make fun of all sorts of things, and it is then that he uses that little weapon, the epigram.

There are two ways of recognizing an epigram: it is always short, and it is always sharp. It is frequently twisted, edged with sarcasm, even tipped with poison. But the chief point is — its point. Samuel Taylor Coleridge described it in two lines:

AN EPIGRAM
What is an epigram? A dwarfish whole:
Its body brevity, and wit its soul.

Here, then, are a few famous epigrams. They range from philosophy to foolery, from grave reason to outright ridicule.

A Reply

Sir, I admit your general rule
That every poet is a fool;
But you yourself may serve to show it,
That every fool is not a poet.

MATTHEW PRIOR

Today and Tomorrow

Happy the man, and happy he alone,
    He who can call today his own;
He who, secure within, can say,
    Tomorrow, do thy worst, for I have lived today!

JOHN DRYDEN

Swan Song

Swans sing before they die—'twere no bad thing
Should certain persons die before they sing.

SAMUEL TAYLOR COLERIDGE

Dust to Dust

After such years of dissension and strife,
Some wonder that Peter should weep for his wife;
But his tears on her grave are nothing surprising—
He's laying her dust, for fear of its rising.

THOMAS HOOD

Dogs

I am his Highness' dog at Kew.
Pray tell me sir—whose dog are you?

ALEXANDER POPE

Boston

Here's to good old Boston,
    The home of the bean and the cod,
Where the Lowells talk only to Cabots,
    And the Cabots talk only to God.

JOHN COLLINS BOSSIDY

Perhaps the shortest yet the most lasting kind of verse is found on tombstones. It is known as an epitaph. An epigram may be written on any subject; an epitaph is something about — and sometimes against—someone who has died. Like the epigram, epitaphs are always pointed and personal. Quaint and queer inscriptions are found in old graveyards the world over.

The first of the following epitaphs is said to be more than two hundred years old. The second was written more recently by the famous novelist and poet, Robert Louis Stevenson, for himself.

Here Lies...

Here lie I, Martin Eldinbrodde,
Ha' mercy on my soul, Lord God,
As I would do, were I Lord God,
An' Thou wert Martin Eldinbrodde.

Requiem

Under the wide and starry sky
Dig the grave and let me lie.
Glad did I live and gladly die,
    And I laid me down with a will.

This be the verse you grave for me:
Here he lies where he longed to be;
Home is the sailor, home from sea,
    And the hunter home from the hill.

ROBERT LOUIS STEVENSON

Although the subject of every epitaph is death, most of the epitaph-makers seem to enjoy their work. In fact, while the topic is deadly, the treatment is often lively. The grave was looked upon—without gravity.

The first epitaph which follows is perhaps one of the most famous ever written; its author was said to have been banished from the seventeenth-century court of Charles II for having written it. The second was one of Benjamin Franklin's little jokes. The third is the work of a living poet who conceals himself under another name. The rest are by unknown writers.

On Charles II

Here lies our Sovereign Lord and King,
  Whose word no man relies on,
Who never said a foolish thing,
  Nor ever did a wise one.

JOHN WILMOT, Earl of Rochester

On Skugg

Here Skugg lies snug
As a bug in a rug.

BENJAMIN FRANKLIN

A Dead Liar Speaks

Even my tombstone gives the truth away.
  It says to all who face this little hill
Hic jacet: Here I lie. Or should it say
  Here I lie—still?

MICHAEL LEWIS

The Optimist

The optimist fell ten stories.
  At each window bar
He shouted to his friends:
  "All right so far."

237

On Leslie Moore

Here lies what's left
Of Leslie Moore.
No Les
No more.

* * *

On a Man Named Merideth

Here lies one blown out of breath,
Who lived a merry life, and died a Merideth.

* * *

On a Thieving Locksmith

A thieving locksmith died of late
And soon arrived at heaven's gate.
He stood outside and would not knock
Because he meant to pick the lock.

* * *

On a Doctor Named Isaac Letsome

When people's ill, they come to I;
   I physics, bleeds, and sweats 'em.
Sometimes they live, sometimes they die;
   What's that to I? I. Letsome.

* * *

Praying and Preaching

My bishop's eyes I've never seen
Though the light in them may shine;
For when he prays, he closes his,
And when he preaches, mine.

On Richard Dent, Landlord

Here lies Richard Dent
In his cheapest tenement.

* * *

On a Dentist

Stranger, approach this spot with gravity:
John Brown is filling his last cavity.

On Prince Frederick

Here lies Fred,
Who was alive and is dead.
Had it been his father,
I had much rather;
Had it been his brother,
Still better than another;
Had it been his sister,
No one would have miss'd her;
Had it been the whole generation,
Still better for the nation;
But since 'tis only Fred,
Who was alive and is dead,
There's no more to be said.

* * *

Speak No Evil

Speak with contempt of none, from slave to king,
The meanest bee has, and will use, a sting.

On a Clergyman's Horse

The steed bit his master;
  How came this to pass?
He heard the good pastor
  Cry, "All flesh is grass."

* * *

On Martha Snell

Poor Martha Snell, she's gone away;
She would have stayed, but could not stay.
She had bad legs and a hacking cough;
It was her legs that carried her off.

On Stubborn Michael Shay

Here lies the body of Michael Shay,
Who died maintaining his right of way.
His case was clear and his will was strong—
But he's as dead as if he'd been wrong.

* * *

On John Bun

Here lies John Bun;
He was killed by a gun.
His name was not Bun, but Wood;
But Wood would not rhyme with gun, and Bun would.

It is hard to believe that the following epitaphs were actually put on any tombstones. Yet they have all been found in various country churchyards in England and America. The first was discovered in an Oxfordshire churchyard; the last was uncovered—I was about to say "unearthed"— in Massachusetts.

Four Country Epitaphs

Here lies me and my three daughters,
Brought here by using seidlitz water:
If we had stuck to Epsom salts
We wouldn't have been in these here vaults.

Here I lie at the chancel door,
Here I lie because I'm poor;
The further in, the more the pay;
But here I lie as warm as they.

* * *

Here lies father, mother, sister, and I;
  We all died within the space of one short year;
They all be buried at Wimble, except I,
  And I be buried here.

Here lies the body of Jonathan Pound,
Who was lost at sea and never found.

239

Closely related to the epigram, the lowly limerick has grown more and more popular. It is a sport—an oddly shaped sort of verse, never more and never less than five short lines—and it is always comic in sense and sound. All sorts of people have enjoyed repeating, and making, limericks. They have been composed by the most serious writers, and they have been put together by housewives for prizes and by schoolboys for fun. Edward Lear was one of the first to use them. Although Lear's limericks were fantastic in idea, they were fairly simple in form. His Complete Book of Nonsense contained more than two hundred laughable limericks. From that volume the following five have been selected.

Lear's Limericks

There was an Old Man in a tree,
Who was horribly bored by a Bee;
    When they said, "Does it buzz?"
    He replied, "Yes, it does!
It's a regular brute of a Bee!"

❂   ❂   ❂

There was an Old Person of Ware,
Who rode on the back of a bear.
    When they asked, "Does it trot?"
    He said, "Certainly *not!*
He's a Moppsikon Floppsikon bear!"

There was an Old Man of Dumbree
Who taught little owls to drink tea;
    For he said, "To eat mice
    Is not proper or nice,"
That amiable Man of Dumbree.

❂   ❂   ❂

There was an Old Man who, when little,
Fell casually into a kettle;
    But growing too stout
    He could never get out—
So he passed all his life in that kettle!

❂   ❂   ❂

There was an Old Man who said, "Hush!
I perceive a young bird in this bush!"
    When they said, "Is it small?"
    He replied, "Not at all!
It is ten times as big as the bush!"

EDWARD LEAR

Since Lear's time the limerick has become more complicated in idea and cleverer in rhyme. Oliver Wendell Holmes was credited with this limerick that is also a pun; it is about Henry Ward Beecher, an author who was also a minister.

Said a great Congregational preacher
To a hen, "You're a beautiful creature."
    The hen, just for that,
    Laid an egg in his hat,
And thus did the hen reward Beecher.

240

The following limericks are more recent. Most of them depend for their humor upon tricks of pronunciation and peculiarities in spelling. They are famous as examples of word-scrambling and tongue-twisting.

Four are by American poets; with the exception of the one by Lewis Carroll, the rest are by unknown but expert limerick fanciers.

Limericks Since Lear

There was a young person named Tate
Who dined with his girl at 8:8.
    But I'd hate to relate
    What that fellow named Tate
And his tête-à-tête ate at 8:8.

CAROLYN WELLS

A tutor who tooted the flute
Tried to tutor two tooters to toot.
    Said the two to the tutor,
    "Is it harder to toot or
To tutor two tooters to toot?"

CAROLYN WELLS

I wish that my room had a floor;
I don't care so much for a door.
    But this walking around
    Without touching the ground
Is getting to be quite a bore.

GELETT BURGESS

As a beauty I am not a star,
There are others more handsome, by far;
    But my face—I don't mind it,
    For I am behind it.
It's the people in front that I jar!

ANTHONY EUWER

There was a young girl of Asturias,
Whose temper was frantic and furious.
    She used to throw eggs
    At her grandmother's legs—
A habit unpleasant, but curious.

There was a faith-healer of Deal
Who said, "Although pain isn't real,
    If I sit on a pin
    And I puncture my skin,
I dislike what I *fancy* I feel."

She frowned and called him Mr.
Because in sport he kr.
    And so, in spite,
    That very night
This Mr. kr. sr.

A cheerful old bear at the Zoo
Could always find something to do.
    When it bored him to go
    On a walk to and fro,
He reversed it, and walked fro and to.

A flea and a fly in a flue
Were imprisoned, so what could they do?
    Said the fly, "Let us flee."
    Said the flea, "Let us fly."
So they flew through a flaw in the flue.

A foolish young fellow named Hyde
In a funeral procession was spied.
    When asked, "Who is dead?"
    He giggled and said,
"I don't know. I just came for the ride."

The bottle of perfume that Willie sent
Was highly displeasing to Millicent.
    Her thanks were so cold
    That they quarreled, I'm told,
Through that silly scent Willie sent Millicent.

241

There was a young lady of station,
"I love man!" was her sole exclamation.
 When men cried, "You flatter!"
 She replied, "What's the matter?
Isle of Man is the true explanation."

LEWIS CARROLL

A collegiate damsel named Breeze,
Weighed down by B. A's and Litt. D.'s,
 Collapsed from the strain.
 Alas, it was plain
She was killing herself—by degrees.

A girl who weighed many an oz.
Used language I dared not pronoz.
 For a fellow unkind
 Pulled her chair out behind
Just to see (so he said) if she'd boz.

There was a young lady from Woosester
Who ussessed to crow like a roosester.
 She ussessed to climb
 Seven trees at a time—
But her sissester ussessed to boosester.

There was a young man of Bengal
Who went to a fancy-dress ball,
 He went, just for fun,
 Dressed up as a bun,
And a dog ate him up in the hall.

There's a girl out in Ann Arbor, Mich.,
To meet whom I never would wich.,
 She'd eat up ice cream
 Till with colic she'd scream,
Then order another big dich.

An opera star named Maria
Always tried to sing higher and higher,
 Till she hit a high note
 Which got stuck in her throat—
Then she entered the Heavenly Choir.

A handsome young noble of Spain,
Met a lion one day in the rain.
 He ran in a fright
 With all of his might,
But the lion, he ran with his mane!

A housewife called out with a frown
When surprised by some callers from town,
 "In a minute or less
 I'll slip on a dress"—
But she slipped on the stairs and came down.

There were three little birds in a wood,
Who always sang hymns when they could.
 What the words were about
 They could never make out,
But they felt it was doing them good!

There was an old man from the Rhine
Who was asked at what hour he would dine.
 He replied, "At eleven,
 At three, six, and seven,
At eight and a quarter of nine."

An epicure dining at Crewe
Once found a large mouse in his stew.
 Said the waiter, "Don't shout
 And wave it about,
Or the rest will be wanting one, too!"

There was a thick-headed marine
Whose musical sense was not keen.
 He said, "It is odd,
 But I cann't tell 'God
Save the Weasel' from 'Pop Goes the Queen.'"

A daring young lady of Guam
Observed, "The Pacific's so calm
 I'll swim out for a lark."
 She met a large shark...
Let us now sing the Ninetieth Psalm.

The Daughter of the Farrier

The daughter of the farrier
Could find no one to marry her,
    Because she said
    She would not wed
A man who could not carry her.

The foolish girl was wrong enough,
And had to wait quite long enough;
    For as she sat
    She grew so fat
That nobody was strong enough!

There are numbers of very short poems that live long lives. No one remembers exactly where they first appeared; usually their authors are forgotten. But these rhymed jokes are reprinted again and again. Here are a few of the most durable.

Rhymed Chuckles

King David and King Solomon
    Lived merry, merry lives,
With many, many lady friends,
    And many, many wives.
But when old age crept up on them,
    With all its many qualms,
King Solomon wrote the Proverbs,
    And King David wrote the Psalms.

      ❋   ❋   ❋

I dreamed a dream next Tuesday week
    Beneath the apple trees:
I thought my eyes were big pork pies,
    And my nose was Stilton cheese.
The clock struck twenty minutes to six
    As a frog jumped on my knee;
I asked him to lend me sevenpence,
    But he borrowed a shilling from me.

This troubled world is sighing now;
    The flu is at the door;
And many folks are dying now
    Who never died before.

      ❋   ❋   ❋

A doctor fell in a deep well
    And broke his collarbone.
The Moral: Doctor, mind the sick
    And leave the well alone.

      ❋   ❋   ❋

Little Willie from his mirror
    Sucked the mercury all off,
Thinking, in his childish error,
    It would cure his whooping-cough.
At the funeral Willie's mother
    Smartly said to Mrs. Brown:
"'Twas a chilly day for William
    When the mercury went down."

WIDE, WONDERFUL WORLD

The world is full of wonder—and we are struck by the beauty in the most minute as well as the most immense things in nature. The great American poet, Walt Whitman, said that "a leaf of grass is no less than the journeywork of the stars—

> And the narrowest hinge in my hand puts to scorn all machinery,
> And the cow crunching with depressed head surpasses any statue...
> And the running blackberry would adorn the parlors of heaven."

It is hard to convey our feelings when we behold a blazing sunset, an apple tree in bloom, a star-filled sky, or a field starred with daisies. It is then that the poet speaks for us. He finds words that release our emotions as well as his own. A poem like "God's World" not only expresses but recreates our moments of rapture—and our hearts leap up again.

God's World

O world, I cannot hold thee close enough!
    Thy winds, thy wide gray skies!
    Thy mists that roll and rise!
Thy woods, this autumn day, that ache and sag
And all but cry with color! That gaunt crag
To crush! To lift the lean of that black bluff!
World, world, I cannot get thee close enough!

Long have I known a glory in it all,
    But never knew I this;
    Here such a passion is
As stretcheth me apart. Lord, I do fear
Thou'st made the world too beautiful this year.
My soul is all but out of me,—let fall
No burning leaf; prithee, let no bird call.

EDNA ST. VINCENT MILLAY

The Rich Earth

The trees of the Lord are full of sap,
The cedars of Lebanon which he hath planted,
Where the birds make their nests;
As for the stork, the fir trees are her house.
The high hills are a refuge for the wild goats,
And the rocks for the conies.
He appointed the moon for seasons;
The sun knoweth his going down.
Thou maketh darkness, and it is night,

Wherein all the beasts of the forest do creep forth.
The young lions roar after their prey,
And seek their meat from God;
The sun ariseth, they gather themselves together,
And lay them down in their dens.
Man goeth forth unto his work
And to his labor until the evening.
O Lord, how manifold are thy works!
In wisdom hast thou made them all;
The earth is full of thy riches.

The Bible: PSALMS, 104

Thanks

Thank you very much indeed,
River, for your waving reed;
Hollyhocks, for budding knobs;
Foxgloves, for your velvet fobs;
Pansies, for your silky cheeks;
Chaffinches, for singing beaks;
Spring, for wood anemones
Near the mossy toes of trees;
Summer, for the fruited pear,
Yellowing crab, and cherry fare;
Autumn, for the bearded load,
Hazelnuts along the road;
Winter, for the fairy-tale,
Spitting log and bouncing hail.

But, blest Father, high above,
All these joys are from Thy love;
And Your children everywhere,
Born in palace, lane, or square,
Cry with voices all agreed,
"Thank you very much indeed."

NORMAN GALE

A Garden

A garden is a lovesome thing,
    God wot!
    Rose plot,
Fringed pool,
    Ferned grot—
    The veriest school
    of peace; and yet the fool
Contends that God is not—
Not God! in gardens!
When the eve is cool?
Nay, but I have a sign;
'Tis very sure God walks in mine.

THOMAS EDWARD BROWN

The Biblical lines which conclude "O Lord, how manifold are thy works...The earth is full of thy riches," might have been the inspiration for Gerard Manley Hopkins's Pied Beauty. *A deeply religious poet who died in 1889, Hopkins loved not only the major manifestations of God's bounty, but the endless variety of design in nature: the pink dots patterned along the sides of trout, the intricate arrangement of a bird's wing, the streaked colors in the sky like those on a spotted (brinded) cow—all things "counter, original, spare, strange." In his effort to capture all the extravagances and oddities of nature, Hopkins's language was also original and strange. He saw the world "barbarous in beauty," and its luxuriant contrasts were a proof of God's grandeur.*

Pied Beauty

Glory be to God for dappled things—
   For skies of couple-color as a brinded cow;
      For rose-moles all in stipple upon trout that swim;
Fresh-firecoal chestnut-falls; finches' wings;
      Landscaped plotted and pieced—fold, fallow, and plow;
      And all trades, their gear and tackle and trim.

All things counter, original, spare, strange;
     Whatever is fickle, freckled (who knows how?)
       With swift, slow; sweet, sour; adazzle, dim;
He fathers-forth whose beauty is past change:
     Praise Him.

GERARD MANLEY HOPKINS

In 1855, when Walt Whitman was thirty-six, an unknown journalist who could not find a publisher, he printed by hand a little volume of twelve poems which he called Leaves of Grass. *The book was a bombshell. It roused its readers to violent extremes. It was attacked for its form and its frankness, and it was praised for its liberating spirit, for what Emerson called its "free and brave thought." Each new edition of* Leaves of Grass *contained additional poems; a complete collection printed in Whitman's seventy-third year disclosed that the original twelve poems had grown to nearly four hundred. In their subject matter, their language, and their construction the poems were unlike anything that had hitherto been written. What started as an experiment in American poetry became a great fulfillment with a world-wide influence.*

   The influence on form is most obvious. What he wanted to say could only be expressed in the flexible and loosely rhythmical lines now known as free verse. More important still was his recognition of "the glory of the commonplace," his insistence that nothing is insignificant.

Miracles

Why, who makes much of a miracle?
As to me I know of nothing else but miracles,
Whether I walk the streets of Manhattan,
Or dart my sight over the roofs of houses toward the sky,
Or wade with naked feet along the beach just in the edge of the water,
Or stand under trees in the woods,
Or sit at table at dinner with the rest,
Or look at strangers opposite me riding in the car,
Or watch honey-bees busy around the hive of a summer forenoon,
Or animals feeding in the fields,
Or birds, or the wonderfulness of insects in the air,
Or the wonderfulness of the sundown, or of stars shining so quiet and bright,
Or the exquisite delicate thin curve of the new moon in spring;
These with the rest, one and all, are to me miracles,
The whole referring, yet each distinct and in its place.

To me every hour of the light and dark is a miracle,
Every cubic inch of space is a miracle,
Every square yard of the surface of the earth is spread with the same,
Every foot of the interior swarms with the same.

To me the sea is a continual miracle,
The fishes that swim—the rocks—the motion of the waves—the ships
        with men in them,
What stranger miracles are there?

WALT WHITMAN

247

Francis Thompson saw through the tiny snowflake to the vast secret of its creation, describing both the snowflake and the spiritual experience with exquisite exactitude. A mystic like William Blake, he sensed God's shaping hand in everything. Thompson's question, "Who hammered you, wrought you, from argentine vapor" (white frozen mist) recalls Blake's questions in The Tiger, *such as "What immortal hand or eye could frame thy fearful symmetry?"*

The Snow

It sifts from leaden sieves,
It powders all the wood,
It fills with alabaster wool
The wrinkles of the road.

It makes an even face
Of mountain and of plain,—
Unbroken forehead from the east
Unto the east again.

It reaches to the fence,
It wraps it, rail by rail,
Till it is lost in fleeces;
It flings a crystal veil

On stump and stack and stem,—
The summer's empty room,
Acres of seams where harvests were,
Recordless, but for them.

It ruffles wrists of posts,
As ankles of a queen,—
Then stills its artisans like ghosts,
Denying they have been.

EMILY DICKINSON

To a Snowflake

What heart could have thought you?
Past our devisal
(O filigree petal!)
Fashioned so purely,
Fragilely, surely,
From what Paradisal
Imagineless metal,
Too costly for cost?
Who hammered you, wrought you,
From argentine vapor?—
"God was my shaper.

Passing surmisal,
He hammered, He wrought me,
From curled silver vapor,
To lust of his mind:—
Thou couldst not have thought me!
So purely, so palely,
Tinily, surely,
Mightily, frailly,
Insculped and embossed,
With His hammer of wind,
And His graver of frost."

FRANCIS THOMPSON

248

The passionate, short-lived Percy Bysshe Shelley, dead at thirty, was a nineteenth-century romantic torn by conflicting impulses. As a rebel, he devoted much of his life to a struggle for political and personal freedom. An equally ardent love of ideal beauty made him yearn for another life and a golden age when men would cease to strive against each other. Away, Away! invites us to escape to a world where "Nature's art harmonises heart to heart."

Away, Away!

From TO JANE: THE INVITATION

Away, away, from men and towns,
To the wild wood and the downs—
To the silent wilderness
Where the soul need not repress
Its music lest it should not find
An echo in another's mind,
While the touch of Nature's art
Harmonises heart to heart.
I leave this notice on my door
For each accustomed visitor: —
"I am gone into the fields
To take what this sweet hour yields.
Reflection, you may come to-morrow,
Sit by the fireside with Sorrow—
You with the unpaid bill, Despair—
You, tiresome verse-reciter, Care—
I will pay you in the grave—
Death will listen to your stave.
Expectation too, be off!
To-day is for itself enough;
Hope, in pity mock not Woe
With smiles, nor follow where I go;
Long having lived on thy sweet food,
At length I find one moment's good
After long pain—with all your love,
This you never told me of."

Radiant Sister of the Day,
Awake! arise! and come away!
To the wild woods and the plains,
And the pools where winter rains
Image all their roof of leaves,
Where the pine its garland weaves
Of sapless green and ivy dun
Round stems that never kiss the sun;
Where the lawns and pastures be,
And the sandhills of the sea;—
Where the melting hoar-frost wets
The daisy-star that never sets,
And wind-flowers, and violets,
Which yet join not scent to hue,
Crown the pale year weak and new;
When the night is left behind
In the deep east, dun and blind,
And the blue moon is over us,
And the multitudinous
Billows murmur at our feet,
Where the earth and ocean meet,
And all things seem only one
In the universal sun.

From the first line of this poem, the scene is unmistakably American and, equally unmistakably, western America. Its author, Charles Erskine Scott Wood, who died in California in 1944, lived his life in the west and loved every picturesque detail of its unique landscape, from the towering and many-turreted (castellated) cliffs to the characteristic cottonwood trees and irrigation ditches, from the black ravens to the red-bird, whose color is intensified by the sunrise and who "cracks" his whip-like notes over the waking world.

Sunrise

The lean coyote, prowler of the night,
Slips to his rocky fastnesses.
Jack-rabbits noiselessly shuttle among the sage-brush,
And, from the castellated cliffs,
Rock-ravens launch their proud black sails upon the day.
The wild horses troop back to their pastures.

The poplar-trees watch beside the irrigation-ditches.
Orioles, whose nests sway in the cottonwood trees by the ditchside, begin to
    twitter.
All shy things, breathless, watch
The thin white skirts of dawn,
The dancer of the sky,
Who trips daintily down the mountain-side
Emptying her crystal chalice....
And a red-bird, dipped in sunrise, cracks from a poplar's top
His exultant whip above a silver world.

CHARLES ERSKINE SCOTT WOOD

I Meant To Do My Work Today

I meant to do my work today—
But a brown bird sang in the apple tree,
And a butterfly flitted across the field,
And all the leaves were calling me.

And the wind went sighing over the land
Tossing the grasses to and fro,
And a rainbow held out its shining hand—
So what could I do but laugh and go?

RICHARD LEGALLIENNE

Any Sunset

There's something about the going down of the sun,
Whether it makes a bonfire of a cloud,
Or, too obscure and lonely to be proud,
Sinks on the nearest rooftop, and is gone.
There's something, not of color nor of size,
In the mere going, in the calm descent,
Half out of heaven and half imminent;
Final, as though it never again would rise.

There's something in its very noiselessness,
Unlike mad waters or the winds that shout
Their end in one last agony of excess;
Something that does not count its days nor deeds,
But trusts itself to darkness and goes out
And finds whatever after-life it needs.

LOUIS UNTERMEYER

You have read other poems by Emily Dickinson and have been charmed by her unusual yet accurate use of words. Here her images are more playful than ever; they become sheer fancy. For example, the colors of sunset suggest to her a host of children clambering over a fence, and the dusk is a pastor (dominie) who shepherds them home. You may not see such things the way Emily Dickinson did, but it is a lovely way of seeing.

A Day

I'll tell you how the sun rose—
A ribbon at a time.
The steeples swam in amethyst,
The news like squirrels ran.

The hills untied their bonnets,
The bobolinks begun.
Then I said softly to myself,
"That must have been the sun!"

But how he set, I know not.
There seemed a purple stile
Which little yellow boys and girls
Were climbing all the while

Till when they reached the other side,
A dominie in gray
Put gently up the evening bars,
And led the flock away.

EMILY DICKINSON

With perfectly ordinary words, but adding detail to detail, Genevieve Taggard evokes the sensations of a happy midsummer day in the country. As you read, you can almost smell the sun on the hills, feel the barbed tangle of weeds, and taste the juice of the strawberries.

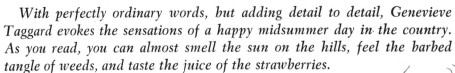

Millions of Strawberries

Marcia and I went over the curve,
Eating our way down
Jewels of strawberries we didn't deserve,
Eating our way down,
Till our hands were sticky, and our lips painted.
And over us the hot day fainted,
And we saw snakes,
And got scratched,
And a lust overcame us for the red unmatched
Small buds of berries,
Till we lay down—
Eating our way down—
And rolled in the berries like two little dogs,
Rolled
In the late gold.
And gnats hummed,
And it was cold,
And home we went, home without a berry,
Painted red and brown,
Eating our way down.

GENEVIEVE TAGGARD

252

In Desert Places

God has a way of making flowers grow;
    He is both daring and direct about it;
If you know half the flowers that I know,
    You do not doubt it.

He chooses some gray rock, austere and high,
    For garden-plot, traffics with sun and weather;
Then lifts an Indian paint brush to the sky,
    Half flame, half feather.

In desert places it is quite the same;
    He delves at petal-plans, divinely, surely,
Until a bud too shy to have a name
    Blossoms demurely.

He dares to sow the waste, to plow the rock.
    Though Eden knew His beauty and His power,
He could not plant in it a yucca stalk,
    A cactus flower.

SISTER MARY MADELEVA

Every Time I Climb a Tree

Every time I climb a tree
Every time I climb a tree
Every time I climb a tree
I scrape a leg
Or skin a knee
And every time I climb a tree
I find some ants
Or dodge a bee
And get the ants
All over me.

And every time I climb a tree
Where have you been?
They say to me
But don't they know that I am free
Every time I climb a tree?

I like it best
To spot a nest
That has an egg
Or maybe three.

And then I skin
The other leg
But every time I climb a tree
I see a lot of things to see
Swallows rooftops and TV
And all the fields and farms there be
Every time I climb a tree
Though climbing may be good for ants
It isn't awfully good for pants
But still it's pretty good for me
Every time I climb a tree.

DAVID McCORD

The Young Dandelion

I am a bold fellow
    As ever was seen,
With my shield of yellow,
    And my blade of green.

You may uproot me
    From field and from lane;
Trample me, cut me,
    I spring up again.

I never flinch, sir,
    Wherever I dwell;
Give me an inch, sir,
    I'll soon take an ell.

Drive me from garden
    In anger and pride,
I'll thrive and harden
    By the roadside.

Not a bit fearful,
    Showing my face,
Always so cheerful,
    In every place.

DINAH MULOCK CRAIK

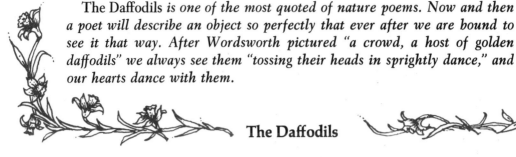

The Daffodils is one of the most quoted of nature poems. Now and then a poet will describe an object so perfectly that ever after we are bound to see it that way. After Wordsworth pictured "a crowd, a host of golden daffodils" we always see them "tossing their heads in sprightly dance," and our hearts dance with them.

The Daffodils

I wandered lonely as a cloud
That floats on high o'er vales and hills,
When all at once I saw a crowd,
A host of golden daffodils,
Beside the lake, beneath the trees
Fluttering and dancing in the breeze.

Continuous as the stars that shine
And twinkle on the milky way,
They stretched in never-ending line
Along the margin of a bay:
Ten thousand saw I at a glance
Tossing their heads in sprightly dance.

The waves beside them danced, but they
Out-did the sparkling waves in glee:
A poet could not but be gay
In such a jocund company!
I gazed—and gazed—but little thought
What wealth the show to me had brought:

For oft, when on my couch I lie
In vacant or in pensive mood,
They flash upon that inward eye
Which is the bliss of solitude;
And then my heart with pleasure fills,
And dances with the daffodils.

WILLIAM WORDSWORTH

The Tree

I love thee when thy swelling buds appear
    And one by one their tender leaves unfold,
As if they knew that warmer suns were near,
    Nor longer sought to hide from winter's cold.
And when with darker growth thy leaves are seen,
    To veil from view the early robin's nest,
I love to lie beneath thy waving screen
    With limbs by summer's heat and toil oppressed.
And when the autumn winds have stripped thee bare,
    And round thee lies the smooth, untrodden snow,
When naught is thine that made thee once so fair,
    I love to watch thy shadowy form below,
And through thy leafless arms to look above
On stars that brighter beam when most we need their love.

JONES VERY

254

Tiger-Lilies

I like not lady-slippers,
Nor yet the sweet-pea blossoms,
Nor yet the flaky roses,
        Red, or white as snow;
I like the chaliced lilies,
The heavy Eastern lilies,
The gorgeous tiger-lilies,
        That in our garden grow!

For they are tall and slender;
Their mouths are dashed with carmine,
And, when the wind sweeps by them,
        On their emerald stalks
They bend so proud and graceful—
They are Circassian women,
The favorites of the Sultan,
        Adown our garden walks!

And when the rain is falling,
I sit beside the window
And watch them glow and glisten—
        How they burn and glow!
O for the burning lilies,
The tender Eastern lilies,
The gorgeous tiger-lilies,
        That in our garden grow!

THOMAS BAILEY ALDRICH

The Cloud-Mobile

Above my face is a map.
Continents form and fade.
Blue countries, made
on a white sea, are erased,
and white countries traced
on a blue sea.

It is a map that moves,
faster than real,
but so slow.
Only my watching proves
that island has being,
or that bay.

It is a model of time.
Mountains are wearing away,
coasts cracking,
the ocean spills over,
then new hills
heap into view
with river-cuts of blue
between them.

It is a map of change.
This is the way things are
with a stone or a star.
This is the way things go,
hard or soft,
swift or slow.

MAY SWENSON

Like Walt Whitman who preceded him by half a century, Carl Sandburg moves naturally in the easy flow of free verse. The six short lines of Fog seem to be made out of the padded quiet of the atmosphere itself.

Fog

The fog comes
on little cat feet.
It sits looking
over harbor and city
on silent haunches
and then moves on.

CARL SANDBURG

255

Once upon a time coal was a living thing. It took millions of years to turn fallen trees into the mineral that goes into stoves and furnaces. Science has shown us that heat from the sun is stored in the tree, retained in the coal, and finally liberated when the fuel is burned. . . . Coal Fire is another instance of how poetry can be made out of seemingly unpoetic material.

Coal Fire

And once, in some swamp-forest, these
Were trees.
Before the first fox thought to run,
These dead black chips were one
Green net to hold the sun.
Each leaf in turn was taught the right
Way to drink light;
The twigs were made to learn
How to catch flame and yet not burn;
Branch and then bough began to eat
Their diet of heat.
And so for years, six million years, or higher,
They held that fire.

And here, out of the splinters that remain,
The fire is loose again.
See how its hundred hands reach here and there,
Finger the air;
Then, growing bolder, twisting free,
It fastens on the remnants of the tree
And, one by one,
Consumes them; mounts beyond them; leaps; is done;
And goes back to the sun.

LOUIS UNTERMEYER

256

Comparatively few people know Emerson's The Rhodora *in its entirety. But practically everyone has heard one line of the poem: the often quoted "Beauty is its own excuse for being."*

The Rhodora

In May, when sea-winds pierced our solitudes,
I found the fresh Rhodora in the woods,
Spreading its leafless blooms in a damp nook,
To please the desert and the sluggish brook.
The purple petals, fallen in the pool,
Made the black water with their beauty gay;
Here might the red-bird come his plumes to cool,
And court the flowers that cheapen his array.

Rhodora! if the sages ask thee why
This charm is wasted on the earth and sky,
Tell them, dear, that if eyes were made for seeing,
Then Beauty is its own excuse for being:
Why thou wert there, O rival of the rose!
I never thought to ask, I never knew:
But in my simple ignorance, suppose
The self-same Power that brought me there brought you.

RALPH WALDO EMERSON

Looking at a few shrivelled grains, we often forget the magic sealed into the tiniest seed. Muriel Stuart makes us aware of the marvel.

The Seed Shop

Here in a quiet and dusty room they lie,
Faded as crumbled stone or shifting sand,
Forlorn as ashes, shrivelled, scentless, dry—
Meadows and gardens running through my hand.

Dead that shall quicken at the call of Spring,
Sleepers to stir beneath June's magic kiss,
Though birds pass over, unremembering,
And no bee seeks here roses that were his.

In this brown husk, a dale of hawthorn dreams;
A cedar in this narrow cell is thrust
That will drink deeply of a century's streams.
These lilies shall make summer on my dust.

Here in their safe and simple house of death,
Sealed in their shells, a million roses leap;
Here I can blow a garden with my breath,
And in my hand a forest lies asleep.

MURIEL STUART

Vachel Lindsay, the midwestern wanderer whose poetry preached "the Gospel of Beauty," wrote more than thirty moon-poems. In the verses the moon was different things to different viewers. A clown saw it as a paper-covered jumping hoop; an old horse saw it as a shining peck of corn; a hyena as a skull; a sexton as a tombstone in the sky...and a little girl saw it as a cooky.

The Moon's the North Wind's Cooky

The Moon's the North Wind's cooky.
He bites it, day by day,
Until there's but a rim of scraps
That crumble all away.

The South Wind is a baker.
He kneads clouds in his den,
And bakes a crisp new moon *that...greedy*
North...Wind...eats...again!

VACHEL LINDSAY

The Wind and the Moon

Said the Wind to the Moon, "I will blow you out;
    You stare
    In the air
  Like a ghost in a chair,
Always looking what I am about;
I hate to be watched; I will blow you out."

The Wind blew hard, and out went the Moon.
    So, deep
    On a heap
  Of clouds to sleep,
Down lay the Wind, and slumbered soon—
Muttering low, "I've done for that Moon."

He turned in his bed; she was there again!
    On high,
    In the sky,
  With her one ghost eye,
The Moon shone white and alive and plain,
Said the Wind, "I will blow you out again."

258

The Wind blew hard, and the Moon grew dim,
    "With my sledge
    And my wedge
  I have knocked off her edge!
If only I blow right fierce and grim,
The creature will soon be dimmer than dim."

He blew and he blew, and she thinned to a thread.
    "One puff
    More's enough
  To blow her to snuff!
One good puff more where the last was bred,
And glimmer, glimmer, glum will go that thread!"

He blew a great blast and the thread was gone.
    In the air
    Nowhere
  Was a moonbeam bare;
Far-off and harmless the shy stars shone;
Sure and certain the Moon was gone!

The Wind he took to his revels once more;
    On down,
    In town,
  Like a merry-mad clown,
He leaped and hallooed with whistle and roar—
"What's that?" The glimmering thread once more!

He flew in a rage; he danced and blew;
    But in vain
    Was the pain
  Of his bursting brain;
For still the broader the Moon-scrap grew
The broader he swelled his big cheeks and blew.

Slowly she grew, till she filled the night,
    And shone
    On her throne
  In the sky alone,
A matchless, wonderful, silvery light,
Radiant and lovely, the Queen of the night.

Said the Wind, "What a marvel of power am I!"
    With my breath,
    Good faith,
  I blew her to death—
First blew her away right out of the sky—
Then blew her right in; what strength have I!"

But the Moon she knew nothing about the affair;
    For high
    In the sky,
  With her one white eye,
Motionless, miles above the air,
She had never heard the great Wind blare.

GEORGE MACDONALD

A Windy Day

This wind brings all dead things to life,
Branches that lash the air like whips
And dead leaves rolling in a hurry
Or peering in a rabbit's bury
Or trying to push down a tree;
Gates that fly open to the wind
And close again behind,
And fields that are a flowing sea
And make the cattle look like ships;

Straws glistening and stiff
Lying on air as on a shelf
And pond that leaps to leave itself;
And feathers too that rise and float,
Each feather changed into a bird,
And line-hung sheets that crack and strain;
Even the sun-greened coat,
That through so many winds has served,
The scarecrow struggles to put on again.

ANDREW YOUNG

Only the Wind Says Spring

The grass still is pale, and spring is yet only a wind stirring
    Over the open field.
There is no green even under the forest leaves.
    No buds are blurring
    The pencil sketch of trees. No meadows yield
The song of larks, nor the buzz of bees conferring.
Only the wind says spring. Everything else shouts winter:
    The whitened beards of grass,
The shriveled legs of corn with their trousers flapping,
    The year-old cuts in the root of the sassafras;
A spruce-cone empty of seeds, the scales unwrapping
    Open to dryness, last year's withered peach,
A stiff tomato-vine begun to splinter,
    The crones of milkweed talking each to each.

The earth stands mute, without a voice to sing.
But the wind is saying spring.

HELEN JANET MILLER

*It does not happen often that a poet writes about nature in a fashion
that is fond and at the same time funny. In* Wind *Leonard Feeney demonstrates that it can be done.*

Wind

Wind is to show
    How a thing can blow,
And especially through trees.
    When it is fast
    It is called a blast,
And it's otherwise known as a breeze.

It begins somewhere in the sky,
    Like a sigh,
Then it turns to a roar,
And returns to a sigh once more.

    Wind is the air
    In your hair,
    When you stand
    On the sand
    By the shore.

Wind will shake the lattices late at night;
It will make the clouds go by.
Anything easy that's hard to do,
It is pretty sure to try:

    Blow down a pine,
    Clothes from a line,
Tumble a chimney top.
    Wind is the general sound
    You hear around,
That suddenly likes to stop.

LEONARD FEENEY

260

The next two poems are variations on a single theme: the unlimited mystery of the sea—the spell of an unfathomed expanse which has lured men from the beginning of time.

The Secret of the Sea

Ah! what pleasant visions haunt me
  As I gaze upon the sea!
All the old romantic legends,
  All my dreams, come back to me.

Sails of silk and ropes of sandal,
  Such as gleam in ancient lore;
And the singing of the sailors,
  And the answer from the shore.

Most of all, the Spanish ballad
  Haunts me oft, and tarries long,
Of the noble Count Arnaldos
  And the sailor's mystic song.

Like the long waves on a sea-beach,
  Where the sand and silver shines,
With a soft, monotonous cadence,
  Flow its unrhymed lyric lines;—

Telling how the Count Arnaldos,
  With his hawk upon his hand,
Saw a fair and stately galley,
  Steering onward to the land;—

How he heard the ancient helmsman
  Chant a song so wild and clear,
That the sailing sea-bird slowly
  Poised upon the mast to hear,

Till his soul was full of longing,
  And he cried, with impulse strong,—
Helmsman! for the love of heaven,
  Teach me, too, that wondrous song!"

"Wouldst thou"—so the helmsman answered,
  "Learn the secret of the sea?
Only those who brave its dangers
  Comprehend its mystery!"

In each sail that skims the horizon,
  In each landward-blowing breeze,
I behold that stately galley,
  Hear those mournful melodies;

Till my soul is full of longing
  For the secret of the sea,
And the heart of the great ocean
  Sends a thrilling pulse through me.

HENRY WADSWORTH LONGFELLOW

The Sea Gypsy

I am fevered with the sunset,
  I am fretful with the bay,
For the wander-thirst is on me
  And my soul is in Cathay.

There's a schooner in the offing,
  With her topsails shot with fire,
And my heart has gone aboard her
  For the Islands of Desire.

I must forth again to-morrow!
  With the sunset I must be
Hull down on the trail of rapture
  In the wonder of the sea.

RICHARD HOVEY

In recent years there have been many scientific explorations of the underwater world. Yet more than a century and a half ago, a Connecticut poet, James Gates Percival, was aware that "life, in rare and beautiful forms" existed in a region observed by few men.

The Coral Grove

Deep in the wave is a coral grove,
Where the purple mullet and gold-fish rove;
Where the sea-flower spreads its leaves of blue
That never are wet with falling dew,
But in bright and changeful beauty shine
Far down in the green and glassy brine.
The floor is of sand, like the mountain drift,
And the pearl-shells spangle the flinty snow;
From coral rocks the sea-plants lift
Their boughs, where the tides and billows flow;
The water is calm and still below,
For the winds and waves are absent there,
And the sands are bright as the stars that glow
In the motionless fields of upper air.

There, with its waving blade of green,
The sea-flag streams through the silent water,
And the crimson leaf of the dulse is seen
To blush, like a banner bathed in slaughter.
There, with a light and easy motion,
The fan-coral sweeps through the clear, deep sea;
And the yellow and scarlet tufts of ocean
Are bending like corn on the upland lea.
And life, in rare and beautiful forms,
Is sporting amid those bowers of stone,
And is safe, when the wrathful spirit of storms
Has made the top of the wave his own.
And when the ship from his fury flies,
Where the myriad voices of ocean roar,
When the wind-god frowns in the murky skies,
And demons are waiting the wreck on shore;
Then, far below, in the peaceful sea,
The purple mullet and gold-fish rove
Where the waters murmur tranquilly,
Through the bending twigs of the coral grove.

JAMES GATES PERCIVAL

Sea Song

To sea! to sea! the calm is o'er,
  The wanton water leaps in sport,
And rattles down the pebbly shore,
  The dolphin wheels, the sea cows snort,
And unseen mermaid's pearly song
Comes bubbling up, the weeds among.
Fling broad the sail, dip deep the oar:
To sea! to sea! the calm is o'er.

To sea! to sea! our white winged bark
  Shall billowing cleave its watery way,
And with its shadow, fleet and dark,
  Break the caved Tritons' azure day,
Like mountain eagle soaring light
O'er antelopes on Alpine height.
The anchor heaves! The ship swings free!
Our sails swell full! To sea! to sea!

THOMAS LOVELL BEDDOES

Silver

Slowly, silently, now the moon
Walks the night in her silver shoon;
This way, and that, she peers, and sees
Silver fruit upon silver trees;
One by one the casements catch
Her beams beneath the silvery thatch;
Couched in his kennel, like a log,
With paws of silver sleeps the dog;
From their shadowy cote the white breasts p
Of doves in a silver-feathered sleep;
A harvest mouse goes scampering by,
With silver claws, and silver eye;
And moveless fish in the water gleam,
By silver reeds in a silver stream.

WALTER DE LA M.

To Blake, the coming of night brought no fear of darkness. He was so sure of heavenly care that the end of a day meant peace—the arrival of protective angels who (according to the last four beautiful lines of Night*) kept watch and "poured" soothing sleep over the heads of any who might be sorrowful.*

Night

The sun descending in the west
The evening star does shine,
The birds are silent in their nest
And I must seek for mine,
The moon, like a flower
In heaven's high bower,
With silent delight
Sits and smiles on the night.

Farewell green fields and happy groves
Where flocks have took delight;
Where lambs have nibbled, silent moves
The feet of angels bright;

Unseen they pour blessing
And joy without ceasing
On each bud and blossom
And each sleeping bosom.

They look in every thoughtless nest
Where birds are covered warm,
They visit caves of every beast
To keep them all from harm;
If they see any weeping
That should have been sleeping,
They pour sleep on their head
And sit down by their bed.

WILLIAM BLAKE

Travel

I should like to rise and go
Where the golden apples grow;—
Where below another sky
Parrot islands anchored lie,
And, watched by cockatoos and goats,
Lonely Crusoes building boats;—
Where in sunshine reaching out
Eastern cities, miles about,
Are with mosque and minaret
Among sandy gardens set,
And rich goods from near and far
Hang for sale in the bazaar;—
Where the Great Wall round China goes,
And on one side the desert blows,
And with bell and voice and drum,
Cities on the other hum;—
Where are forest, hot as fire,
Wide as England, tall as a spire,

Full of apes and cocoa-nuts
And the Negro hunters' huts ...
Where among the desert sands
Some deserted city stands,
All its children, sweep and prince,
Grown to manhood ages since,

Not a foot in street or house,
Not a stir of child or mouse,
And when kindly falls the night,
In all the town no spark of light.
There I'll come when I'm a man
With a camel caravan;
Light a fire in the gloom
Of some dusty dining-room;
See the pictures on the walls,
Heroes, fights, and festivals;
And in a corner find the toys
Of the old Egyptian boys.

ROBERT LOUIS STEVENSON

Out in the Fields with God

The little cares that fretted me,
    I lost them yesterday,
Among the fields above the sea,
    Among the winds at play,
Among the lowing of the herds,
    The rustling of the trees,
Among the singing of the birds,
    The humming of the bees.

The foolish fears of what might pass
    I cast them all away
Among the clover-scented grass
    Among the new-mown hay,
Among the hushing of the corn
    Where drowsy poppies nod,
Where ill thoughts die and good are born—
    Out in the fields with God.

Long before anyone thought seriously of space-travel, William Words-worth imagined a trip in a flying ship that took him beyond the strato-sphere. It was in 1798 that he wrote the long narrative poem Peter Bell, *from which* Among the Stars *is taken. Even at that time, Wordsworth suggested that Mars was inhabited by a "red-haired race," that Jupiter was full of forests, and that there were towns on Saturn. But nothing out among the stars could compare with the green globe of Earth, and the space-traveler returned home with a rush of delight.*

Among the Stars

There's something in a flying horse,
There's something in a huge balloon;
But through the clouds I'll never float
Until I have a little boat,
Shaped like the crescent-moon.

And now I *have* a little boat,
In shape a very crescent-moon:
Fast through the clouds my boat can sail;
And if perchance your faith should fail,
Look up—and you shall see me soon!

The woods, my friends, are round you roaring,
Rocking and roaring like a sea;
The noise of danger's in your ears,
And ye have all a thousand fears
Both for my little boat and me!

Meanwhile untroubled I admire
The pointed horns of my canoe;
And, did not pity touch my breast,
To see how ye are all distrest,
Till my ribs ached, I'd laugh at you!

Away we go, my boat and I—
Frail man ne'er sat in such another;
Whether among the winds we strive,
Or deep into the clouds we dive,
Each is contented with the other.

Away we go—and what care we
For treason, tumults, and for wars?
We are as calm in our delight
As is the crescent-moon so bright
Among the scattered stars.

Then back to Earth, the dear green Earth: —
Whole ages if I here should roam,
The world for my remarks and me
Would not a whit the better be;
I've left my heart at home.

Up goes my boat among the stars
Through many a breathless field of light,
Through many a long blue field of ether,
Leaving ten thousand stars beneath her:
Up goes my little boat so bright!

The Crab, the Scorpion, and the Bull—
We pray among them all; have shot
High o'er the red-haired race of Mars,
Covered from top to toe with scars;
Such company I like it not!

The towns in Saturn are decayed,
And melancholy spectres throng them;—
The Pleiads, that appear to kiss
Each other in the vast abyss,
With joy I sail among them.

Swift Mercury resounds with mirth,
Great Jove is full of stately bowers;
But these, and all that they contain,
What are they to that tiny grain,
That little Earth of ours?

See! There she is, the matchless Earth!
There spreads the famed Pacific Ocean!
Old Andes thrusts yon craggy spear
Through the grey clouds; the Alps are here,
Like waters in commotion!

Yon tawny slip is Libya's sands;
That silver thread the river Dnieper;
And look, where clothed in brightest green
Is a sweet Isle, of isles the Queen;
Ye fairies, from all evil keep her!

And see the town where I was born!
Around those happy fields we span
In boyish gambols;—I was lost
Where I have been, but on this coast
I feel I am a man.

Never did fifty things at once
Appear so lovely, never, never;—
How tunefully the forests ring!
To hear the earth's soft murmuring,
Thus could I hang forever!

WILLIAM WORDSWORTH

The following poem might have been written by an old and experienced poet. The central idea—a love for all the beauties of this world—is simple and yet universal. The choice of words is sharp and exact; the reader's attention is arrested by such phrases as "the square aggressiveness of new-cut hedges"...."the way grass cuddles"...."porch steps leaned upon by time" ...."dandelions nudge the stones."

But Altar Smoke *is not the work of a mature professional. It is a poem which, in 1946, won first prize in an annual Inter-High School Contest, and its author, Rosalie Grayer, was a student at Abraham Lincoln High School in Brooklyn, New York. She was then seventeen years old.*

Altar Smoke

Somewhere inside of me
There must have always been
A tenderness
For the little, lived-with things
A man crowds upon his worn fistful of earth.
Somewhere inside of me
There must have always been
A love
Made to fill the square aggressiveness of new-cut hedges,
And feed the pursed green mouths of baby leaves;
A love made to understand
The way grass cuddles up to porch steps leaned upon by time,
And why dandelions nudge the stones along the walk;
A love for garden hose curled sleeping in the noon hush,
Coolness trickling lazily from its open mouth,
For shingles starched and saucy in white paint,
And an old rake rusty with dreams of tangled grass and butterflies.
A love
For candle flames, like pointed blossoms on their ghostly stems,
And frost-forests breathing wonder on the parlor windows.
Somewhere inside of me
There must have always been
An altar of hewn stones
Upon which my love casts these—
Burnt offerings—
To make a sweet savor
Unto my soul.

Give me the strength, my God,
To scatter my fires and tumble the altar stones in confusion;
Give me the strength to raise my eyes,
So that hard and sharp across my heart
Like shadow cut on mountain rock,
Will fall the agony of sunset—
So that I can see
The laughter of clouds spun into the blue web of infinity,
So that my soul can reach out
And melt in the sweep of forever
Above all these.

ROSALIE GRAYER

266

AROUND THE YEAR

One of my favorite lines of poetry is Shelley's "If winter comes, can spring be far behind?" I repeated the words over and over to myself long before I understood why one season inevitably must succeed another.

It is the perpetual change which the earth needs and which creates in us a sense of anticipation the whole year round. Every month has its own mood —and its own particular delights.

267

A Calendar

January brings the snow,
Makes our feet and fingers glow.

February brings the rain,
Thaws the frozen lake again.

March brings breezes, loud and shrill,
To stir the dancing daffodil.

April brings the primrose sweet,
Scatters daisies at our feet.

May brings flocks of pretty lambs
Skipping by their fleecy dams.

June brings tulips, lilies, roses,
Fills the children's hands with posies.

Hot July brings cooling showers,
Apricots, and gillyflowers.

August brings the sheaves of corn,
Then the harvest home is borne.

Warm September brings the fruit;
Sportsmen then begin to shoot.

Fresh October brings the pheasant;
Then to gather nuts is pleasant.

Dull November brings the blast;
Then the leaves are whirling fast.

Chill December brings the sleet,
Blazing fire, and Christmas treat.

SARA COLERIDGE

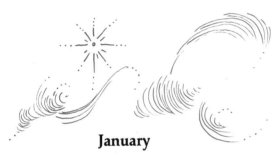

January

SKIING SONG

A silver sky is faintly etched;
White against white the world is stretched;
The silence beats through a distant hum,
And down the slopes the skiers come.

Then it's hi! ho! hi!
When the woods all lie
A-huddling close toward a wintry sky.
And it's ho! hi! ho!
When the white winds blow,
And the whole world sweeps
Down the steeps
Of the snow.

MICHAEL LEWIS

268

February

Around, above the world of snow
The light-heeled breezes breathe and blow;
Now here, now there, they wheel the flakes,
And whistle through the sun-dried brakes,
Then, growing faint, in silence fall
Against the keyhole in the hall.

Then dusky twilight spreads around,
The last soft snowflake seeks the ground,
And through unshaded window panes
The lamp-rays strike across the plains,
While now and then a shadow tall
Is thrown upon the whitewashed wall.

The hoar frost crackles on the trees,
The rattling brook begins to freeze,
The well sweep glistens in the light
As if with dust of diamonds bright;
And spreading o'er the crusted snow
A few swift-footed rabbits go.

Then the night silence, long and deep,
When weary eyes close fast in sleep;
The hush of Nature's breath, until
The cock crows loud upon the hill;
And shortly through the eastern haze
The red sun sets the sky ablaze.

JAMES BERRY BENSEL

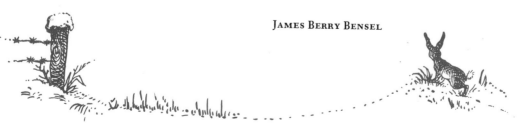

March

I wonder what spendthrift chose to spill
Such bright gold under my window-sill!
Is it fairy gold? Does it glitter still?
Bless me! It is a daffodil!

And look at the crocuses, keeping tryst
With the daffodil by the sunshine kissed!
Like beautiful bubbles of amethyst
They seem, blown out of the earth's snow-mist.

And snowdrops, delicate fairy bells,
With a pale green tint like the ocean swells;
And the hyacinths weaving their perfumed spells!
The ground is a rainbow of asphodels!

Who said that March was a scold and a shrew?
Who said she had nothing on earth to do
But tempests and furies and tempests to brew?
Why, look at the wealth she has lavished on you!

O March that blusters and March that blows,
What color under your footsteps glows!
Beauty you summon from winter snows,
And you are the pathway that leads to the rose.

CELIA THAXTER

Written in March

The cock is crowing,
The stream is flowing,
The small birds twitter,
The lake doth glitter,
The green field sleeps in the sun;
The oldest and youngest
Are at work with the strongest;
The cattle are grazing,
Their heads never raising;
There are forty feeding like one!

Like an army defeated
The snow hath retreated,
And now doth fare ill
On the top of the bare hill;
The ploughboy is whooping—anon—anon:
There's joy in the mountains;
There's life in the fountains;
Small clouds are sailing,
Blue sky prevailing;
The rain is over and gone!

WILLIAM WORDSWORTH

Scarcely Spring

Nothing is real. The world has lost its edges;
The sky, uncovered, is the one thing clear.
The earth is little more than atmosphere
Where yesterday were rocks and naked ridges
Nothing is fixed. Tentative rain dislodges
Green upon green or lifts a coral spear
That breaks in blossom, and the hills appear
Too frail to be the stony fruit of ages.

Nothing will keep. Even the heavens waver.
Young larks, whose first thought is to cry aloud
Have spent their bubble notes. And here or the
A few slow-hearted boys and girls discover
A moon as insubstantial as a cloud
Painted by air on washed and watery air.

LOUIS UNTERMEY

Spring

Sound the flute!
Now it's mute.
Birds delight
Day and Night;
Nightingale
In the dale,
Lark in Sky,
Merrily,
Merrily, merrily, to welcome in the Year.

Little Boy,
Full of joy;
Little Girl,
Sweet and small;
Cock does crow,
So do you;
Merry voice,
Infant noise,
Merrily, merrily, to welcome in the Year.

Little Lamb
Here I am;
Come and lick
My white neck;
Let me pull
Your soft Wool;
Let me kiss
Your soft face;
Merrily, merrily, we welcome in the Year.

WILLIAM BLAKE

271

E. E. Cummings (who sometimes signs himself e e cummings) is one of the modern poets who has stressed attention-getting devices. The appearance of the page inevitably draws the eye and the curiosity.

Cummings is equally surprising—and equally successful—in what he does with words. "Mud-luscious" and "puddle-wonderful" become new experiences for the reader as these adjectives recall childhood precisely and with great relish. The running of names together like "eddieandbill" accentuates the quick way the playmates act in unison.

Quite distinctly, as though the scene were being animated, Cummings shows you the baloonman limping down the road, the children running to him from their games. Then the poet hints that the baloonman is more than he seems. He is lame, goat-footed—like Pan, the spirit of eternal spring.

In Just—

in Just—
spring   when the world is mud—
luscious the little
lame baloonman

whistles   far   and wee
and eddieandbill come
running from marbles and
piracies and it's
spring

when the world is puddle-wonderful

the queer
old baloonman whistles
far   and   wee
and bettyandisbel come dancing
from hop-scotch and jump-rope and

it's
spring
and
    the
        goat-footed
baloonman   whistles
far
and
wee

E. E. CUMMINGS

272

Spring Song

From PIPPA PASSES

The year's at the spring
And day's at the morn;
Morning's at seven;
The hillside's dew-pearled;
The lark's on the wing;
The snail's on the thorn;
God's in his heaven—
All's right with the world!

ROBERT BROWNING

April

April, April,
Laugh thy girlish laughter;
Then, the moment after,
Weep thy girlish tears!
April, that mine ears
Like a lover greetest,
If I tell thee, sweetest,
All my hopes and fears,
April, April,
Laugh thy golden laughter;
But, the moment after,
Weep thy golden tears!

WILLIAM WATSON

William Watson's April *which you have just read, personifies the month of capricious sun and rain "like a lover." On the other hand, Ted Robinson is not quite so enthralled. He too responds to the contrast of warmth and wet weather—but his mimicking rhymes make merry with it.*

April

So here we are in April, in showy, blowy April,
   In frowsy, blowsy April, the rowdy, dowdy time;
In soppy, sloppy April, in wheezy, breezy April,
   In ringing, stinging April, with a singing swinging rhyme!

The smiling sun of April on the violets is focal,
   The sudden showers of April seek the dandelions out;
The tender airs of April make the local yokel vocal,
   And he raises rustic ditties with a most melodious shout.

So here we are in April, in tipsy gypsy April,
   In showery, flowery April, the twinkly, sprinkly days;
In tingly, jingly April, in highly wily April,
   In mighty, flighty April with its highty-tighty ways!

The duck is fond of April, and the clucking chickabiddy
   And other barnyard creatures have a try at caroling;
There's something in the air to turn a stiddy kiddy giddy,
   And even I am forced to raise my croaking voice and sing.

TED ROBINSON

273

May-Day Song

The moon shines bright; the stars give a light
    A little before 'tis day:
So God bless you all, both great and small,
    And send you a joyful May.

We have been rambling all the night,
    And almost all the day;
And now, returning back again,
    We have brought you a branch of May.

A branch of May we have brought you,
    And at your door it stands;
It is but a sprout, but it's well budded out
    By the work of our Lord's hands.

The hedges and trees they are so green,
    As green as any leek;
Our heavenly Father He watered them
    With His heavenly dew so sweet.

The heavenly gates are open wide,
    Our paths are beaten plain;
And if a man be not too far gone,
    He may return again.

The moon shines bright; the stars give a light,
    A little before 'tis day:
So God bless you all, both great and small,
    And send you a joyful May!

The nineteenth-century New England poet, James Russell Lowell, never could decide what kind of poet he wanted to be. In one vein, he wrote half-humorous, half-serious dialect verse; in another, he composed deeply religious poetry. The Vision of Sir Launfal is a legend of King Arthur's Round Table which is also a sermon, and it is from the prologue to this poem that the following famous description is taken.

June

And what is so rare as a day in June?
    Then, if ever, come perfect days;
Then Heaven tries the earth if it be in tune,
    And over it softly her warm ear lays:
Whether we look, or whether we listen,
We hear life murmur, or see it glisten;
Every clod feels a stir of might,
    An instinct within it that reaches and towers,
And, groping blindly above it for light,
    Climbs to a soul in grass and flowers;
The flush of life may well be seen
    Thrilling back over hills and valleys;
The cowslip startles in meadows green,
The buttercup catches the sun in its chalice,
And there's never a leaf nor a blade too mean
    To be some happy creature's palace;
The little bird sits at his door in the sun,
    Atilt like a blossom among the leaves,
And lets his illumined being o'errun
    With the deluge of summer it receives;

His mate feels the eggs beneath her wings,
And the heart in her dumb breast flutters and sings;
He sings to the wide world, and she to her nest,—
In the nice ear of Nature which song is the best?

Now is the high-tide of the year,
    And whatever of life hath ebbed away
Comes flooding back with a ripply cheer,
    Into every bare inlet and creek and bay;
Now the heart is so full that a drop overfills it,
We are happy now because God wills it;

No matter how barren the past may have been,
'T is enough for us now that the leaves are green;
We sit in the warm shade and feel right well
How the sap creeps up and the blossoms swell;
We may shut our eyes, but we cannot help knowing
That skies are clear and grass is growing;
The breeze comes whispering in our ear,
That dandelions are blossoming near,
    That maize has sprouted, that streams are flowing,
That the river is bluer than the sky,
That the robin is plastering his house hard by;
And if the breeze kept the good news back,
For other couriers we should not lack;
    We could guess it all by yon heifer's lowing,—
And hark! how clear bold chanticleer,
Warmed with the new wine of the year,
    Tells all in his lusty crowing!

JAMES RUSSELL LOWELL

July

Loud is the Summer's busy song,
The smallest breeze can find a tongue,
While insects of each tiny size
Grow teasing with their melodies,
Till noon burns with its blistering breath
Around, and day lies still as death.

The busy noise of man and brute
Is on a sudden lost and mute;
Even the brook that leaps along,
Seems weary of its bubbling song.
And, so soft its waters creep,
Tired silence sinks in sounder sleep;

The cricket on its bank is dumb;
The very flies forget to hum;
And, save the wagon rocking round,
The landscape sleeps without a sound.
The breeze is stopped, the lazy bough
Hath not a leaf that danceth now;

The taller grass upon the hill,
And spider's threads, are standing still;
The feathers, dropped from moorhen's wing
Which to the water's surface cling,
Are steadfast, and as heavy seem
As stones beneath them in the stream;

Noon swoons beneath the heat it made,
And flowers e'en within the shade;
Until the sun slopes in the west,
Like weary traveller, glad to rest
On pillowed clouds of many hues.
Then Nature's voice its joy renews,

And checkered field and grassy plain
Hum with their summer songs again,
A requiem to the day's decline,
Whose setting sunbeams coolly shine
As welcome to day's feeble powers
As falling dews to thirsty flowers.

JOHN CLARE

August

The city dwellers all complain
When August comes and brings no rain.
The pavements burn upon their feet;
Temper and temperature compete.
They mop their brows, they slow their pace,
And wish they were some other place.

But farmers do not mind the heat;
They know it ripens corn and wheat.
They love to see the sun rise red,
Remembering what their fathers said:
"An August month that's dry and warm
Will never do the harvest harm."

MICHAEL LEWIS

September

The golden-rod is yellow,
    The corn is turning brown;
The trees in apple orchards
    With fruit are bending down.

The gentian's bluest fringes
    Are curling in the sun;
In dusty pods the milkweed
    Its hidden silk has spun.

The sedges flaunt their harvest,
    In every meadow-nook;
And asters by the brookside
    Make asters in the brook.

By all these lovely tokens
    September days are here,
With summer's best of wealth
    And autumn's best of cheer.

HELEN HUNT JACKSON

A Vagabond Song

There is something in the autumn that is native to my blood—
Touch of manner, hint of mood;
And my heart is like a rhyme,
With the yellow and the purple and the crimson keeping time.

The scarlet of the maples can shake me like a cry
Of bugles going by.
And my lonely spirit thrills
To see the frosty asters like a smoke upon the hills.

There is something in October sets the gypsy blood astir;
We must rise and follow her,
When from every hill of flame
She calls and calls each vagabond by name.

BLISS CARMAN

277

Indian Summer

These are the days when birds come back,
A very few, a bird or two,
To take a backward look.

These are the days when skies put on
The old, old sophistries of June,—
A blue and gold mistake.

Oh, fraud that cannot cheat the bee,
Almost thy plausibility
Induces my belief,

Till ranks of seeds their witness bear,
And softly through the altered air
Hurries a timid leaf!

Oh, sacrament of summer days,
Oh, last communion in the haze,
Permit a child to join,

Thy sacred emblems to partake,
Thy consecrated bread to break,
Taste thine immortal wine!

EMILY DICKINSON

October

October turned my maple's leaves to gold;
    The most are gone now; here and there one lingers.
Soon these will slip from out the twig's weak hold,
    Like coins between a dying miser's fingers.

THOMAS BAILEY ALDRICH

Thanksgiving Day

Over the river and through the wood,
    To grandfather's house we go;
        The horse knows the way
        To carry the sleigh
Through the white and drifted snow.

Over the river and through the wood—
    Oh, how the wind does blow!
        It stings the toes
        And bites the nose,
As over the ground we go.

Over the river and through the wood,
    To have a first-rate play.
        Hear the bells ring,
        "Ting-a-ling-ding!"
Hurrah for Thanksgiving Day!

Over the river and through the wood
    Trot fast, my dapple-gray!
        Spring over the ground,
        Like a hunting-hound!
For this is Thanksgiving Day.

Over the river and through the wood,
    And straight through the barn-yard gate.
        We seem to go
        Extremely slow,—
It is so hard to wait!

Over the river and through the wood—
    Now grandmother's cap I spy!
        Hurrah for the fun!
        Is the pudding done?
Hurrah for the pumpkin-pie!

L. MARIA CHILD

Many people believe that John Keats, the marvelous genius who died before he was twenty-six, composed the most perfect poetry ever written. To Autumn is perhaps his most flawless poem. The mood is faintly melancholy and the music is in a minor key. But there is a richness and a ripeness—a sense of "mellow fruitfulness"—which poetry has never surpassed.

To Autumn

Season of mists and mellow fruitfulness,
    Close bosom-friend of the maturing sun;
Conspiring with him how to load and bless
    With fruit the vines that round the thatch-eaves run;
To bend with apples the mossed cottage-trees,
    And fill all fruit with ripeness to the core;
      To swell the gourd, and plump the hazel shells
    With a sweet kernel; to set budding more,
And still more, later flowers for the bees,
Until they think warm days will never cease,
      For Summer has o'er-brimmed their clammy cells.

Who hath not seen thee oft amid thy store?
    Sometimes whoever seeks abroad may find
Thee sitting careless on a granary floor,
    Thy hair soft-lifted by the winnowing wind;
Or on a half-reaped furrow sound asleep,
    Drowsed with the fume of poppies, while thy hook
      Spares the next swath and all its twinèd flowers;
And sometimes like a gleaner thou dost keep
    Steady thy laden head across a brook;
Or by a cider-press, with patient look,
      Thou watchest the last oozings, hours by hours.

Where are the songs of Spring? Ay, where are they?
    Think not of them, thou hast thy music too,—
While barred clouds bloom the soft-dying day,
    And touch the stubble-plains with rosy hue;
Then in a wailful choir, the small gnats mourn
    Among the river sallows,[1] borne aloft
      Or sinking as the light wind lives or dies;
And full-grown lambs loud bleat from hilly bourn;
    Hedge-crickets sing; and now with treble soft
    The redbreast whistles from a garden-croft,
      And gathering swallows twitter in the skies.

[1] Sallows: willows   JOHN KEATS

Sometimes a serious poet, as in I Remember, I Remember *on Page 95, sometimes a comic versifier, Thomas Hood always liked to sport with words. Even when he wrote about a somber season he could not restrain his pleasure in a pun. For example, each of the following lines begins with the word "No," but no one is prepared for what happens in Hood's last line.*

No!

No sun—no moon!
No morn—no noon—
No dawn—no dusk—no proper time of day—
No sky—no earthly view—
No distance looking blue—
No road—no street—no "t'other side the way"—
No top to any steeple—
No recognitions of familiar people—
No courtesies for showing 'em—
No knowing 'em!
No travelling at all—no locomotion—
No inkling of the way—no notion—
"No go"—by land or ocean—
No mail—no post—
No news from any foreign coast—
No park—no ring—no afternoon gentility—
No company—no nobility—
No warmth, no cheerfulness, no healthful ease,
No comfortable feel in any member—
No shade, no shine, no butterflies, no bees,
No fruits, no flowers, no leaves, no birds.
November!

THOMAS HOOD

Winter-Time

Late lies the wintry sun abed
A frosty, fiery sleepy-head;
Blinks but an hour or two; and then,
A blood-red orange, sets again.

Before the stars have left the skies,
At morning in the dark I rise;
And shivering in my nakedness,
By the cold candle, bathe and dress.

Close by the jolly fire I sit
To warm my frozen bones a bit;
Or with a reindeer-sled, explore
The colder countries round the door.

When to go out, my nurse doth wrap
Me in my comforter and cap;
The cold wind burns my face, and blow
Its frosty pepper up my nose.

Black are my steps on silver sod;
Thick blows my frosty breath abroad;
And tree and house, and hill and lake,
Are frosted like a wedding-cake.

ROBERT LOUIS STEVENSO

William Wordsworth lived most of his life in the lovely Lake District of England. In his long poem, The Prelude, *which he subtitled "The Growth of a Poet's Mind," he wrote about himself with charm and candor. He was particularly happy remembering his favorite sports: rambling among the mountains, rowing, fishing, and skating.*

Skating

nd in the frosty season, when the sun
'as set, and visible for many a mile
he cottage windows blazed through twilight gloom,
eeded not their summons: happy time
was indeed for all of us—for me
was a time of rapture! Clear and loud
he village clock tolled six,—I wheeled about
roud and exulting like an untired horse
hat cares not for his home. All shod with steel,
'e hissed along the polished ice in games
onfederate, imitative of the chase
nd woodland pleasures,—the resounding horn,
he pack loud chiming, and the hunted hare.

So through the darkness and the cold we flew,
And not a voice was idle; with the din
Smitten, the precipices rang aloud;
The leafless trees and every icy crag
Tinkled like iron; while far distant hills
Into the tumult sent an alien sound
Of melancholy not unnoticed, while the stars
Eastward were sparkling clear, and in the west
The orange sky of evening died away.
Not seldom from the uproar I retired
Into a silent bay, or sportively
Glanced sideway, leaving the tumultuous throng,
To cut across the reflex of a star
That fled, and, flying still before me, gleamed
Upon the glassy plain; and oftentimes,
When we had given our bodies to the wind,
And all the shadowy banks on either side
Came sweeping through the darkness, spinning still
The rapid line of motion, then at once
Have I, reclining back upon my heels,
Stopped short; yet still the solitary cliffs
Wheeled by me—even as if the earth had rolled
With visible motion her diurnal[1] round!
Behind me did they stretch in solemn train,
Feebler and feebler, and I stood and watched
Till all was tranquil as a dreamless sleep.

WILLIAM WORDSWORTH

November

The shepherds almost wonder where they dwell
And the old dog for his right journey stares:
The path leads somewhere, but they cannot tell
And neighbour meets with neighbour unawares
The maiden passes close beside her cow,
And wanders on, and thinks her far away;
The ploughman goes unseen behind his plough
And seems to lose his horses half the day.
The lazy mist creeps on in journey slow;
The maidens shout and wonder where they go;
So dull and dark are the November days.
The lazy mist high up the evening curled,
And now the morn quite hides in smoke and ha
The place we occupy seems all the world.

JOHN CLA

[1] Diurnal: daily

December is a companion piece to James Russell Lowell's June. It, too, is from The Vision of Sir Launfal, *the prelude to the second part of that poem.*

December

Down swept the chill wind from the mountain peak,
    From the snow five thousand summers old;
On open wold and hill-top bleak
    It had gathered all the cold,
And whirled it like sleet on the wanderer's cheek;
It carried a shiver everywhere
From the unleafed boughs and pastures bare;
The little brook heard it and built a roof
Neath which he could house him, winter-proof;
All night by the white stars' frosty gleams
He groined his arches and matched his beams;
Slender and clear were his crystal spars
As the lashes of light that trim the stars:
He sculptured every summer delight
In his halls and chambers out of sight;
Sometimes his tinkling waters slipt
Down through a frost-leaved forest-crypt,
Long, sparkling aisles of steel-stemmed trees
Bending to counterfeit a breeze;
Sometimes the roof no fretwork knew
But silvery mosses that downward grew;
Sometimes it was carved in sharp relief
With quaint arabesques of ice-fern leaf;
Sometimes it was simply smooth and clear
For the gladness of heaven to shine through, and here
He had caught the nodding bulrush-tops
And hung them thickly with diamond drops,
That crystalled the beams of moon and sun,
And made a star of every one:
No mortal builder's most rare device
Could match this winter-palace of ice;
'T was as if every image that mirrored lay
In his depth serene through the summer day,
Each fleeting shadow of earth and sky,
    Lest the happy model should be lost,
Had been mimicked in fairy masonry
    By the elfin builders of the frost.

JAMES RUSSELL LOWELL

Robert Frost has been a farmer as well as a poet most of his life. I have lived on a farm in the Adirondack Mountains. Both of us have experienced the deep concern country people feel at the coming of winter. Both of us have written poems about it. In Good-bye and Keep Cold, *Frost addresses his orchard in a spirit which is half-playful, half-prayerful. In somewhat the same key, I talk about (and to) the farm, opening and closing* Last Words Before Winter *with a children's jingle because it seemed both amusing and appropriate.*

Good-bye and Keep Cold

This saying good-bye on the edge of the dark
And the cold to an orchard so young in the bark
Reminds me of all that can happen to harm
An orchard away at the end of the farm
All winter, cut off by a hill from the house.
I don't want it girdled by rabbit and mouse,
I don't want it dreamily nibbled for browse
By deer, and I don't want it budded by grouse.
(If certain it wouldn't be idle to call
I'd summon grouse, rabbit, and deer to the wall
And warn them away with a stick for a gun.)
I don't want it stirred by the heat of the sun.
(We made it secure against being, I hope,
By setting it out on a northerly slope.)
No orchard's the worse for the wintriest storm.
But one thing about it, it mustn't get warm.
How often already you've had to be told,
"Keep cold, young orchard. Good-bye and keep cold.
Dread fifty above more than fifty below."
I have to be gone for a season or so.
My business awhile is with different trees,
Less carefully nurtured, less fruitful than these,
And such as is done to their wood with an axe—
Maples and birches and tamaracks.
I wish I could promise to lie in the night
And think of an orchard's arboreal plight
When slowly (and nobody comes with a light)
Its heart sinks lower under the sod.
But something has to be left to God.

ROBERT FROST

284

Last Words Before Winter

All my sheep
Gather in a heap,
For I spy the woolly, woolly wolf.

Farewell, my flocks,
Farewell. But let me find you
Safe in your stall and barn and box
With your winter's tale behind you.

Farewell, my cattle (both);
I leave you just as loath
As though you were a hundred head,
Instead
Of two-and-a-half—
Two cows and a calf.

Farewell, my apple-trees;
You have learned what it is to freeze,
With the drift on your knees.
But, oh, beware
Those first kind days, the snare
Of the too promising air,
The cost
Of over-sudden trust—
And then the killing frost.

Farewell, beloved acres.
I leave you in the hands
Of one whose earliest enterprise was lands—
Your Maker's.

Yard, hutch, and house, farewell.
It is for you to tell
How you withstood the great white wolf, whose fell
Is softer than a lambkin's
But whose breath
Is death.
Farewell, hoof, claw, and wing,
Finned, furred, and feathered thing,
Till Spring—

All my sheep
Gather in a heap,
For I spy the woolly, woolly wolf.

LOUIS UNTERMEYER

285

COME CHRISTMAS

Christmas means many things. It is a sacred day and a happy celebration. It is also a season — a season which combines reverence and merriment, glory and gift-giving, solemnity and song.

Christmas Daybreak

Before the paling of the stars,
    Before the winter morn,
Before the earliest cockcrow,
    Jesus Christ was born:
Born in a stable,
    Cradled in a manger,
In the world His hands had made,
    Born a stranger.

Priest and king lay fast asleep
    In Jerusalem,
Young and old lay fast asleep
    In crowded Bethlehem:

Saint and angel, ox and ass,
    Kept a watch together,
Before the Christmas daybreak
    In the winter weather.

Jesus on His Mother's breast
    In the stable cold,
Spotless Lamb of God was He,
    Shepherd of the fold.
Let us kneel with Mary Maid,
    With Joseph bent and hoary,
With saint and angel, ox and ass,
    To hail the King of Glory.

CHRISTINA GEORGINA ROSSETTI

Painters and poets have pictured the Nativity in countless ways. The setting is always the same, but the treatment differs with every generation. The sixteenth-century English poet, Robert Southwell, describes the scene in the classical manner of his period, while Elizabeth Coatsworth's The Barn *is written in the everyday speech of our own time and place.*

Humble Pomp

Behold, a silly tender Babe
    In freezing winter night
In homely manger trembling lies, ·
    Alas, a piteous sight!

The inns are full; no man will yield
    This little pilgrim bed,
But forced he is with silly beasts
    In crib to shroud his head.

Despise him not for lying there,
    First, what he is inquire;
An orient pearl is often found
    In depth of dirty mire.

Weigh not his crib, his wooden dish,
    Nor beasts that by him feed;
Weigh not his Mother's poor attire,
    Nor Joseph's simple weed.[1]

This stable is a Prince's court,
    This crib his chair of state;
The beasts are parcel of his pomp,
    The wooden dish his plate.

The persons in that poor attire
    His royal liveries wear;
The Prince himself is come from heaven;
    This pomp is prized there.

With joy approach, O Christian wight,[2]
    Do homage to thy King;
And highly praise his humble pomp,
    Which he from heaven doth bring.

[1] Weed: clothing
[2] Wight: person
       ROBERT SOUTHWELL

The Barn

"I am tired of this barn!" said the colt.
"And every day it snows.
 Outside there's no grass any more
 And icicles grow on my nose.
 I am tired of hearing the cows
 Breathing and talking together.
 I am sick of these clucking hens.
 I *hate* stables and winter weather!"

"Hush, little colt," said the mare
"And a story I will tell
 Of a barn like this one of ours
 And the wonders that there befell.
 It was weather much like this,
 And the beasts stood as we stand now
 In the warm good dark of the barn—
 A horse and an ass and a cow."

"And sheep?" asked the colt. "Yes, sheep,
 And a pig and a goat and a hen.
 All of the beasts of the barnyard,
 The usual servants of men.
 And into their midst came a lady
 And she was cold as death,
 But the animals leaned above her
 And made her warm with their breath.

"There was her baby born
 And laid to sleep in the hay,
 While music flooded the rafters
 And the barn was as light as day.
 And angels and kings and shepherds
 Came to worship the babe from afar,
 But we looked at him first of all creatures
 By the bright strange light of a star!"

ELIZABETH COATSWORTH

I Sing of a Maiden *is one of the earliest and one of the very loveliest of English songs. It dates from the fifteenth century; its age is revealed in archaic words like "makeles," which means "matchless," and "ches," which means "chose." Most of the other words have been modernized.*

I Sing of a Maiden

I sing of a maiden
  That is makeles;
King of all kings
  To her son she ches.

He came all so still
  There his mother was,
As dew in April
  That falleth on the grass.

He came all so still
  To His mother's bower,

As dew in April
  That falleth on the flower.

He came all so still
  There His mother lay,
As dew in April
  That falleth on the spray.

Mother and maiden
  Was never none but she;
Well may such a lady
  God's mother be.

Elizabeth Madox Roberts was born in Kentucky, a descendant of pioneers who had been in that state since the days of Daniel Boone. A little over fifty when she died, she had crowded an immense amount of feeling into her poems, short stories, and novels. All her work glows with the warmth of the soil and shines with the beauty of simple but colorful speech.

Her Christmas Morning describes the Nativity with loving exactness. All the details are those we would see through the eyes of a child; the very words are a child's words. Although the scene is Bethlehem, the place could be anywhere in the American countryside.

Christmas Morning

If Bethlehem were here today,
Or this were very long ago,
There wouldn't be a winter time
Nor any cold or snow.

I'd run out through the garden gate,
And down along the pasture walk;
And off beside the cattle barns
I'd hear a kind of gentle talk.

I'd move the heavy iron chain
And pull away the wooden pin;
I'd push the door a little bit
And tiptoe very softly in.

The pigeons and the yellow hens
And all the cows would stand away;
Their eyes would open wide to see
A lady in the manger hay,

If this were very long ago
And Bethlehem were here today.

And Mother held my hand and smiled—
I mean the lady would—and she
Would take the woolly blankets off
Her little boy so I could see.

His shut-up eyes would be asleep,
And he would look like our John,
And he would be all crumpled too,
And have a pinkish color on.

I'd watch his breath go in and out.
His little clothes would all be white.
I'd slip my finger in his hand
To feel how he could hold it tight.

And she would smile and say, "Take care,"
The mother, Mary, would, "Take care";
And I would kiss his little hand
And touch his hair.

While Mary put the blankets back
The gentle talk would soon begin.
And when I'd tiptoe softly out
I'd meet the wise men going in.

ELIZABETH MADOX ROBERTS

The Three Kings

Three Kings came riding from far away,
  Melchior and Gaspar and Baltasar;
Three Wise Men out of the East were they.
And they travelled by night and they slept by day,
  For their guide was a beautiful, wonderful star.

The star was so beautiful, large, and clear,
  That all the other stars of the sky
Became a white mist in the atmosphere,
And by this they knew that the coming was near
  Of the Prince foretold in the prophecy.

Three caskets they bore on their saddle-bows,
  Three caskets of gold with golden keys;
Their robes were of crimson silk with rows
Of bells and pomegranates and furbelows,
  Their turbans like blossoming almond-trees.

And so the Three Kings rode into the West,
  Through the dusk of night, over hill and dell,
And sometimes they nodded with beard on breast,
And sometimes talked, as they paused to rest,
  With the people they met at some wayside well.

"Of the child that is born," said Baltasar,
  "Good people, I pray you, tell us the news;
For we in the East have seen his star,
And have ridden fast, and have ridden far,
  To find and worship the King of the Jews."

And the people answered, "You ask in vain;
  We know of no king but Herod the Great!"
They thought the Wise Men were men insane,
As they spurred their horses across the plain,
  Like riders in haste, and who cannot wait.

And when they came to Jerusalem,
  Herod the Great, who had heard this thing,
Sent for the Wise Men and questioned them;
And said, "Go down unto Bethlehem,
  And bring me tidings of this new king."

290

So they rode away; and the star stood still,
  The only one in the gray of morn;
Yes, it stopped,—it stood still of its own free will,
Right over Bethlehem on the hill,
  The city of David, where Christ was born.

And the Three Kings rode through the gate and the guard,
  Through the silent street, till their horses turned
And neighed as they entered the great inn-yard;
But the windows were closed, and the doors were barred,
  And only a light in the stable burned.

And cradled there in the scented hay,
  In the air made sweet by the breath of kine,
The little child in the manger lay,
The child, that would be king one day
  Of a kingdom not human but divine.

His mother Mary of Nazareth
  Sat watching beside his place of rest,
Watching the even flow of his breath,
For the joy of life and the terror of death
  Were mingled together in her breast.

They laid their offerings at his feet:
  The gold was their tribute to a King,
The frankincense, with its odor sweet,
Was for the Priest, the Paraclete,
  The myrrh for the body's burying.

And the mother wondered and bowed her head,
  And sat as still as a statue of stone;
Her heart was troubled yet comforted,
Remembering what the Angel had said
  Of an endless reign and of David's throne.

Then the Kings rode out of the city gate,
  With a clatter of hoofs in proud array;
But they went not back to Herod the Great,
For they knew his malice and feared his hate,
  And returned to their homes by another way.

HENRY WADSWORTH LONGFELLOW

291

Most of us know the following poem, and most of us know it as The Night Before Christmas. *But that was not its title when it appeared more than a hundred years ago. Its author did not think much of it. He was Clement Clarke Moore, an eminent teacher, an interpreter of the Bible, a professor of Greek Literature. He called his lines* A Visit from Saint Nicholas *and he wrote them only for his children; he never meant to publish them. However, a friend of the family heard the poem, copied it in her "album," and a year later sent it (without the author's permission) to the Troy (New York)* Sentinel. *The poem appeared, unsigned. Dr. Moore was not pleased but he said nothing. Other writers claimed that they had written the poem—it became more and more popular—and finally Dr. Moore told the story of how it happened to be printed.*

All the many works of the learned scholar have been forgotten. But everybody remembers the happy jingle that the professor wrote one Christmas day for his children's amusement—it is the only thing of his which has survived to this day.

A Visit from St. Nicholas

'Twas the night before Christmas, when all through the house
Not a creature was stirring, not even a mouse;
The stockings were hung by the chimney with care,
In hopes that St. Nicholas soon would be there;
The children were nestled all snug in their beds,
While visions of sugar-plums danced in their heads;
And mamma in her kerchief, and I in my cap,
Had just settled our brains for a long winter nap—
When out on the lawn there arose such a clatter,
I sprang from my bed to see what was the matter.
Away to the window I flew like a flash,
Tore open the shutters and threw up the sash.
The moon, on the breast of the new-fallen snow,
Gave a lustre of midday to objects below;
When what to my wondering eyes should appear
But a miniature sleigh and eight tiny reindeer,
With a little old driver, so lively and quick,
I knew in a moment it must be St. Nick.

More rapid than eagles his coursers they came,
And he whistled, and shouted, and called them by name:
"Now, Dasher! now, Dancer! now, Prancer and Vixen!
On, Comet! on, Cupid! on, Donder and Blitzen!
To the top of the porch, to the top of the wall!
Now, dash away, dash away, dash away all!"
As dry leaves that before the wild hurricane fly,
When they meet with an obstacle, mount to the sky,
So up to the house-top the coursers they flew,
With the sleigh full of toys—and St. Nicholas too.
And then in a twinkling I heard on the roof
The prancing and pawing of each little hoof.
As I drew in my head, and was turning around,
Down the chimney St. Nicholas came with a bound.
He was dressed all in fur from his head to his foot,
And his clothes were all tarnished with ashes and soot;
A bundle of toys he had flung on his back,
And he looked like a peddler just opening his pack.
His eyes how they twinkled! his dimples how merry!
His cheeks were like roses, his nose like a cherry;
His droll little mouth was drawn up like a bow,
And the beard on his chin was as white as the snow.
The stump of a pipe he held tight in his teeth,
And the smoke it encircled his head like a wreath.
He had a broad face and a little round belly
That shook, when he laughed, like a bowl full of jelly.
He was chubby and plump,—a right jolly old elf,
And I laughed, when I saw him, in spite of myself.
A wink of his eye and a twist of his head
Soon gave me to know I had nothing to dread.
He spoke not a word, but went straight to his work,
And filled all the stockings; then turned with a jerk,
And laying his finger aside of his nose,
And giving a nod, up the chimney he rose.
He sprang to his sleigh, to his team gave a whistle,
And away they all flew like the down of a thistle;
But I heard him exclaim, ere he drove out of sight,
"Happy Christmas to all, and to all a good-night!"

CLEMENT CLARKE MOORE

I Saw Three Ships

I saw three ships come sailing in
    On Christmas day, on Christmas day;
I saw three ships come sailing in
    On Christmas day in the morning.

And what was in those ships all three
    On Christmas day, on Christmas day;
And what was in those ships all three
    On Christmas day in the morning?

Our Saviour Christ and his ladie,
    On Christmas day, on Christmas day;
Our Saviour Christ and his ladie,
    On Christmas day in the morning.

Pray whither sailed those ships all three
    On Christmas day, on Christmas day;
Pray whither sailed those ships all three
    On Christmas day in the morning?

O they sailed into Bethlehem
    On Christmas day, on Christmas day;
O they sailed into Bethlehem
    On Christmas day in the morning.

And all the bells on earth shall ring
    On Christmas day, on Christmas day;
And all the bells on earth shall ring
    On Christmas day in the morning.

And all the angels in heaven shall sing
    On Christmas day, on Christmas day;
And all the angels in heaven shall sing
    On Christmas day in the morning.

And all the souls on earth shall sing
    On Christmas day, on Christmas day;
And all the souls on earth shall sing
    On Christmas day in the morning.

Then let us all rejoice amain
    On Christmas day, on Christmas day;
Then let us all rejoice amain
    On Christmas day in the morning.

Awake! Glad Heart!

Awake! glad heart! get up and sing!
It is the birthday of thy King.
    Awake! awake!
    The sun doth shake
Light from his locks, and, all the way
Breathing perfumes, doth spice the day.

Awake! awake! hark how th'wood rings,
Winds whisper, and the busy springs
    A concert make!
    Awake! awake!
Man is their high-priest, and should rise
To offer up the sacrifice.

I would I were some bird, or star,
Fluttering in woods, or lifted far
    Above this inn,
    And roar of sin!
Then either star or bird should be
Shining or singing still to thee.

HENRY VAUGHAN

Christmas Bells

I heard the bells on Christmas Day
Their old, familiar carols play,
    And wild and sweet
    The words repeat
Of peace on earth, good-will to men!

And thought how, as the day had come,
The belfries of all Christendom
    Had rolled along
    The unbroken song
Of peace on earth, good-will to men!

Till, ringing, singing on its way,
The world received from night to day,
    A voice, a chime,
    A chant sublime
Of peace on earth, good-will to men!

Then from each black, accursed mouth
The cannon thundered in the South,
    And with the sound
    The carols drowned
Of peace on earth, good-will to men!

It was as if an earthquake rent
The hearth-stones of a continent,
    And made forlorn
    The households born
Of peace on earth, good-will to men!

And in despair I bowed my head;
"There is no peace on earth," I said;
    "For hate is strong,
    And mocks the song
Of peace on earth, good-will to men!"

Then pealed the bells more loud and deep:
"God is not dead; nor doth he sleep!
    The Wrong shall fail,
    The Right prevail,
With peace on earth, good-will to men!"

HENRY WADSWORTH LONGFELLOW

Christmas Everywhere

Everywhere, everywhere, Christmas to-night!
Christmas in lands of the fir tree and pine,
Christmas in lands of the palm tree and vine,
Christmas where snow peaks stand solemn and white,
Christmas where cornfields lie sunny and bright!

Christmas where children are hopeful and gay,
Christmas where old men are patient and gray,
Christmas where peace, like a dove in his flight,
Broods o'er brave men in the thick of the fight,
Everywhere, everywhere, Christmas to-night.

For the Christ Child who comes is the Master of all;
No palace too great and no cottage too small.

PHILLIPS BROOKS

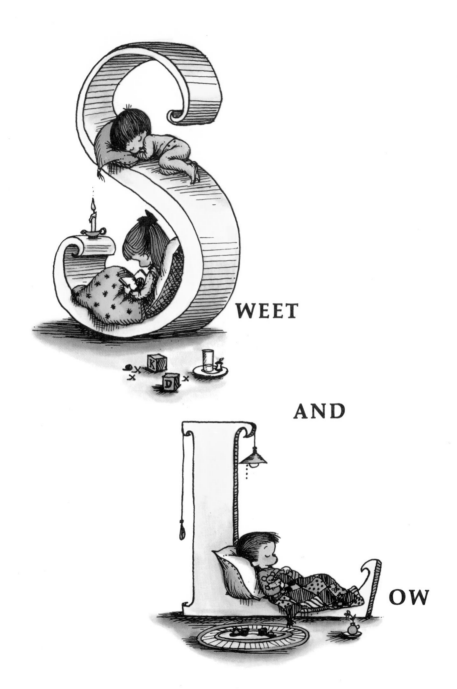

SWEET

AND

LOW

Most of us look forward, not backward. But when we think of our childhood, we recall the quiet bedtime hour, the low light in the shaded room, and a voice soothing us into dreams. Even after we are grown, we remember and cherish those early slumber-songs. They comfort us like little lulling tunes, or reassure us with reminders of eternal love.

296

Sleepy Song

Ere the moon begins to rise
  Or a star to shine,
All the bluebells close their eyes—
  So close thine,
    Thine, dear, thine!

Birds are sleeping in the nest
  On the swaying bough,
Thus, against the mother's breast—
  So sleep thou—
    Sleep, sleep, thou!

THOMAS BAILEY ALDRICH

Lullaby of an Infant Chief

Oh, hush thee, my baby, thy sire was a knight,
Thy mother a lady, both lovely and bright;
The woods and the glens, from the towers we see,
They all are belonging, dear baby, to thee.

Oh, fear not the bugle, though loudly it blows,
It calls but the warders that guard thy repose;
Their bows would be bended, their blades would be red,
Ere the step of a foeman draws near to thy bed.

Oh, hush thee, my baby, the time will soon come
When thy sleep shall be broken by trumpet and drum;
Then hush thee, my darling, take rest while you may,
For strife comes with manhood, and waking with day.

SIR WALTER SCOTT

Fairy Lullaby

First Fairy

You spotted snakes with double tongue,
  Thorny hedgehogs, be not seen;
Newts, and blind-worms, do no wrong;
  Come not near our fairy queen.

Chorus

Philomel with melody
  Sing in our sweet lullaby;
Lulla, lulla, lullaby; lulla, lulla, lullaby!
Never harm, nor spell, nor charm,
  Come our lovely lady nigh!
  So good-night, with lullaby.

Second Fairy

Weaving spiders, come not here;
  Hence, you long-legg'd spinners, hence;
Beetles black, approach not near;
  Worm, nor snail, do no offence.

Chorus

Philomel with melody
  Sing in our sweet lullaby;
Lulla, lulla, lullaby; lulla, lulla, lullaby!
Never harm, nor spell, nor charm,
  Come our lovely lady nigh!
  So good-night, with lullaby.

From *A Midsummer Night's Dream*
WILLIAM SHAKESPEARE

297

The Fly-Away Horse is half song, half story—a kind of enlarged lullaby. It is full of delightfully unreal things: a moon that gallops; stars that hide their faces in the lap of their old grandmother Night; trees made of candy, streams of honey, cornfields that ripen into popcorn; lions that offer free rides; bears that playfully beg you to wrestle—just the sort of fancies a child might have as it slides into sleep. Only here the child does not "slide" into slumber. He rides off, rides proudly into dreams on the back of the magical Fly-Away Horse.

The Fly-Away Horse

Oh, a wonderful horse is the Fly-Away Horse—
    Perhaps you have seen him before;
Perhaps, while you slept, his shadow has swept
    Through the moonlight that floats on the floo
For it's only at night, when the stars twinkle bright
    That the Fly-Away Horse, with a neigh
And a pull at his rein and a toss of his mane,
    Is up on his heels and away!
        The Moon in the sky,
        As he gallopeth by,
Cries: "Oh! what a marvelous sight!"
        And the Stars in dismay
        Hide their faces away
In the lap of old Grandmother Night.

It is yonder, out yonder, the Fly-Away Horse
     Speedeth ever and ever away—
Over meadows and lanes, over mountains and plains,
     Over streamlets that sing at their play;
And over the sea like a ghost sweepeth he,
     While the ships they go sailing below,
And he speedeth so fast that the men at the mast
     Adjudge him some portent of woe.
        "What ho, there!" they cry,
        As he flourishes by
With a whisk of his beautiful tail;
       And the fish in the sea
       Are as scared as can be,
From the nautilus up to the whale!

And the Fly-Away Horse seeks those far-away lands
     You little folk dream of at night—
Where candy-trees grow, and honey-brooks flow,
     And corn-fields with popcorn are white;
And the beasts in the wood are ever so good
     To children who visit them there—
What glory astride of a lion to ride,
     Or to wrestle around with a bear!
        The monkeys, they say:
        "Come on, let us play,"
And they frisk in the coconut-trees:
       While the parrots, that cling
       To the peanut-vines, sing
Or converse with comparative ease!

Off! scamper to bed—you shall ride him to-night!
     For, as soon as you've fallen asleep,
With a jubilant neigh he shall bear you away
     Over forest and hillside and deep!
But tell us, my dear, all you see and you hear
     In those beautiful lands over there,
Where the Fly-Away Horse wings his far-away course
     With the wee one consigned to his care.
        Then grandma will cry
        In amazement: "Oh, my!"
And she'll think it could never be so.
       And only we two
       Shall know it is true—
You and I, little precious! shall know!

EUGENE FIELD

You would scarcely expect to find a tender lullaby in a half-serious poem about a princess whose aim in life is to found a college for women and is defeated by a prince who gains admission into the college and disguises himself as a girl. Love (of course) conquers all in Tennyson's long poem The Princess, *where* Sweet and Low *first appeared.*

Orkney Lullaby

A moonbeam floateth from the skies,
    Whispering, "Heigho, my dearie!
I would spin a web before your eyes,—
A beautiful web of silver light,
Wherein is many a wondrous sight
Of a radiant garden leagues away,
Where the softly tinkling lilies sway,
And the snow-white lambkins are at play,—
    Heigho, my dearie!"

A brownie stealeth from the vine
    Singing, "Heigho, my dearie!
And will you hear this song of mine,—
A song of the land of murk and mist
Where bideth the bud the dew hath kissed?
Then let the moonbeam's web of light
Be spun before thee silvery white,
And I shall sing the livelong night,—
    Heigho, my dearie!"

The night wind speedeth from the sea,
    Murmuring, "Heigho, my dearie!
I bring a mariner's prayer for thee;
So let the moonbeam veil thine eyes,
And the brownie sing thee lullabies;
But I shall rock thee to and fro,
Kissing the brow *he* loveth so,
And the prayer shall guard thy bed, I trow,—
    Heigho, my dearie!"

EUGENE FIELD

Sweet and Low

Sweet and low, sweet and low,
    Wind of the western sea,
Low, low, breathe and blow,
    Wind of the western sea!
    Over the rolling waters go,
    Come from the dying moon, and blow,
    Blow him again to me;
While my little one, while my pretty one sleeps.

Sleep and rest, sleep and rest,
    Father will come to thee soon;
Rest, rest, on mother's breast,
    Father will come to thee soon;
    Father will come to his babe in the nest,
    Silver sails all out of the west
    Under the silver moon;
Sleep, my little one, sleep, my pretty one, sleep.

ALFRED, LORD TENNYSON

Welsh Lullaby

Sleep, my babe, lie still and slumber,
    All through the night;
Guardian angels God will lend thee,
    All through the night;
Soft the drowsy hours are creeping,
Hill and vale in slumber sleeping,
Mother dear her watch is keeping,
    All through the night.

God is here, thou'lt not be lonely,
    All through the night;
'Tis not I who guards thee only,
    All through the night.
Night's dark shades will soon be over,
Still my watchful care shall hover,
God with me His watch is keeping,
    All through the night.

Holy Lullaby

Sleep, baby, sleep.
    Thy father guards the sheep;
Thy mother shakes the dreamland tree,
Down falls a little dream for thee:
    Sleep, baby, sleep.

Sleep, baby, sleep.
    The large stars are the sheep;
The little stars are the lambs, I guess;
And the gentle moon is the shepherdess:
    Sleep, baby, sleep.

Sleep, baby, sleep.
    Our Saviour loves His sheep;
He is the Lamb of God on high,
Who for our sakes came down to die:
    Sleep, baby, sleep.

Cradle Hymn

Away in a manger, no crib for a bed,
The little Lord Jesus laid down His sweet head.
The stars in the bright sky looked down where He lay—
The little Lord Jesus asleep on the hay.

The cattle are lowing, the baby awakes,
But little Lord Jesus no crying He makes.
I love Thee, Lord Jesus! look down from the sky,
And stay by my cradle till morning is nigh.

Be near me, Lord Jesus, I ask Thee to stay
Close by me for ever and love me, I pray;
Bless all the dear children in Thy tender care,
And fit us for Heaven, to live with Thee there.

From the German of MARTIN LUTHER

German Slumber Song

Go to sleep and good night;
In a rosy twilight,
With the moon overhead
Snuggle deep in your bed.
God will watch, never fear,
While Heaven draws near.

Go to sleep and good night;
You are safe in the sight
Of the angels who show
Christmas trees all aglow.
So to sleep, shut your eyes,
In a dream's Paradise.

From the German by Karl Simrock
Adapted by LOUIS UNTERMEYER

Wynken, Blynken, and Nod

Wynken, Blynken, and Nod one night
   Sailed off in a wooden shoe,—
Sailed on a river of crystal light
   Into a sea of dew.
"Where are you going, and what do you wish?"
   The old moon asked the three.
"We have come to fish for the herring-fish
   That live in this beautiful sea;
   Nets of silver and gold have we,"
      Said Wynken,
      Blynken,
      And Nod.

The old moon laughed and sang a song,
   As they rocked in the wooden shoe;
And the wind that sped them all night long
   Ruffled the waves of dew;
The little stars were the herring-fish
   That lived in the beautiful sea.
"Now cast your nets wherever you wish,—
   Never afraid are we!"
   So cried the stars to the fishermen three,
      Wynken,
      Blynken,
      And Nod.

All night long their nets they threw
   To the stars in the twinkling foam,—
Then down from the skies came the wooden shoe,
   Bringing the fishermen home:
'Twas all so pretty a sail, it seemed
   As if it could not be;
And some folk thought 'twas a dream they'd dreamed
   Of sailing that beautiful sea;
   But I shall name you the fishermen three:
      Wynken,
      Blynken,
      And Nod.

Wynken and Blynken are two little eyes,
　　And Nod is a little head,
And the wooden shoe that sailed the skies
　　Is a wee one's trundle-bed;
So shut your eyes while Mother sings
　　Of wonderful sights that be,
And you shall see the beautiful things
　　As you rock in the misty sea
Where the old shoe rocked the fishermen three:—
　　　　Wynken,
　　　　Blynken,
　　　　And Nod.

EUGENE FIELD

The Land of Nod

From breakfast on through all the day
At home among my friends I stay,
But every night I go abroad
Afar into the land of Nod.

All by myself I have to go,
With none to tell me what to do—
All alone beside the streams
And up the mountain-sides of dreams.

The strangest things are there for me,
Both things to eat and things to see,
And many frightening sights abroad
Till morning in the land of Nod.

Try as I like to find the way,
I never can get back by day,
Nor can remember plain and clear
The curious music that I hear.

ROBERT LOUIS STEVENSON

Nod

Softly along the road of evening,
　　In a twilight dim with rose,
Wrinkled with age, and drenched with dew
　　Old Nod, the shepherd, goes.

His drowsy flock streams on before him,
　　Their fleeces charged with gold,
To where the sun's last beam leans low
　　On Nod the shepherd's fold.

The hedge is quick and green with briar,
　　From their sand the conies creep;
And all the birds that fly in heaven
　　Flock singing home to sleep.

His lambs outnumber a noon's roses,
　　Yet, when night's shadows fall,
His blind old sheep-dog, Slumber-soon,
　　Misses not one of all.

His are the quiet steps of dreamland,
　　The waters of no-more-pain;
His ram's bell rings 'neath an arch of stars,
　　"Rest, rest, and rest again."

WALTER DE LA MARE

303

GUIDING STARS

This book ends with a group of poems which are inspirational in nature, flashes of guidance. Most of them are short, but their very brevity gives them power. In a few lines they tell us sharply and unforgettably what volumes of prose may fail to say.

304

To See a World

To see a world in a grain of sand
And a heaven in a wild flower,
Hold Infinity in the palm of your hand
And Eternity in an hour.

WILLIAM BLAKE

Prayer for Miracle

O God, no more Thy miracle withhold;
To us in tents give palaces of gold;
And while we stumble among things that are,
Give us the solace of a guiding star.

ANNA WICKHAM

Dare To Be True

Dare to be true;
    Nothing can need a lie.
The fault that needs one most
    Grows two thereby.

GEORGE HERBERT

Standards

You cannot choose your battlefields,
    The Gods do that for you.
But you can plant your standard
    Where a standard never flew.

NATHALIA CRANE

He Who Knows

He who knows not, and knows not that he knows not, is a fool. Shun him;
He who knows not, and knows that he knows not, is a child. Teach him.
He who knows, and knows not that he knows, is asleep. Wake him.
He who knows, and knows that he knows, is wise. Follow him.

From the Persian

For Every Evil

For every evil under the sun
There is a remedy or there is none.
If there is one, seek till you find it;
If there be none, never mind it.

Destiny

The wind doth wander up and down
Forever seeking for a crown;
The rose in stillness on a stem
Inherits love's own diadem.

NATHALIA CRANE

Four Things

Four things a man must learn to do
If he would make his record true:
To think without confusion clearly;
To love his fellow-men sincerely;
To act from honest motives purely;
To trust in God and Heaven securely.

HENRY VAN DYKE

Tremendous Trifles

For want of a nail, the shoe was lost;
For want of the shoe, the horse was lost;
For want of the horse, the rider was lost;
For want of the rider, the battle was lost;
For want of the battle, the kingdom was lost;
And all from the want of a horseshoe nail.

Three Things

Three things there are that will never come back:
The arrow shot forth on its destined track;
The appointed hour that could not wait;
And the helpful word that was spoken too late.

From the Persian: Paraphrased by L. U.

*　*　*

Humility

Humble we must be, if to heaven we go;
High is the roof there, but the gate is low.

ROBERT HERRICK

*　*　*

Precious Stones

An emerald is as green as grass;
  A ruby red as blood;
A sapphire shines as blue as heaven;
  A flint lies in the mud.

A diamond is a brilliant stone,
  To catch the world's desire;
An opal holds a fiery spark;
  But a flint holds fire.

CHRISTINA GEORGINA ROSSETTI

Little Things

Little drops of water,
  Little grains of sand,
Make the mighty ocean
  And the pleasant land.

Thus the little minutes,
  Humble though they be,
Make the mighty ages
  Of eternity.

JULIA FLETCHER CARNEY

*　*　*

Certainty

I never saw a moor,
I never saw the sea;
Yet know I how the heather looks,
And what a wave must be.

I never spoke with God,
Nor visited in heaven;
Yet certain am I of the spot
As if the chart were given.

EMILY DICKINSON

In each of the following poems, Walt Whitman develops an idea to illuminate the truth of what it means to be an individual. In I Hear America Singing *he speaks up not only for the dignity of labor but for the joy that each man or woman feels in his own particular work. In* There Was a Child Went Forth *he points out that each person is the sum of everything he sees and touches and feels.*

I Hear America Singing

I hear America singing, the varied carols I hear,
  Those of mechanics, each one singing his as it should be blithe
      and strong,
  The carpenter singing his as he measures his plank or beam,

306

The mason singing his as he makes ready for work,
    or leaves off work,
The boatman singing what belongs to him in his boat,
    the deckhand singing on the steamboat deck,
The shoemaker singing as he sits on his bench,
    the hatter singing as he stands,
The wood-cutter's song, the ploughboy's on his way
    in the morning, or at noon intermission or at sundown,
The delicious singing of the mother, or of the young wife
    at work, or of the girl sewing or washing,
Each singing what belongs to him or her and to none else,
The day what belongs to the day—at night
    the party of young fellows, robust, friendly,
Singing with open mouths their strong melodious songs.

WALT WHITMAN

There Was a Child Went Forth

There was a child went forth every day;
And the first object he looked upon, that object he became.
And that object became part of him for the day, or a certain
    part of the day, or for many years, or stretching cycles of years:
The early lilacs became part of this child . . . .
And the apple-trees covered with blossoms, and the fruit
    afterward, and wood-berries, and the commonest weeds by the road;
And the schoolmistress that passed on her way to the school . . . .

The blow, the quick loud word, the tight bargain, the crafty lure,
The family usages, the language, the company, the furniture
    —the yearning and swelling heart . . . .

The doubts of day-time and the doubts of night-time—the
    curious whether and how,
Whether that which appears is so, or is it all flashes and specks?
Men and women crowding fast in the streets—if they are
    not flashes and specks, what are they?

These became part of that child who went forth every day,
And who now goes, and will always go forth every day.

WALT WHITMAN

John Bunyan, author of the next poem, spent much of his life in jail. He was a seventeenth-century preacher who, because of his refusal to accept the conventions, was sentenced to prison for more than twelve years. During his confinement he wrote nine books, including a great part of his most famous work, The Pilgrim's Progress. *With this background in mind, the poem takes on added meaning.*

The Shepherd Boy Sings in the Valley of Humiliation

He that is down needs fear no fall,
   He that is low, no pride;
He that is humble ever shall
   Have God to be his guide.

I am content with what I have,
   Little be it or much:
And, Lord, contentment still I crave,
   Because Thou savest such.

Fullness to such a burden is
   That go on pilgrimage:
Here little, and hereafter bliss,
   Is best from age to age.

JOHN BUNYAN

The Celestial Surgeon

If I have faltered more or less
In my great task of happiness;
If I have moved among my race
And shown no shining morning face;
If beams from happy human eyes
Have moved me not; if morning skies,
Books, and my food, and summer rain
Knocked on my sullen heart in vain:—
Lord, thy most pointed pleasure take
And stab my spirit broad awake.

ROBERT LOUIS STEVENSON

Prayer

God, though this life is but a wraith,
   Although we know not what we use,
Although we grope with little faith,
   Give me the heart to fight—and lose.

Ever insurgent let me be,
   Make me more daring than devout;
From sleek contentment keep me free,
   And fill me with a buoyant doubt.

Open my eyes to visions girt
   With beauty, and with wonder lit—

But let me always see the dirt,
   And all that spawn and die in it.

Open my ears to music; let
   Me thrill with Spring's first flutes and drums—
But never let me dare forget
   The bitter ballads of the slums.

From compromise and things half-done,
   Keep me, with stern and stubborn pride.
And when, at last, the fight is won,
   God, keep me still unsatisfied.

LOUIS UNTERMEYER

Where Is Heaven?

Where is Heaven? Is it not
Just a friendly garden plot,
Walled with stone and roofed with sun,
Where the days pass one by one
Not too fast and not too slow,
Looking backward as they go
At the beauties left behind
To transport the pensive mind.

Does not Heaven begin that day
When the eager heart can say,
Surely God is in this place,
I have seen Him face to face
In the loveliness of flowers,
In the service of the showers,
And His voice has talked to me
In the sunlit apple tree.

BLISS CARMAN

Music

Let me go where'er I will
I hear a sky-born music still:
It sounds from all things old,
It sounds from all things young;
From all that's fair, from all that's foul,
Peals out a cheerful song.
It is not only in the rose,
It is not only in the bird,
Not only where the rainbow glows,
Nor in the song of woman heard,
But in the darkest, meanest things
There always, always something sings.
'Tis not in the high stars alone,
Nor in the cups of budding flowers,
Nor in the redbreast's mellow tone,
Nor in the bow that smiles in showers,
But in the mud and scum of things
There always, always something sings.

RALPH WALDO EMERSON

Words

Bright is the ring of words
  When the right man rings them,
Fair the fall of songs
  When the singer sings them.
Still they are carolled and said—
  On wings they are carried—
After the singer is dead
  And the maker buried.

ROBERT LOUIS STEVENSON

Treasures in Heaven

Lay not up for yourselves treasures upon earth,
Where moth and rust doth corrupt,
And where thieves break through and steal:

But lay up for yourselves treasures in heaven,
Where neither moth nor rust doth corrupt,
And where thieves do not break through nor steal.
For where your treasure is, there will your heart be also.

The Bible: ST. MATTHEW, 6

Opportunity

This I beheld, or dreamed it in a dream:
There spread a cloud of dust along a plain;
And underneath the cloud, or in it, raged
A furious battle, and men yelled, and swords
Shocked upon swords and shields. A prince's banner
Wavered, then staggered backward, hemmed by foes.
A craven hung along the battle's edge
And thought, "Had I a sword of keener steel—
That blue blade that the king's son bears—but this
Blunt thing——!" He snapt and flung it from his hand,
And, lowering, crept away and left the field.

Then came the king's son, wounded, sore bestead,
And weaponless, and saw the broken sword,
Hilt-buried in the dry and trodden sand,
And ran and snatched it, and with battle-shout
Lifted afresh, he hewed his enemy down,
And saved a great cause that heroic day.

EDWARD ROWLAND SILL

Advice

He that sweareth
Till no man trust him;
He that lieth
Till no man believe him;

He that borroweth
Till no man will lend him;
Let him go where
No man knoweth him.

HUGH RHODES

At the height of the War between the States, Julia Ward Howe was in Washington where her husband was a doctor with the Union troops. One day the Howes were in the outskirts of the city during an artillery skirmish. On the way back, the Union soldiers tramped by the side of their carriage singing. One song especially, John Brown's Body, with its triumphant chorus "Glory, Glory, Hallelujah!" impressed Mrs. Howe and repeated itself over and over in her mind. She could not get the tune out of her head, but she was not satisfied with the lyrics. If she could only find new words to fit that ringing melody!

The next morning just as dawn was breaking, she got up and hurriedly jotted down lines that became the Battle-Hymn of the Republic. It was the greatest marching song of the Civil War, perhaps of all wars, and it was also a most majestic plea for the freedom of men.

Battle-Hymn of the Republic

Mine eyes have seen the glory of the coming of the Lord:
He is trampling out the vintage where the grapes of wrath are stored;
He hath loosed the fateful lightning of his terrible swift sword:
      His truth is marching on.

I have seen Him in the watch-fires of a hundred circling camps:
They have builded Him an altar in the evening dews and damps;
I can read his righteous sentence by the dim and flaring lamps.
      His day is marching on.

He has sounded forth the trumpet that shall never call retreat;
He is sifting out the hearts of men before his judgment seat;
Oh! be swift, my soul, to answer Him! be jubilant, my feet!
      Our God is marching on.

In the beauty of the lilies Christ was born across the sea,
With a glory in his bosom that transfigures you and me:
As He died to make men holy, let us die to make men free,
      While God is marching on.

JULIA WARD HOWE

From: The Sermon on the Mount

Blessed are the poor in spirit:
For theirs is the kingdom of heaven.

Blessed are they that mourn:
For they shall be comforted.

Blessed are the meek:
For they shall inherit the earth.

Blessed are they which do hunger and thirst after righteousness:
For they shall be filled.

Blessed are the merciful:
For they shall obtain mercy.

Blessed are the pure in heart:
For they shall see God.

Blessed are the peacemakers:
For they shall be called the children of God.

Blessed are they which are persecuted for righteousness' sake:
For theirs is the kingdom of heaven.

The Bible: ST. MATTHEW, 5

The startling name of Ozymandias is said to have been that of an ancient Egyptian king. Shelley was apparently struck by the resonance of the name and, in a fabulous sonnet, made it a symbol of human vanity and futility.

Ozymandias

I met a traveller from an antique land
Who said: Two vast and trunkless legs of stone
Stand in the desert... Near them, on the sand,
Half sunk, a shattered visage lies, whose frown,
And wrinkled lip, and sneer of cold command,
Tell that its sculptor well those passions read
Which yet survive, stamped on these lifeless things,
The hand that mocked them, and the heart that fed:
And on the pedestal these words appear:
"My name is Ozymandias, king of kings:

Look on my works, ye Mighty, and despair!"
Nothing beside remains. Round the decay
Of that colossal wreck, boundless and bare
The lone and level sands stretch far away.

PERCY BYSSHE SHELLEY

The following sonnet is an intensely personal one. In it, the tubercular poet, John Keats, sensing that he might soon die, confessed his ambitions to write, his delight in beauty, and his unfulfilled love for a girl. Unlike that of The Minstrel-Boy *and other poems that call for courage, action, and resistance, Keats' philosophy is a deeply quiet one. It is an acceptance of his place in the universe.*

When I Have Fears That I May Cease To Be

When I have fears that I may cease to be
   Before my pen has gleaned my teeming brain,
Before high-piled books, in charactery,
   Hold like rich garners the full ripened grain;
When I behold, upon the night's starred face,
   Huge cloudy symbols of a high romance,
And think that I may never live to trace
   Their shadows, with the magic hand of chance;
And when I feel, fair creature of an hour,
   That I shall never look upon thee more,
Never have relish in the faery power
   Of unreflecting love;—then on the shore
Of the wide world I stand alone, and think
Till love and fame to nothingness do sink.

JOHN KEATS

The Minstrel-Boy

The Minstrel-boy to the war is gone,
   In the ranks of death you'll find him;
His father's sword he has girded on,
   And his wild harp slung behind him.—
"Land of song!" said the warrior-bard,
   "Though all the world betrays thee,
One sword, at least, thy rights shall guard,
   One faithful harp shall praise thee!"

The Minstrel fell! But the foeman's chain
   Could not bring his proud soul under;
The harp he loved ne'er spoke again,
   For he tore its cords asunder;
And said "No chains shall sully thee,
   Thou soul of love and bravery!
Thy songs were made for the brave and free,
   They shall never sound in slavery!"

THOMAS MOORE

313

Rudyard Kipling was one of the great story-tellers of modern times. His fiction ranges from the realistic Plain Tales from the Hills, *which reflect his years in India, to the fanciful* Just So Stories *and* The Jungle Books. *His poetry is equally varied. It includes such favorites as the rousing* Gunga Din, *the sentimental* Mandalay, *and the memorable* If—.

If—

If you can keep your head when all about you
    Are losing theirs and blaming it on you;
If you can trust yourself when all men doubt you,
    But make allowance for their doubting too;
If you can wait and not be tired by waiting,
    Or, being lied about, don't deal in lies,
Or, being hated, don't give way to hating,
    And yet don't look too good, nor talk too wise;

If you can dream—and not make dreams your master;
    If you can think—and not make thoughts your aim;
If you can meet with triumph and disaster
    And treat those two impostors just the same;
If you can bear to hear the truth you've spoken
    Twisted by knaves to make a trap for fools,
Or watch the things you gave your life to broken,
    And stoop and build 'em up with wornout tools;

If you can make one heap of all your winnings
    And risk it on one turn of pitch-and-toss,
And lose, and start again at your beginnings
    And never breathe a word about your loss;
If you can force your heart and nerve and sinew
    To serve your turn long after they are gone,
And so hold on when there is nothing in you
    Except the Will which says to them: "Hold on";

If you can talk with crowds and keep your virtue,
    Or walk with kings—nor lose the common touch;
If neither foes nor loving friends can hurt you;
    If all men count with you, but none too much;
If you can fill the unforgiving minute
    With sixty seconds' worth of distance run—
Yours is the Earth and everything that's in it,
    And—which is more—you'll be a Man, my son!

RUDYARD KIPLING

The Fountain

Into the fountain
    Full of the light,
Leaping and flashing
    From morn till night!

Into the moonlight
    Whiter than snow,
Waving so flower-like
    When the winds blow!

Into the starlight,
    Rushing in spray,
Happy at midnight,
    Happy by day!

Ever in motion,
    Blithesome and cheery,
Still climbing heavenward,
    Never aweary;

Glad of all weathers,
    Still seeming best
Upward or downward
    Motion thy rest;

Full of a nature
    Nothing can tame,
Changed every moment,
    Ever the same;

Ceaseless aspiring,
    Ceaseless content,
Darkness or sunshine
    Thy element;

Glorious fountain!
    Let my heart be
Fresh, changeful, constant,
    Upward like thee!

JAMES RUSSELL LOWELL

Abou Ben Adhem

Abou Ben Adhem (may his tribe increase!)
Awoke one night from a deep dream of peace,
And saw within the moonlight in his room,
Making it rich, and like a lily in bloom,
An Angel, writing in a book of gold;
Exceeding peace had made Ben Adhem bold,
And to the presence in the room he said,
"What writest thou?"—The vision raised its head,
And with a look made of all sweet accord,
Answer'd, "The names of those who love the Lord."
"And is mine one?" said Abou. "Nay, not so,"
Replied the angel. Abou spoke more low,
But cheerily still; and said, "I pray thee, then,
Write me as one that loves his fellowmen."
The angel wrote and vanish'd. The next night
It came again, with a great wakening light,
And show'd the names whom love of God had bless'd,
And, lo! Ben Adhem's name led all the rest.

LEIGH HUNT

It is natural to want to be popular but, as No Enemies *points out, popularity may be a sign of weakness rather than of strength. The phrase "dashed no cup from perjured lip" refers to the ancient custom of kissing a cup of wine when taking an oath. It was anyone's duty to prevent at any cost a perjured, or lying, lip from touching the cup.*

No Enemies

You have no enemies, you say?
Alas, my friend, the boast is poor.
He who has mingled in the fray
Of duty, that the brave endure,
Must have made foes. If you have none,
Small is the work that you have done.
You've hit no traitor on the hip,
You've dashed no cup from perjured lip,
You've never turned the wrong to right,
You've been a coward in the fight.

CHARLES MACKAY

*No matter how often it has been repeated—and it has been reprinted and recited endlessly—*Invictus *remains a stirring statement of the courageous and heroic spirit. The very title means invincible.*

Invictus

Out of the night that covers me,
   Black as the Pit from pole to pole,
I thank whatever gods may be
   For my unconquerable soul.

In the fell clutch of circumstance
   I have not winced nor cried aloud.
Under the bludgeonings of chance
   My head is bloody, but unbowed.

Beyond this place of wrath and tears
   Looms but the horror of the shade,
And yet the menace of the years
   Finds, and shall find me, unafraid.

It matters not how strait the gate,
   How charged with punishments the scroll,
I am the master of my fate:
   I am the captain of my soul.

WILLIAM ERNEST HENLEY

INDEX OF TITLES

318

319

INDEX OF FIRST LINES

322

INDEX OF AUTHORS

QRS